BELLINI
MANTEGNA

MASTERPIECES
FACE-TO-FACE

The Presentation
of Jesus at the Temple

BELLINI
MANTEGNA

SilvanaEditoriale

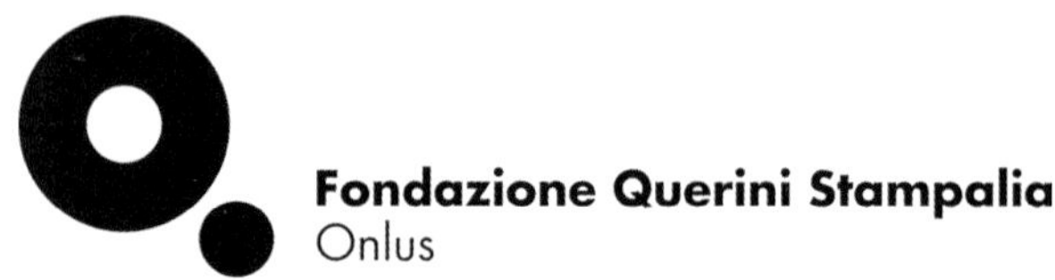
Fondazione Querini Stampalia
Onlus

MASTERPIECES FACE-TO-FACE
BELLINI / MANTEGNA
The Presentation of Jesus at the Temple
March 21 – July 1, 2018

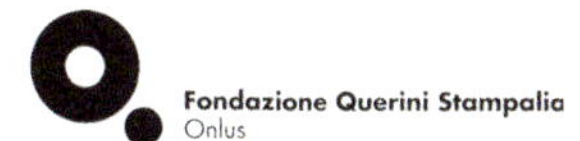

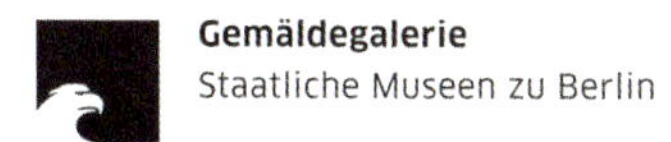

Curated by
Brigit Blass-Simmen
Neville Rowley
Giovanni Carlo Federico Villa

Exhibition Scientific Commettee
Brigit Blass-Simmen
Caroline Campbell
Michael Eissenhauer
Gabriele Finaldi
Babette Hartwieg
Marigusta Lazzari
Neville Rowley
Babet Trevisan
Giovanni Carlo Federico Villa
Stefan Weppelmann

Exhibition Design
Mario Botta
with Mario Gemin

Head of Conservation
Babette Hartwieg
Babet Trevisan

Organizational Coordination
Tiziana Bottecchia
Lara Marchese
Marta Savaris
Babet Trevisan

Learning, Promotion and Development
Associazione Barchetta Blu
Dora De Diana
Neda Furlan
with Elisa Campana, Valentina Zocca

Archival Research
Angela Munari

Exhibition Content Development
Elisabetta Dal Carlo
Nicole Moolhuijsen
Angela Munari *with* Giulia Ferrari

Graphic Design
We Exhibit Srl *with* Studio Visuale

Communication
Studio ESSECI
Sara Bossi, Fondazione Querini Stampalia

Social Media
Barbara Colli *with* Marta Corazza,
Elisa Rampazzo,
Francesca Piran

Administration
Federico Acerboni
Andrea Bellemo
Barbara Rossi

Technical Support
Alessandro Marinello
with Margherita Olivieri,
Lisa Pierantoni

Set-up and Information Material
We exhibit Srl

Translations
Jo Ann Titmarsh

Lighting
ERCO
Spazioluce

Transports
Hasenkamp Internationale
Transporte GmbH

Insurance
KUHN & BÜLOW
Versicherungsmakler GmbH

Security
Archeoclub d'Italia onlus
Associazione Nazionale Carabinieri
Ekos Club
BiEvent

With the scientic collaboration of

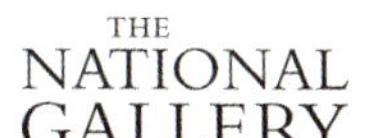

MEDAL OF THE PRESIDENT OF THE REPUBLIC

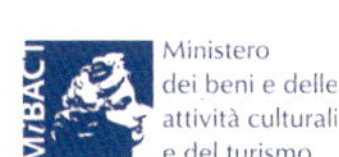

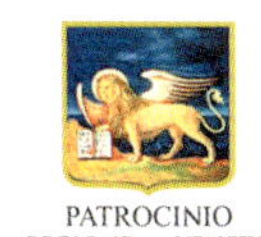

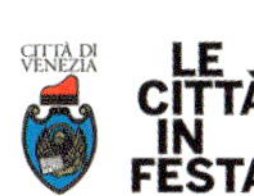

With the support of

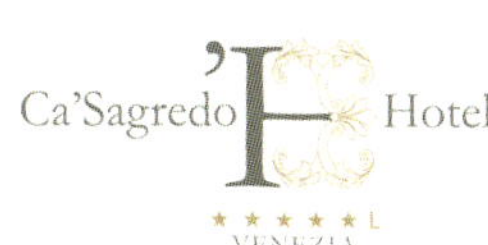

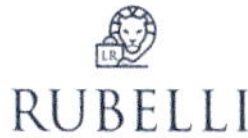

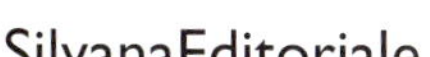

Nunc dimittis servum tuum, Domine,
secundum verbum tuum in pace:
quia viderunt oculi mei salutem tuam,
quam parasti ante faciem omnium populorum,
lumen ad revelationem gentium
et gloriam plebis tuae Israel.
Lc 2,29-32

An initiative is coming into being during the European Year of Cultural Heritage; one, at length lingering in the vision of our Foundation, whose sense is bringing to light an important chapter of European culture: namely Italian Renaissance. A period that led to the great events of modern times which, setting off from Europe, would have involved the entire world.
Two works by Andrea Mantegna and Giovanni Bellini have been juxtaposed, having in common a central event for the history of Europe and of mankind as a whole: the Presentation of Jesus at the Temple, *the consignment of the Saviour to the prophet Simeon, and in turn to the universal Church, to men of all times. The fulfilment of such a long awaited event, which would have left its mark in history, led the elderly Simeon into releasing his extraordinary canticle.*
This singular occasion that witnesses the collaboration of two Italian and German museums (ours and the Gemäldegalerie in Berlin) in the said endeavour is also European. Important scientific collaborations have also been established with the National Gallery in London: a comparison between the two works will in fact be at the heart of exhibitions of the two artists scheduled at the National Gallery from October 1st this year and at the Gemäldegalerie from March 1st next year.
The panel by Bellini has always been one of the most important paintings initially belonging to the collection of the Querini Stampalia family and subsequently to the Foundation. Early inventories mentioned it as being by Andrea Mantegna and then it was definitely restored to Bellini during the twentieth century; the artistic and communicative power of the painting is such that it attracts throngs of scholars and art enthusiasts. Even contemporary artists, perceiving the charge of the said artwork,

have felt the need to engage with it: within the sphere of our programme for the appreciation of ancient art through contemporary art, entitled Conservare il Futuro *(Preserving the Future) that has been conceived and curated by Chiara Bertola, artists such as Georges Adeagbo, Elisabetta Di Maggio, Jimmie Durham, Marisa Merz have chosen to pay their tribute and relate themselves to this Renaissance master.*
Hence for some time now, following new studies on the paintings and being reassured that they may be moved without any risks to their preservation, an idea has arisen for an exhibition comparing these two artists. And so we have captured this extraordinary opportunity for being the first to present the two masterpieces side-by-side – as they have always been illustrated in books, but never in reality.
Our gratitude goes to all those who have made the presence of this illustrious guest in Venice possible: Professor Michael Eissenhauer, Director of the Gemäldegalerie; the exhibition curators, Brigit Blass-Simmen, Neville Rowley, Professor Giovanni Carlo Federico Villa; the entire scientific committee; staff working with the three museums involved in the event; the sponsors, who have been fundamental in the establishment of the initiative; and the sponsoring organizations that have recognized the great cultural value of this operation. Special thanks go to the Director of the Fondazione Scientifica Querini Stampalia, Marigusta Lazzari, who has strongly willed this exhibition and who has worked tenaciously in overcoming the many organizational difficulties that it has entailed; to all our collaborators and to the architect Mario Botta who has seen to its outfitting with the same skills and availability employed over the past two decades in designing the new aspect of our Palazzo.

MARINO CORTESE
President Fondazione Querini Stampalia of Venice

Since the late nineteenth century, the two Presentations of Jesus at the Temple *by Andrea Mantegna and Giovanni Bellini have often been compared to one another – occasionally to appraise Mantegna's version at the Gemäldegalerie in Berlin or, on the other hand, Bellini's version at the Fondazione Querini Stampalia in Venice. Until now, this at times heated debate could only rely on photographs, as the two works were never physically together. The Fondazione Querini Stampalia and the Gemäldegalerie have been collaborating for a few years with the aim of bringing these two masterpieces together. This ambitious project finally became possible when the National Gallery in London and the abovementioned Gemäldegalerie began developing a project for a wide-ranging exhibition on the overall relationship between Andrea Mantegna and Giovanni Bellini. The two* Presentations *will be exhibited side-by-side in London in autumn 2018, moving to Berlin in spring 2019, but it was only fitting that their reunion first take place in Venice, the birthplace of Giovanni Bellini – and more precisely, at the institution that houses Bellini's masterpiece. Aside from this epoch-making comparison, the exhibition and catalogue present the results of studies aimed at establishing the relationship between the two paintings, by revealing some of their secrets. Yet some questions still remain: why did Bellini decide to mechanically copy Mantegna's painting without, however, being faithful to his model, replacing Mantegna's self-portrait and the likeness of his wife (Bellini's own sister) with four mysterious figures? There is still much we do not know, but this mystery is part of the allure of the two masterpieces brought together here for the very first time in over five centuries.*

MICHAEL EISSENHAUER
Director Gemäldegalerie Staatliche Museen zu Berlin

GABRIELE FINALDI
Director The National Gallery, London

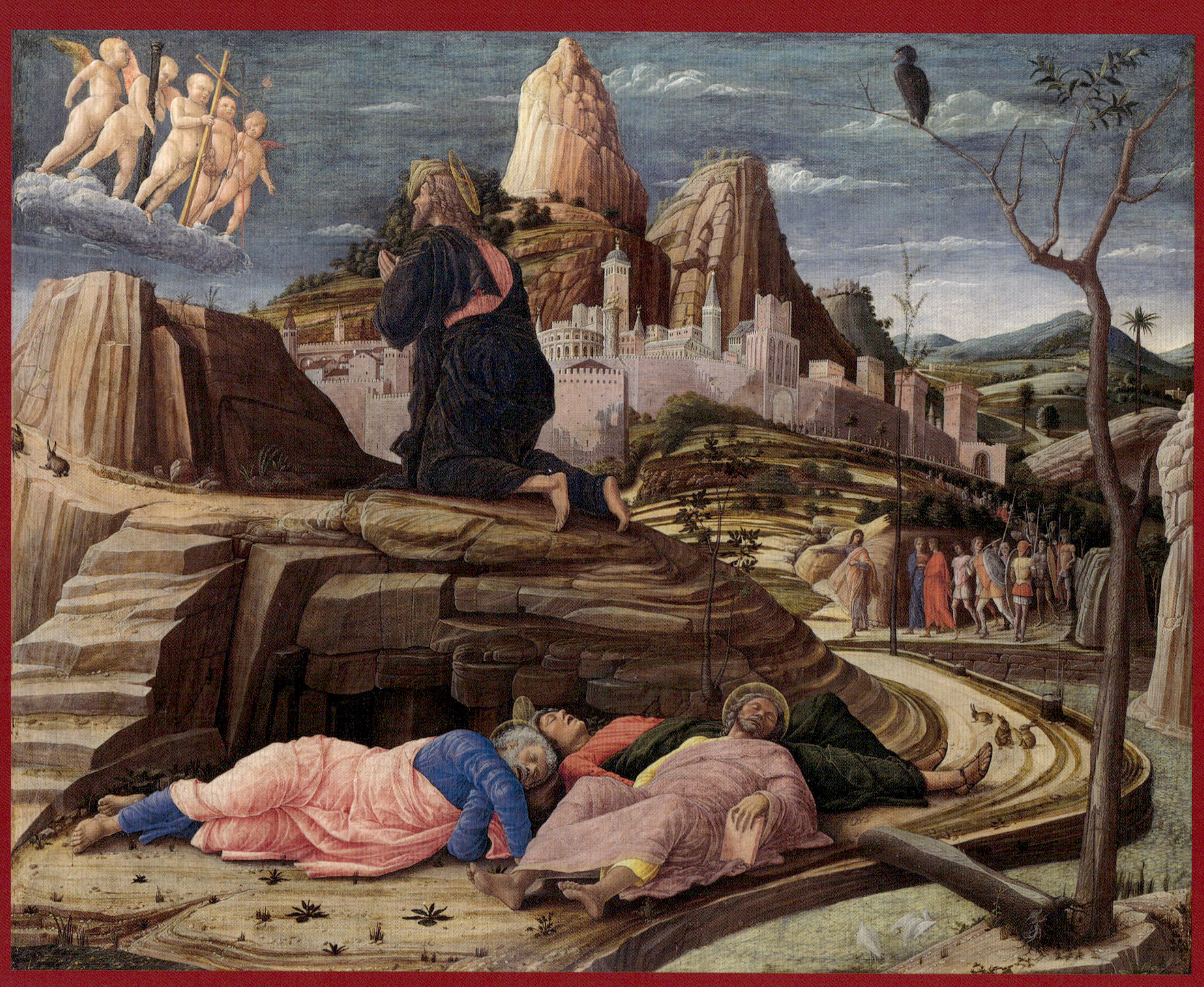

Becoming Bellini and Maintaining Mantegna: The Art of Repetition

CAROLINE CAMPBELL

1. Andrea Mantegna, *The Agony in the Garden*. London, The National Gallery

Introduction[1]

One of the greatest ironies of Renaissance art history – at least for those who want to believe in a Vasarian teleological progression – is that Giovanni Bellini, one of the most innovative and influential of European painters of the fifteenth century, was also one of the most innately conservative. Roberto Longhi, one of the greatest art historians and critics of the twentieth century, struggled with this. Longhi argued that Giovanni Bellini must have been born earlier than his brother-in-law Andrea Mantegna, because his idea of Bellini as a transformative genius could not conceive of him ever following in the path of Mantegna.[2]

Longhi's anxiety concerning the relationship between innovation and imitation is still relevant in the early twenty-first century. Today, when originality is valued more than any other quality in judging the relative worth of an artist, it is particularly hard to comprehend the intrinsic connection that can exist between copying and innovation, whether in historic or contemporary art. On a macro level, this may explain why Renaissance painting – except, of course, the incontrovertible individualism of a Leonardo – is probably less revered today by a wide public (in the Anglo-Saxon world at least) than at any time since the fifteenth and sixteenth centuries. In this short essay, I will explore the role that copying played in Giovanni Bellini's artistic development. I will argue that it was through repeating or honing the ideas of others, whether his father Jacopo or – in particular – his brother-in-law Andrea Mantegna that Giovanni Bellini found his own artistic identity. This was far from being a novel or radical idea in the context of the fifteenth century. The classical revival or 'Re-naissance' of the fifteenth and sixteenth centuries was based on the assumption that it was only by following and imitating the expressive forms established by ancient Greek and Roman thinkers – whether in literature or art – that a creative writer or practitioner could become truly himself. Copying, or replicating another's idea, did not necessarily imply a lack of creativity.

Bellini, born in Venice, probably in the late 1430s (the date is contentious and has been much discussed[3]), to a father who was a *cittadino originario*, started his life with great social and professional advantages. His father Jacopo was a successful painter who combined business sense with talent to an unusual degree. By the time of Giovanni's birth, Jacopo was one of the leading painters not merely of Venice but of north-eastern Italy, and his good luck to produce not one but two talented painter-sons meant that the family firm was likely to continue for at least another generation.[4] Giovanni's career, like that of his brother Gentile, fitted into a typical Venetian pattern, which depended on family.[5] Well into the eighteenth century, Venetian artists tended to work in dynasties, for the practical reason that employing close relatives reduced the need to pay your assistants. Daughters, although less likely to be employed in the family business, also had their uses. By the late 1440s Andrea Mantegna was the most promising young artist in north-eastern Italy, and Jacopo Bellini would have viewed Mantegna's marriage with his daughter Nicolosia as an attractive possibility. The match took place in 1453,[6] and in the middle years of the 1450s, it would have looked likely to be producing exactly the artistic results that Jacopo Bellini had envisaged: domination not just of the painterly production of Venice, but of its nearby neighbour, the university and cultural centre of Padua.[7]

Jacopo Bellini's well-laid plans, however, went awry, when Mantegna's exceptional talent meant that he was persuaded to accept the post of Court Artist to the Gonzaga, the ruling family of Mantua.[8] Despite this, Mantegna's marriage had a long lasting impact on the Bellini dynasty of painters, as it transformed Giovanni Bellini's artistic development. Although the creative stimulus of Mantegna was present throughout Bellini's career, it was never more significant than during his first years as an independent painter. It was through Bellini's intense study of and admiration for Mantegna that he discovered his own voice, one that it is distinct both from that of his father, and from that of his brother-in-law. Most of Bellini's first independent paintings are hard to separate completely from Mantegna. Some use the same motifs, or replicate forms and features that Mantegna had invented. Some are so closely connected with Mantegna that they have been called copies – although they are more accurately reprises – of his compositions. Other works take up Mantegnesque subjects, and reinvent them in a Bellinian form.[9] And even in the works that Giovanni made with his father Jacopo and his brother Gentile, including the Carità altarpieces, and the canvases of the Lives of Christ and the Virgin for the Scuola di San Giovanni Evangelista, we can discern his personal style for the first time, through his integration of Mantegna's manner into paintings made in Jacopo Bellini's image.[10]

St Jerome: Asserting Artistic Independence?

The painting which has the best case to be Giovanni Bellini's first independent painting is the St Jerome in the Barber Institute, Birmingham.[11] Painted around 1460, this tiny panel shows the eremitical saint in a bleak mountainous desert, accompanied by his titular lion. Almost as important as any pictorial motif is the inscription, IHOVANES BELINVS, in the centre of the foreground. Giovanni is here asserting his authorship and invention, in a way that was separate to the shared artistic enterprise of the Bellini family workshop, as represented in the Gattemelata altarpiece, painted at the same time for the former Paduan *condottiere*'s funerary chapel.[12]

The subject of St Jerome became one which Giovanni Bellini was to make his own, as much as the Virgin and Child. In these compositions, over the course of his career, infinite variety is found within particular pictorial choices, for instance of colour, and of details of the land- and sky-scape.[13] The initial inspiration was Jacopo Bellini, as the subject occurs in a painting (Verona, Museo di Castelvecchio) and on several occasions in the drawing albums. As Giovanni Villa has demonstrated, the underdrawing closely follows these precedents.[14] However, there are important elements in the Birmingham picture which signal how Mantegna's example allowed Giovanni to express an artistic voice different to that of his father, even when depicting a subject associated with Jacopo. One is in the very Mantegnesque description of the rocks that form Jerome's hermitage, and the linear decoration of some of their forms, at the extreme left, with lines of silver and gold. This is similar to Bellini's outlining of Christ's draperies in his London *Agony*

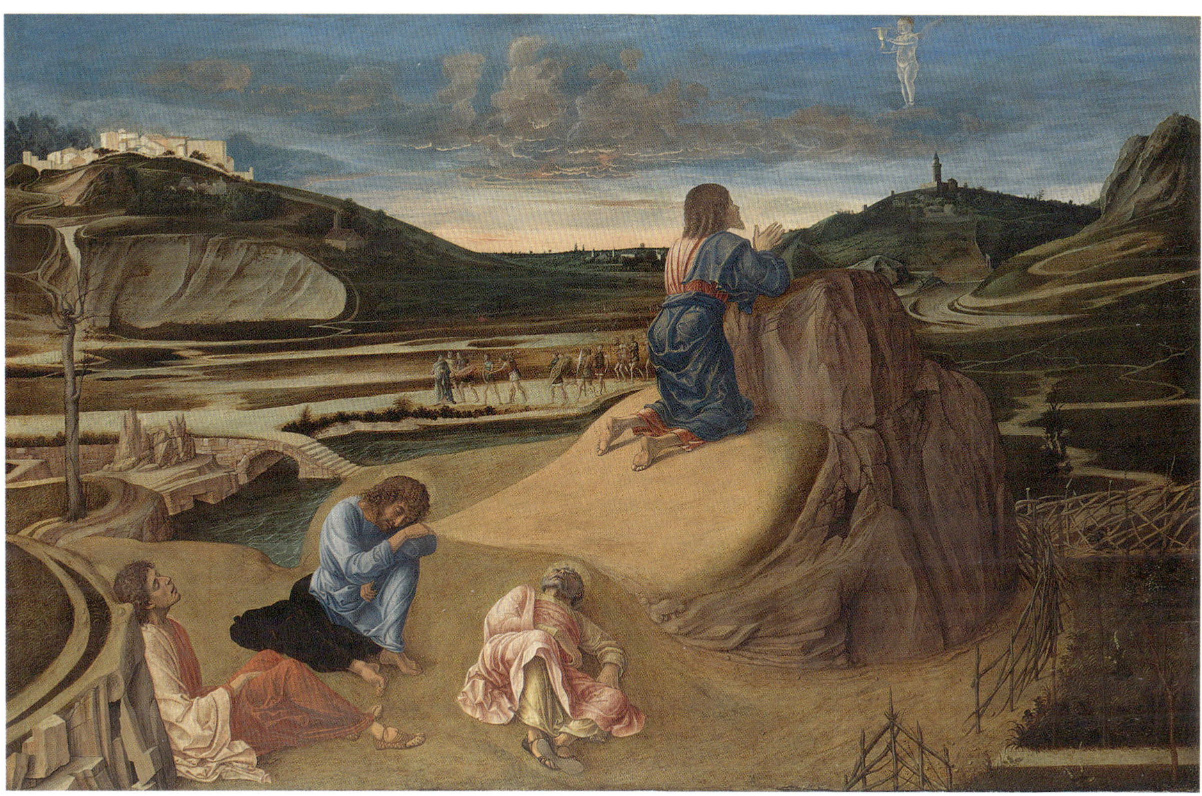

2. Giovanni Bellini, *The Agony in the Garden*. London, The National Gallery

in the Garden. Another is the perspectival device by which the far landscape can be glimpsed through the 'window' in Jerome's rocky cave. This is analogous to Mantegna's *St Jerome* of around 10 years earlier,[15] and, as has been demonstrated, it is very different to the artificial, bleak background of Jacopo Bellini's Verona *St Jerome*.

A third and perhaps the most important Mantegnesque element is the inscription. As Mauro Lucco has argued, this should be connected to Mantegna's use of a *cartellino* or scroll to proclaim his creation of the *St Mark* (Frankfurt, Städel Museum),[16] which – like Bellini's *St Jerome* in Birmingham – is one of Mantegna's earliest independent works.[17] For Lucco, the inscription on the *cartellino* in Bellini's picture is a 'genial homage' to Mantegna's example.[18] To carry the analogy further, the *St Mark* dates from the period of Mantegna's formal manumission from the authority of his master and adopted father Squarcione. As Neville Rowley has observed, it is telling that in this *cartellino* Mantegna does not sign himself as a student of Squarcione, unlike Squarcione's other exceptional pupils Marco Zoppo and Carlo Crivelli.[19] Just as the pictorial format of the *St Mark* recalls some of Squarcione's inventions,[20] so Giovanni Bellini uses his *St Jerome* – a painting similar, in terms of what it represents, to his father's work – to proclaim his artistic autonomy, inscribing his name for the first time on a work that he conceived and created independent of any other painter.

The Agony in the Garden: Repetition, Mimesis and Invention[21]

A different aspect of Bellini's indebtedness to Mantegna, as it also shows Mantegna's response to Bellini, is illustrated by their linked versions of the *Agony in the Garden*, which have hung side by side in the National Gallery since 1893 (fig. 1).[22] Mantegna's *Agony*, with its elaborate and antiquarian-inspired

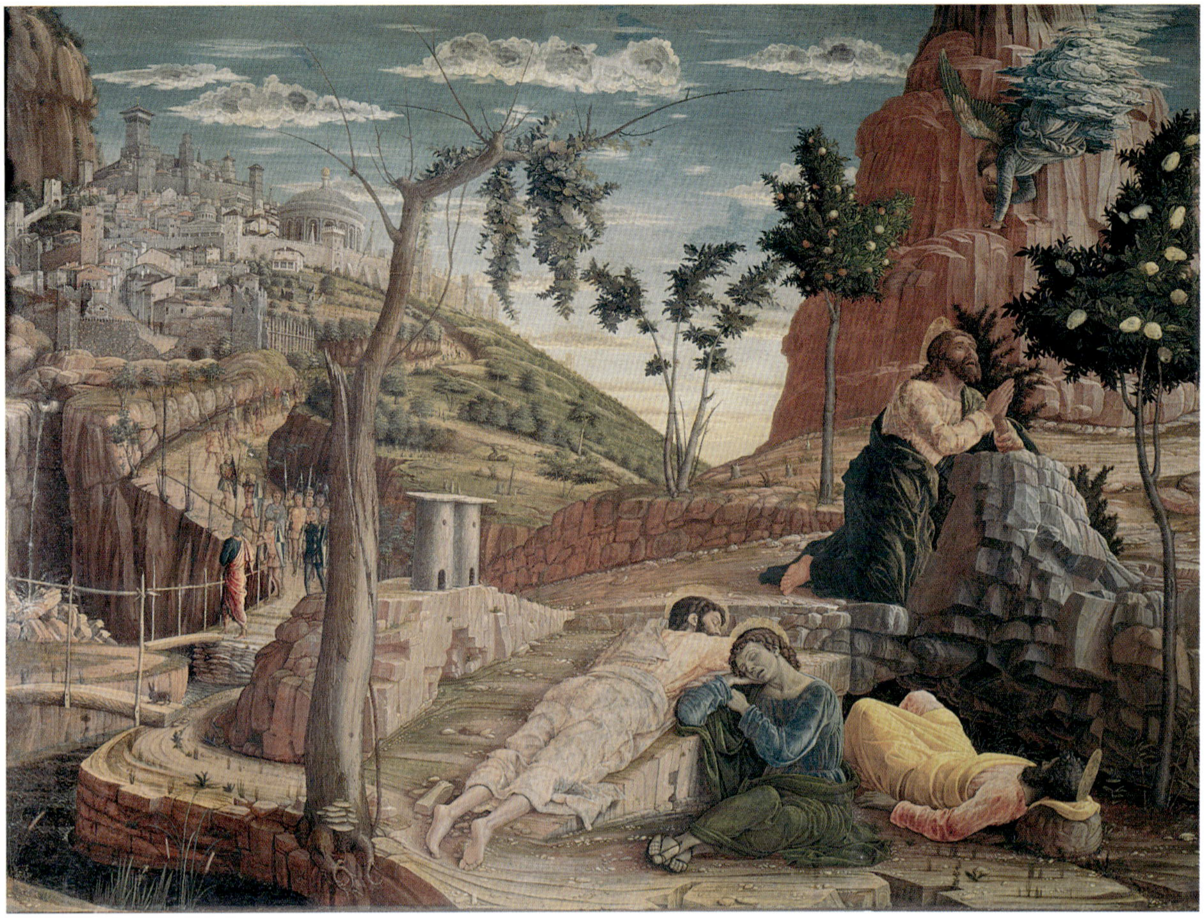

3. Andrea Mantegna, *The Agony in the Garden*. Tours, Musée des beaux-arts

details,[23] and Bellini's, a landscape suffused with the light of dawn,[24] exemplify the key characteristics of each artist. Their evident relationship, as well as their connection to Mantegna's *predella* panel of the same subject for the San Zeno altarpiece (Tours, Musée des Beaux-Arts) has been explored by many scholars, and the paintings have been exhaustively studied, in the individual contexts of Mantegna and Bellini's oeuvre, and their wider relationship to the changing nature of painting in the fifteenth century.[25] Thanks to this work, and to the forthcoming studies of Jill Dunkerton, Babette Hartwieg and Marika Spring,[26] it is now possible to establish a satisfactory chronology and order for the production of these three paintings.

Mantegna's first *Agony in the Garden* was painted perhaps as much as a decade before Bellini's, probably in the early 1450s when his marriage to Nicolosia Bellini would have given him regular access for the first time to Jacopo's Sketchbooks.[27] Yet the expression and execution of the composition is more fundamentally about Mantegna than the Bellini family. The figures of the sleeping disciples in the foreground – their mouths open as they snore – are supreme examples of Mantegna's interest in perspective, and in the human form. They are mirrored in drawn studies of a similar date, from the dazzling *di sotto in su* of the sketch for *St James taken to his Execution* for the Ovetari chapel and the *Three studies of a human body* (both London, British Museum). Mantegna's justifiable pride can be seen in the placement of his signature OPVS ANDREAE

MANTEGNA on the three rocks behind the heads of the dreaming apostles. The miniaturist style of this *Agony* – seen particularly in the gnarled roots of the tree trunk in the foreground, and the individual bricks of the city wall – has close affinities with other paintings by Mantegna of the middle 1450s, particularly the *Adoration of the Magi* (New York, Metropolitan Museum of Art).[28] But the feature of the painting that has attracted special comment is the idealised view of Jerusalem. As Andrea De Marchi has written, it is 'one of the first urban fantasies conceived by Mantegna': an area of invention in which the artist excelled.[29]

Forty years ago, Michael Vickers argued that the city in Mantegna's London *Agony* was an ideal city, based on the Constantinople of the fifteenth century (as known by Ciriaco d'Ancona, whose presence in and impact on Padua is well-documented),[30] intended to represent the Jerusalem of the New Testament.[31] Faietti, in her convincing analysis of the buildings and the sources, argues that Mantegna's desire to depict Jerusalem as the Heavenly City led him to combine buildings from Rome herself, and the 'new Rome', Constantinople, and that this was tied to the circulation and dissemination of Manuel Crysorlas's *Synkrisis*, or *Elogio delle due città* of 1411 (written in Rome).[32] Mantegna's Jerusalem is a consciously catholic mixture of buildings that are both imagined and real, from the half-collapsed gate tower that recalls the Torre delle Milizie (still believed by many in the fifteenth century to have been the tower from which Nero watched Rome burn),[33] the recently repaired city walls (looking forward to the future destruction of Jerusalem in 70 CE), the Colosseum-type structure familiar from the many 'picture-postcard' views of Rome depicted in *cassone* paintings, a bell tower topped with a weathervane in the shape of a crescent, and an equestrian statue that has variously been described as the Monument of Theodosius,[34] an invention of Mantegna, or based on a drawing by Jacopo Bellini.[35] The venerable nature of the city is suggested not by structures that accurately recall Jerusalem, but ones that evoke its symbolic value as the Eternal City, Christ's heavenly bride. Mantegna has combined a number of textual and visual sources, devotional, Christian, and classical, to create a unique *historia* which takes a pictorial form.[36]

What Mantegna's London *Agony* does not have, however, is the emotional connection between landscape and figures that we see in the three predella scenes for the San Zeno altarpiece, documented between 1456 and 1459.[37] This characteristic was the result of prolonged exposure to the work of his brother-in-law Giovanni.[38] In the *Agony* for San Zeno, the figure of Christ is integrated into the landscape, rather than towering over the rock on which he prays and his sleeping disciples. The clouds no longer scud aimlessly in the sky, but are organised to draw attention to the vanishing point on the horizon, from where the sun begins to rise. Probably at no other moment was Mantegna so close to Bellini.[39]

Bellini's *Agony* (fig. 2) is a faithful copy of neither of Mantegna's Agonies, although it is impossible not to see it in relationship to these paintings.[40] Bellini's figural composition is based on Mantegna's National Gallery *Agony*, and infra-red reflectography has revealed the meticulous underdrawing of the figures in both works.[41] The audacious – and not wholly successful – foreshortening of St Peter shows Bellini's awareness of Mantegna's studies of the human body from life. Bellini's unusual use of shell gold to delineate the drapery folds and halo of the figure of Christ is based on Mantegna's employment of the same technique in his National Gallery *Agony* (figs. 1-2). Again, Mantegna used this throughout his career, but it is very rarely found in Bellini's work.[42]

Yet, for all these influences and impressions, the picture is wholly Bellini's own. It is physically larger, and in its atmosphere more expansive than Mantegna's two *Agonies*. While Mantegna contracts and minimises, Bellini expands. Rather than dominating the landscape, Bellini's view of Jerusalem is only a composite part of it. The contours of the city merge with that of the hill on which it sits. And the landscape, although imagined, is more rooted in the reality of fifteenth-century Italy than Mantegna's Holy Land. The built environment is at one with the natural world: the outlines of the roads which go to and from Jerusalem meander organically, like rivers, and the tall tower in the hill town at the right, leads Christ (and the viewer's eyes) to the angel standing on a cloud, as insubstantial as a cloud himself, who holds the chalice of sacrifice and of salvation. The viewer is encouraged to 'wander at will' through the painting just as, many years later, Pietro Bembo was to describe Giovanni Bellini's intentions in making paintings to Isabella d'Este.[43] And the whole landscape is lit by the glowing dawn, which rises from the distant horizon, and is reflected in the clouds above. In Bellini's picture, the narrative of Christ's sacrifice and ultimate salvation is told as much through the rosy light of day break, as it is by the details of Christ, his sleeping companions, or the figures of Judas and the Roman soldiers approaching in the distance. If Mantegna's painting is about how mimesis takes us back to Christ's lifetime, Bellini's makes it part and parcel of the viewer's world and lived experiences. Both are effective – although very different – means of enabling Christ's *Agony* to be recreated by their beholders.

The Descent into Limbo

A group of works depicting the Descent into Limbo shows how Mantegna and Bellini's interaction – and by this stage, cross-fertilisation of compositions, motifs and ideas – continued long after Mantegna's departure for Mantua. The subject of Christ's descent into Limbo to rescue the virtuous pagans, immediately after His resurrection,[44] was of particular interest to Mantegna over a period of more than twenty years. As in the case of the Agony in the Garden, the initial compositional idea was probably invented by Mantegna, but we have no clear sense of what this looked like. The subject, like the Agony, was more normally part of a narrative cycle than a free-standing work of art, but it was explored by Jacopo Bellini in each of the British Museum and Louvre albums.[45] It was also one of the predella panels for the Gattamelata altarpiece, that Jacopo Bellini, together with his sons Gentile and Giovanni, painted in 1459–1460.[46] This panel, which has remained in Padua, is horizontal in format, and repeats motifs from both of Jacopo's drawings.

We have no trace of the painting of Christ's Descent into Limbo that Mantegna was commissioned to produce by Lodovico Gonzaga in 1468.[47] It may have been a vertical composition; however, there is no evidence to conclusively prove or disprove its relationship to a drawing which is at least partially by Mantegna, now in the Lehman Collection at the Metropolitan Museum of Art, New York.[48] As Dagmar Korbacher argues, Mantegna may have drawn inspiration for his first depiction of the subject from Donatello as well as Jacopo Bellini.[49] Despite the connections which have been noted with Mantegna's last *Descent into Limbo*, a painting of the early 1490s, an earlier date is more plausible for the drawing because it concentrates on individual motifs rather than on establishing a convincing compositional whole.[50] Some years later, Mantegna embarked on a further version of the Descent into Limbo. A drawing on parchment (Paris, École nationale supérieure des beaux-arts) may reflect Mantegna's earlier painting; it is evidently related to the engraving made in the late 1470s, although the quantity of significant compositional differences suggest it was not made in preparation for it.[51] The existence of the engraving shows Mantegna's pride in his technical and narrative powers of invention. It is a bold composition. Christ is shown in the centre, holding the banner of Resurrection. He is depicted from behind, trampling on the door into hell which lies shattered under his feet. Winged demons blow trumpets and terrify the group of souls, including Adam and Eve, who have just climbed out of their torment in the underworld.[52]

Sometime around 1480, Giovanni Bellini embarked on a painting of the *Descent into Limbo* which is evidently indebted to Mantegna's print. In fact, its underdrawing, which is probably by a studio assistant of Mantegna's, copies it directly.[53] Why did Bellini paint it? It was, for sure, a precious item made for a private patron, who would have appreciated both the high quality of the materials (it is painted on paper, subsequently attached to a panel support), and the source of the invention. But why would Bellini, at this stage in his career an established and respected painter, want to copy his brother-in-law's invention? Imitation is of course the sincerest form of flattery. We know that Bellini knew and admired Mantegna's invention of the Descent into Limbo, as he repeated the rocky foreground of his *Transfiguration* (Venice, Museo Correr).[54] But Bellini had no need to flatter Mantegna. Rather this work may have been carried out in the spirit of a *paragone* between works in one media, although this may have been more the idea of Bellini's patron than the artist himself. The figural elements of the painting follow the underdrawing, based on Mantegna's design. Yet in the landscape, and especially the rocky cliff that houses the door to hell, Bellini has let his imagination and skill run away with him. The outcrops, festooned with ivy and hanging plants, are much more in the manner of Bellini's Uffizi and National Gallery paintings of St Jerome of the 1470s[55] than anything that Mantegna ever painted. Here Bellini is using a direct comparison with the work of his brother-in-law to assert not only his admiration of Mantegna, but also his confidence in the different worth and value of his own work. If Bellini's *Agony in the Garden* is about showing that Bellini is as good as Mantegna, his *Descent into Limbo* hints – at the very least – that Bellini could be better. When Mantegna tackled the subject again, in the early 1490s, probably for a member of the Gonzaga family,[56] he took a different approach. As might be expected from an artist who never made a full-scale copy of any work, Mantegna's last *Descent into Limbo* is radically different to its predecessors. It is equally tiny, but it adopts a cropped, more horizontal format. Here, attention is focused on the figures, highlighting the emotional strength and confidence of Christ, who strides purposefully into the cave where the souls in Limbo are imprisoned. The doors of hell are not beneath his feet: they have completely disappeared due to the power of his wrath. This message that would not have been lost on Mantegna himself, a famously confrontational individual who never balked at the defence of his intellectual property and artistic ideas.[57]

The Presentation of Jesus at the Temple: The Endurance of Admiration

Mantegna's *Presentation of Jesus at the Temple* has been convincingly dated to the middle of the 1450s. This is on stylistic grounds, and because the head of the man at the far right is certainly (on the basis of comparison with the self-portrait in the Ovetari Chapel) Mantegna himself.[58] The woman at the far left, has on the grounds of symmetry and probability, been identified as Nicolosia Bellini. Some writers have gone so far as to identify this picture as the commemoration of a birth; the inference being that this is the child hoped for from the union of Nicolosia and Andrea Mantegna.[59]

Some years later, probably in the 1470s, Giovanni Bellini made a second *Presentation*, which is not merely based on Mantegna's painting, but is a full-scale, accurate tracing of the figures that appear in it.[60] It is still not clear why, after a gap of twenty years, Bellini felt it necessary to make a mechanical copy of his brother-in-law's painting. The painting appears, however, quite different to Mantegna's precedent. Bellini may have made a copy, but he has been unable to reprise the quiet colours and plastic form of Mantegna. The colours are stronger and less subtle, the marble frame has been reduced to a simple parapet, and the figures on the sides of the sacred grouping of Simeon and the Holy Family have been increased from two to four.

Bellini's 'copy' of Mantegna, nonetheless, had an enduring impact on his production as a painter. Two half-length figural compositions, set against a monochrome background, and based on the Presentation at the Temple, were made in substantial quantities by members of the painter's workshop.[61] The first of these compositions also represents the Presentation of the Temple, but here the importance of Christ's body and future sacrifice is underlined by his nakedness. The second is the subsequent story from the New Testament, Christ's circumcision by the High Priest Simeon, following his presentation. Multiple versions of this invention survive, the best of which is the painting in the National Gallery, London (NG 145).[62] Mantegna, who detested repeating himself, never returned to this subject in this form, and only once painted a half-length narrative composition, *The Adoration of the Magi* (Los Angeles, J. Paul Getty Museum).[63]

The essential difference between Mantegna and Bellini, therefore, is revealed in their attitude to copying. For Mantegna, invention and the idea was everything. A painted or drawn copy was not only unnecessary: it was antithetical to his artistic ethos. He could never 'just' repeat a composition; although he could and would vary it, sometimes – as we have seen – in response to the creative stimulus of his brother-in-law's work. The proper medium for repetition was not painting, or drawing, but printmaking, which Mantegna did so much to develop. Not only did this enable the spread of Mantegna's ideas, it also meant that the artist, who retained the plate from which prints were made, maintained total control. Bellini, on the other hand, could enhance his reputation by multiplying and repeating his pictorial ideas, so that they became better known. Not only did this enhance the devotional power of his work,[64] it was also commercially astute, and a sensible approach for a painter active in a Republic rather than a princely court, with a varied and more volatile client base, and more threatening competition from other painters. If Mantegna's genius lay in the uniqueness of his painted ideas, that of Bellini lay – at least in part – in the power and value of repetition.

[1] I am grateful to Giovanni Villa and Neville Rowley for their advice and suggestions; and to Mariagusta Lazzari, Giovanni Villa, Brigit Blass-Simmen, Neville Rowley and Babet Trevisan for inviting my collaboration in this project.

[2] Longhi 1949 [1978], p. 102.

[3] For a summary of this, see Christiansen 2004a, pp. 52–53; Lucco 2008, pp. 20–24; Maze 2017, pp. 37–56; De Marchi 2018 (forthcoming). For a clear explanation of why this matters, see Villa, in this volume, and Rowley in London-Berlin 2018.

[4] Fletcher 2004, pp. 26, 42.

[5] For a summary, see Campbell 2018 (forthcoming).

[6] See Barausse 2008, no. 14, p. 334, for the granting of a dowry for Nicolosia Bellini from the Scuola grande di San Giovanni Evangelista.

[7] Jacopo Bellini had long had contacts with Padua. For his first documented work in Padua, of 1430, see most recently Blass-Simmen 2017, p. 15.

[8] M. Tanzi in Paris 2008, p. 179.

[9] For a good summary see De Marchi 2018 (forthcoming).
[10] For the contentious San Giovanni Evangelista paintings, see Hammond 2016 and Mazzotta 2018 (forthcoming). I agree with Mazzotta's identification of Giovanni Bellini's hand in the faces of St Anne's attendants in *The Birth of the Virgin* (Turin, Galleria Sabauda).
[11] See Gentili 2004, pp. 167–168; Los Angeles 2017, cat. 1 (entry written by Davide Gasparotto), pp. 58–63.
[12] Marcantonio Michiel recorded that the altarpiece was inscribed with the names of three members of the Bellini family. The date of the inscription, transcribed in the sixteenth century as 1409 has generally been agreed to be a mistake, and the real date should be 1459. See Boskovits, Brown 2003, p. 18, n. 17. For a recent summary of the Bellini family's work in the Gattemelata chapel, see Blake-McHam 2017, pp. 37–38.
[13] See Gasparotto 2017.
[14] Cited by M. Lucco in Rome 2008, cat. 2, pp. 136–138.
[15] A. Galli in Paris 2008, cat. 7, pp. 72–74.
[16] A. Galli in Paris 2008, cat. 6, pp. 70–72.
[17] M. Lucco in Rome 2008, cat. 2, p. 138.
[18] Ibid.
[19] I am very grateful to Neville Rowley for this observation (written communication).
[20] Rowley correctly observes that some apparently 'Squarcionesque' motifs are first found in the work of Mantegna and Pizzolo, following the example of Donatello. I am grateful to Neville Rowley for this.
[21] This section of my text is indebted to discussions with Jill Dunkerton, Marika Spring, Rachel Billinge and Gabriele Finaldi.
[22] Davies 1961, pp. 58–60; 335–38 (who gives references to all the literature on both paintings to this date); Dunkerton *et al.* 1991, pp. 292–295; Andrea De Marchi in Paris 2008–2009, cat. 48, pp. 158–159.
[23] Davies 1961, pp. 335–338; Vickers 1976; Faietti 2014; De Marchi 2008, p. 155.
[24] Davies 1961, pp. 58–60; Dunkerton *et al.* 1991, pp. 294–295; Christiansen 2004a, pp. 58–59; Bellosi 2008, p. 106.
[25] As well as the references cited in note 21 above, also see Lucco in Rome 2008, p. 25; Gasparotto 2017, p. 15; Campbell 2018 (forthcoming).
[26] See Dunkerton, Hartwieg 2018 (forthcoming) and Dunkerton *et al.* 2018 (forthcoming).
[27] Jacopo Bellini, Sketchbook (British Museum), 1855,0811.41 v. and 1855,0811.43 r. Jacopo Bellini, Sketchbook (Musée du Louvre), *St Jerome in the Wilderness*, fol. 18v. and *St Christopher*, fols. 21r and 51v. See Paris 2008, p. 158 and London-New York 1992, cat. 8.
[28] Paris 2008, cat. 50, pp. 162–163 .
[29] A. De Marchi in Paris 2008, p. 159.
[30] See Blass-Simmen 2017, pp. 4, 9.
[31] Vickers 1976. For an excellent summary of the scholarship on this subject, see Faietti 2014.
[32] Faietti 2014, p. 129.
[33] Vickers 1976.
[34] Casu 2004, p. 10
[35] A. De Marchi in Paris 2008, p. 159.
[36] Ibid., p. 164.
[37] A. De Marchi, in Paris 2008, p. 159.
[38] Ibid., p. 164.
[39] Ibid., pp. 164–167, nos. 51–53.
[40] Mantegna was in Mantua by the 21 June 1460. For the first documentary evidence of Mantegna in Mantua, see Dall'Acqua 1980, p. 310. Dating of the *Agony* has conventionally been to the early 1460s. See Dunkerton *et al.* 1991, p. 292; also, for a summary, M. Lucco in Rome 2008, p. 25, and further references thereof.
[41] See essay by Dunkerton, Hartwieg in 2018 (forthcoming).
[42] Ibid.
[43] "Di sempre vagare a sua voglia nelle pitture." See Barausse 2008, doc. 99, p. 352 (letter of Pietro Bembo to Isabella d'Este, from Venice, 11 January 1506, Gregorian calendar.
[44] The subject, not found in the *New Testament*, was an established element of Christian doctrine by the fifteenth century.
[45] Jacopo Bellini Paris album, fol. 21 v; Jacopo Bellini, London album, fols. 25 v. and 26.
[46] See Blake-McHam 2017, pp. 37–38.
[47] "[Q]uadro dove fo la instoria del linbo," in a letter from Mantegna to Ludovico of 28 June 1468. See Kristeller 1902, p. 525, doc. 40, and David Ekserdjian in London-New York 1992, pp. 258–259.
[48] D. Ekserdjian in London-New York 1992, cat. 66, pp. 261–263.
[49] D. Korbacher in London-Berlin 2018 (forthcoming); where she argues that Mantegna could have seen Donatello's bronze relief of the Descent into Limbo for the pulpit of San Lorenzo, Florence on his visit to the city in 1466.
[50] D. Korbacher in London-Berlin 2018 (forthcoming); D. Ekserdjian in London-New York 1992, cat. 65, p. 261.
[51] Paris 2008, cat. 68, pp. 196–198.
[52] D. Landau in London-New York 1992, cat. 67 and 67 b, pp. 263–265.
[53] See essay by Neville Rowley in this volume; also Dunkerton, Hartwieg 2018 (forthcoming).
[54] This was recorded by M. Lucco in Rome 2008, cat. 6, p. 150, and M. Servi in Paris 2008 (citing an observation by Antonio Mazzotta).
[55] See Gentili 2004, pp. 168–172; Belting 2017; Los Angeles 2017, cats. 7 (written by Antonio Mazzotta) and 12 (written by Susannah Rutherglen), pp. 92–97, 126–130.
[56] K. Christiansen in London-New York 1992, p. 271.
[57] D. Landau in London-New York 1992, pp. 48–51.
[58] See Rowley 2018 (forthcoming), where this idea is developed more fully.
[59] See Villa 2017, p. 82.
[60] See essay by B. Hartwieg in this volume.
[61] For the versions of the two subjects by Bellini and his followers, see Heinemann 1962, I, pp. 41–44.
[62] See Davies 1961, pp. 68–70.
[63] In the early twentieth century, some writers considered that the Getty painting was the pendant of the Berlin *Presentation of Jesus at the Temple*; for others of this period it was a copy. For an excellent account of this, see K. Christiansen in London-New York 1992, cat. 56, p. 237. For the fullest single publication on the painting see Carr 1997.
[64] For stimulating analyses of Bellini's devotional art, see Goffen 1989, especially pp. 23–24 and Christiansen 2004.

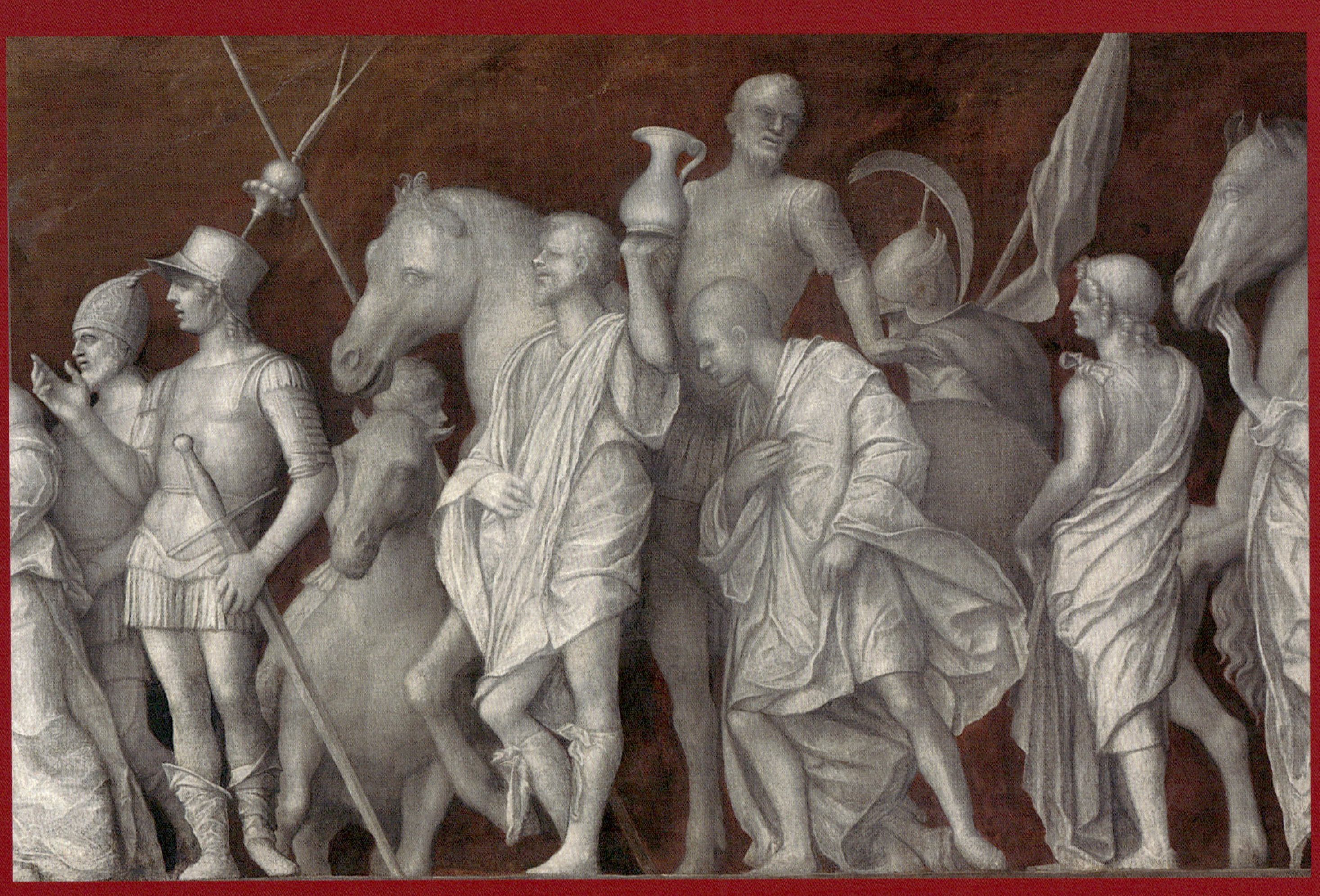

Andrea Mantegna and Giovanni Bellini. *Presentations* in Dialogue

GIOVANNI C.F. VILLA

When the time came for the purification rites required by the Law of Moses, Joseph and Mary took him to Jerusalem to present him to the Lord (as it is written in the Law of the Lord, "Every firstborn male is to be consecrated to the Lord," and to offer a sacrifice in keeping with what is said in the Law of the Lord: "a pair of doves or two young pigeons." Now there was a man in Jerusalem called Simeon, who was righteous and devout. He was waiting for the consolation of Israel, and the Holy Spirit was on him. It had been revealed to him by the Holy Spirit that he would not die before he had seen the Lord's Messiah. Moved by the Spirit, he went into the temple courts. When the parents brought in the child Jesus to do for him what the custom of the Law required, Simeon took him in his arms and praised God, saying: "Sovereign Lord, as you have promised, you may now dismiss your servant in peace. For my eyes have seen your salvation, which you have prepared in the sight of all nations: a light for revelation to the Gentiles, and the glory of your people Israel." The child's father and mother marveled at what was said about him. Then Simeon blessed them and said to Mary, his mother: "This child is destined to cause the falling and rising of many in Israel, and to be a sign that will be spoken against, so that the thoughts of many hearts will be revealed. And a sword will pierce your own soul to."

1. Giovanni Bellini, *The Continence of Scipio*, detail. Washington, D.C., National Gallery of Art

This passage from the Gospel of Luke (2: 22-35) is at the basis of one of the most engaging dialogues in the history of art and is also apparent in the debate that has divided historians for over a century: the relationship between Andrea Mantegna (1431-1506) and Giovanni Bellini (1438/40-1516), substantiated by the iconographic subject taken from the text, the *Presentation of Jesus at the Temple* by the former, now at the Gemäldegalerie in Berlin, and the Venetian *Presentation of Jesus at the Temple* by Giovanni Bellini.[1] "Scolpì in pittura propria viva et vera"[2] (he sculpted in real and living paint): the sonnet by Ulisse (degli Aleotti?) conveys a profound picture of the sense of Mantegna's art, which can easily be associated with the action in the *Presentation*, arranged like a classical bas-relief transformed into painting, with the figures enclosed in autonomous isolation, the gestures reduced to the narrative essence, the composition built upon a precise hierarchy of characters. The scene is painted on very thin linen canvas, with the dark background serving to profile the figures and give them sculptural relief, surrounded by mixed marble with antique veins – white, pink and green – that frame them rhetorically and from a strictly central perspective, only partially separating them from the space of the believer. The marble cornice, which acts as a formal threshold between the real and the pictorial space, is interpreted as a specific illusion of continuity between the two fields, crossed by the Virgin's elbow that rests on the window-

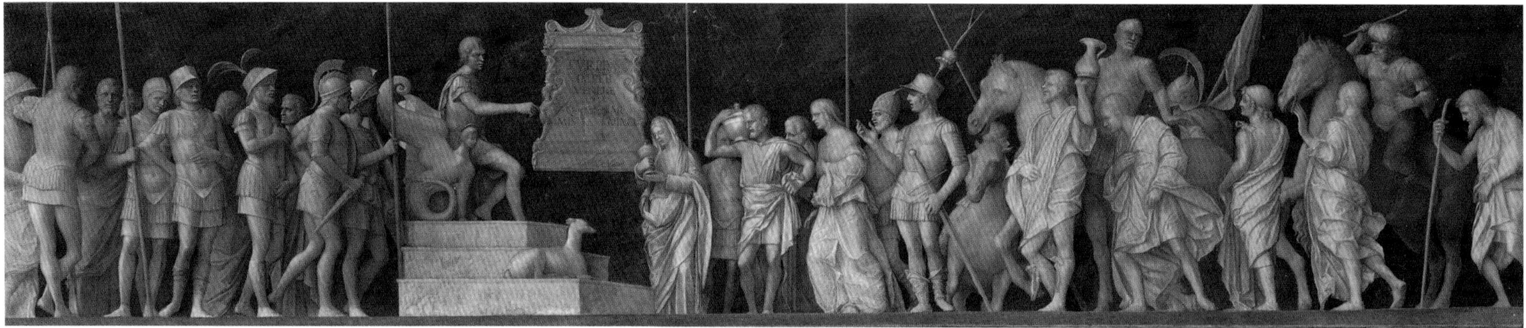

2. Giovanni Bellini, *The Continence of Scipio*. Washington, D.C., National Gallery of Art

sill, almost as if to measure the depth of the space and support the swaddled Christ Child – taken from an altar relief by Donatello in Sant'Antonio and transformed into a column here – upright on a rich velvet cushion of honour. With its lavish gold and pearl tassel, this cushion also seems to protrude from the picture and enter our space, as does the left hand of the high priest Simeon, ready to support the weight of the Child. It is a canvas in which the extremely delicate hues of colour, accompanied by the light arriving from the left, defines the figures in a fiercely descriptive manner, with every detail individually sculpted. We therefore admire the robes of the highly elegant Virgin in dark velvet brocade interwoven with gold and the stiff, heavy cloak of Simeon, a "voided" velvet that "appears to be engraved in the pile of the velvet", evoking the motifs of the "gratings" that embellished windows and doors. The horizontal decorative theme, comprised of sequences of polylobate corollas containing pomegranates, pine cones or cardoons,[3] is enhanced by a masterful use of light that allows Mantegna the virtuosity of the swaddling of the Child, all orchestrated on opaque whites that change into the greys of the areas of shadow. Three other figures stand out against the indistinct background: Joseph in the centre, a formal and severe observer of the act, aware of the funereal announcement of the elderly priest; on opposite sides, a man and a woman, both turned to the left, looking towards an undefined point. They are the result of a later addition, as demonstrated by the X-rays carried out on the work,[4] and an inclusion able to offer a plausible approach to dating the work: 1454, in keeping with the style of the *St Luke Polyptych* for Santa Giustina in Padua,[5] and around the time of the marriage between Mantegna and Nicolosia Bellini, as noted by Wolfgang Prinz on the basis of Giovanni de Lazara and Wilhelm Bode.[6] This very convincing theory seems to be supported by the male portrait with the image that Andrea painted of himself several times, starting with his self-portrait in the Ovetari Chapel, and consequently making it possible to link it to that of his wife, with the canvas conceived as a votive image, perhaps to give thanks for the safe delivery of the couple's first child.

It is a substantially faithful representation of the religious text and an archetypal model for the dramatic close-up in Venetian art. However, despite its compactness and solemnity, the work also highlights Bellinian instances in details such as the overlapping of the Mother and Child's faces,[7] a feature close to the style of Jacopo adopted by Giovanni who, starting with a highly taut line, provided a decidedly antithetical interpretation of the theme almost twenty years later, despite preserving the same composition, copied exactly from the cartoon of Mantegna's painting, as so sharply conjectured in this book by Brigit Blass-Simmen. While the spontaneous question arises as to why Giovanni Bellini used a subject painted by his brother-in-law of some years now, we firstly need to explore the fundamental common denominator: Jacopo Bellini, father-in-law of one and father of the other, whose papers – now in the *Sketchbooks* in the Louvre and the British Museum – offer a direct account of the original transformation in Venetian painting, which took place in the 1430s. At the time everything revolved around three recently established painting workshops: those run by Francesco Squarcione, Antonio Vivarini and Jacopo Bellini. Their management, sometimes family-run, would go on to influence the protagonists of a high-impact generational experience: Andrea Mantegna, the brilliant and very young pupil of Squarcione, who went on to become the son-in-law of Jacopo, his brothers-in-law Gentile and Giovanni Bellini, and the more compact Vivarini family. Jacopo Bellini's activity made him a central figure in the run-up to the Renaissance, partly because of his interest in archaeology and his erudite exploration of Roman epigraphy, as demonstrated by his notebooks, precisely at a time when activity was intensifying in the humanist courts and a passion for antiquity was spreading across the Veneto region. From the middle of the century onwards, the Bellini family's Venetian workshop became an innovative reference point on the city's art scene. Jacopo succeeded in combining the best teachings of the international language of his early teacher Gentile da Fabriano with the perspective developments of the Tuscan, or Florentine avant-garde and the innovations introduced by the febrile group working around Squarcione, while borrowing all Donatello's new developments and his re-reading of antiquity and Tuscan chiaroscuro. Forging a close bond, united by family, with his son-in-law Andrea Mantegna – in the clear yet deluded intention of creating an absolutely exceptional workshop – Jacopo could not do otherwise than educate his children and drive them in technical and stylistically open directions. And it would be Mantegna, firstly in Verona and then definitively in Mantua, to dictate the developments of the discourse initiated in Padua, in an intellectual relationship with Donatello that immediately led to highly effective linguistic autonomy. Despite making his debut among the horde of Francesco Squarcione's one hundred and thirty-seven "sons",[8] Andrea soon worked himself free, becoming an artist much loved by scholars and strongly influenced by the literary elite of the university-city of Patavium, which boasted of and gloried in its Roman vestiges, with a revival of interest in its son Livy and with a temperament that cannot even have escaped the painter who, centuries later, was celebrated in the city's temple of fame, the elliptical square of Prato della Valle, "portrayed completely in the nude, in the Greek style, denoting in this way the extent to which the marvellous value of his art has drawn near to the taste and sublime genius of Greek masters, singularly in painting."[9] A citywide cultural humus of great inspiration for the *enfant prodige*, which he added to everything he learned in the master's studio, abundant in drawings and reliefs so that the education for the pupils ranged from portraying life to modulating tones by observing sculpture, in accordance with an accepted manner of learning primarily based on Alberti and so masterfully described by Roberto Longhi:

> However fanciful it might seem, I profoundly sense that everything that happened between Padua, Ferrara and Venice between the 1950s and 1970s - from the ferocious passions of [Cosmè] Tura and [Carlo] Crivelli to the dolorous elegance of the young Bellini, to the apparently rigorous grammar of the Mantegnesque - had its origins in that brigade of vagabond sons of tailors, barbers, shoemakers, and peasants, that passed through the studio of Squarcione in those twenty years. Really, an indescribable studio, or only to be imagined by the hand of a painter along the lines of de Chirico – in a vespertine and menacing little painting where decapitated classical busts can be seen holding up the twisted mouldings ready for the made-to-measure triptychs for the bishops of the Polesine; Florentine plaquettes serving as trays for the odd ounce of German azurite; the little Chinese carpets ferocious with monsters beside the rolls of dagged cloth thrown there by Squarcione, 'tailor and embroidere'; and some panel of refined Nordic rendering placed like a miracle close to a Tuscan foreshortening *per figura de isomatria* or to a shield with crest painted for some petty lord from the country nearby. Here and there, thinly scattered, is the pale powder of recent plaster casts and, going on all day, the tumultuous and ironical visits of Donatello's workers.[10]

This is the context within which Mantegna grew up and trained, before his life became intertwined with that of Bellini. As we know from an important receipt, issued by the Scuola Grande of San Giovanni Evangelista, when a Francesco *de Lorenzo* received twenty ducats: "Io Francesco de Lorenzo strazariol ò reziudo adì 25 de febraro 1453 ducari vinti per nome di ser Iachomo Belin depintor per sovinzion del maridare di Nicholoxa sua fia."[11] Therefore Jacopo, a brother at the Scuola Grande since 1437, obtained twenty ducats for the marriage of his daughter. These were grants, also known as *grazie*, given to girls by confraternities: the income from bequests were used to provide girls in need with a dowry for marriage or to help them enter a nunnery, but they also provided a contribution for brothers who were not in need. Nicolosia was no more than twenty-three years old at the time if she was the eldest child, or around twenty years old if not. Hers was to be a long marriage, far from the city where she was born, spent almost entirely on the margins of the highly erudite court of Mantua, where her husband was the artist, decorator and, even more so, the advisor to the duke for all art-related matters. We can only imagine the relationship between the brothers-in-law and brothers: there are no documents revealing their affection and familiarity with one another. Only their works speak for them, to those who want to interpret them as sentimental expressions, as well as indications of style, technique and iconographical construction.

The *Presentation* composed by Andrea Mantegna seems to owe a major debt, in the close-up canonized by Sixten Ringbom,[12] to a model borrowed from the sheet 53 in Jacopo Bellini's *Libro* and now in Paris: a *Lamentation over the Dead Christ* in which the holy characters emerge from a sarcophagus, portrayed as half-busts. In the evanescent silverpoint lines, partly gone over in ink, we can recognize an exceptionally important composition, a starting point for exemplary works by Giovanni Bellini, Antonello da Messina and Mantegna, from which the idea of overlapping the face of the Virgin with that of the Child derived. Bellini draws an iconographical arrangement from this *Lamentation*, and from the *Presentation of Jesus at the Temple* by his brother-in-law, while making radical changes to it in the key elements of the composition, so as to focus on the emotional aspects of the image. In the place of the marble frame around the scene, we see a cropped antique green breccia parapet, separating us from it, constructed so as to elongate the field horizontally and enable the painter to include two additional figures, at opposite ends of the composition, creating an original sentimental proximity formed of gestures, gazes and the affectionate sweetness that inevitably involves a group of people around a baby. An emotive logic coordinated by a light that differs significantly from that used by Mantegna, oriented towards a perspectival two-dimensionality that intones the flesh of the figures, with Bellini instead working towards precise three-dimensional analysis rendered with chiaroscuro. This enables us to perceive the innovation of this approach, with its softened colours and focus on sentiments that are alien to the severe austerity of Mantegna's piece, with the format becoming the starting point for the birth of that half-figure *sacra conversazione* that went on to be such a success in Venetian art. Here it is arranged according to heterodox rules of composition: the unpainted space plays a considerable role, with the shadows creating a void above the heads that suspends the intertwined gazes in an eternal and silent time. The Child looks towards the undefined horizon without anyone looking directly at him, adding sacral longevity to a moment that would otherwise be lost within an everyday ritual. But the ritual is present and absolute: the process of handing over a Child, wrapped in swaddling bands, with a foreboding of what is to come. At the same time, Bellini dissolves the still and motionless tone of Mantegna's characters through his flowing atmospheric modulation, with the light defining an extremely soft pictorial ensemble accompanied by the rendering of fabrics, with the striking crimson velvet interwoven with gold thread worn by the priest, "'the two-pile' 'brocade', enriched with '*allucciolature*', or rather loops obtained using additional gold thread that embellished the fabric thanks

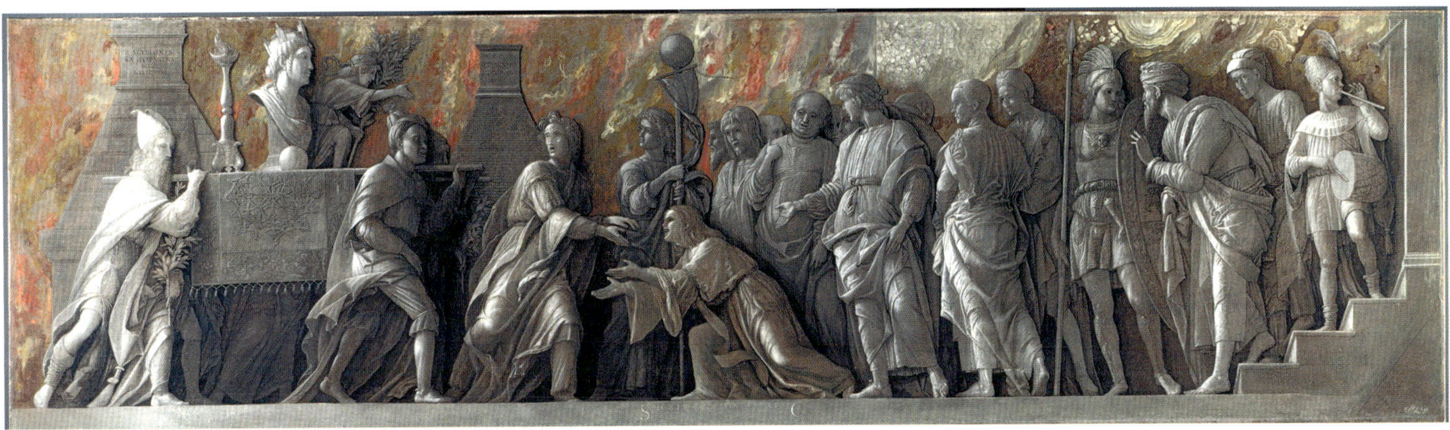

3. Andrea Mantegna, *Introduction of the Cult of Cybele at Rome.* London, The National Gallery

to their bright sparkle and also offered a contrasting texture against the gold brocade background, whose threads can be seen clearly in the painting. The decorative motif is that of the '*griccia*', a pattern comprised of a thick sinuous trunk decorated with Oriental, Persian and Indian-inspired motifs, interrupted by a polylobate corolla within which is the image of a pomegranate or a stylized cardoon", as Isabella Campagnol so well describes it.[13]

But how does the perceptive sensation of Bellini's work change on a communicative level, thereby also significantly varying the proportions of the composition measurements? By developing what is expressed in the *Agony in the Garden* at the National Gallery in London, completed in around 1470 and therefore at least a decade after the same subject painted by Mantegna, it becomes apparent that Bellini prefers to extend the narrative in a horizontal direction, giving it greater spatial breadth for a slower and more extensive interpretation. In an alteration of Mantegna's composition that does not entail any loss of concentration, the visual perception is skilfully kept within the confines of the work with the addition of two figures and a frame: the young man on the right controls and closes the scene, inviting us to look upon it intensely, while the woman on the left checks the potential flight of our and other painted gazes, redirecting them back to the centre. These expert revisions are also accompanied on a structural level: Bellini substantially respects his brother-in-law's golden section, replacing the firm composition offered by Mantegna's marble frame with new geometric relationships between the parts, raising the horizontal line of the parapet so that it forms the base of a new golden rectangle, whose top marks the upper limit of the figures. While, in Mantegna's work, we are enclosed within a world delimited by a sign that becomes a sculpted narrative, unalterable over time, Bellini creates a suspension and an iconic fascination in the message channelled by the warm and enveloping colour, whose light reflects the expert geometric proportions.

Two compositions with a slow and suspended pace, achieved by means of different visual codes, in a perceptive logic of reading time that can be linked to the specific style of the two artists. With Mantegna, the brush becomes the diamond tip for chiselling out the composition of the volumes, step by step. We proceed cautiously and carefully, from contour to contour, won over by the specificity of the forms that leave no room for doubt. Forms of stone, veils, velvets, gestures and gazes, whose invincible substance captures us and holds us there. In Bellini, the brush instead caresses the canvases, reaching out to create soft surfaces, accompanying the gaze between one coloured confine and the next. Our interpretation is more casual, welcomed initially by a coloured light that draws us in and decants itself in forms that reveal themselves softly in all their importance.

We have mentioned that Bellini's version contains more figures than the prototype, a condition followed by significant changes to the physiognomic features of the secondary characters: while the features of the young woman behind the Virgin have remained almost unchanged, the boy on the right is evidently different from the one painted by Mantegna, while the other young man and the older woman seem to be Bellini's invention. Critics have studied these new characters, who are not included in the religious text, in great depth, primarily focusing on the extended Bellini family. According to one theory,[14] which is no longer accepted today, the four characters at the sides, starting from the right, are Giovanni and Gentile Bellini; Jacopo Bellini appears in the character of Joseph or the priest; then we have Ginevra Bocheta, wife of Giovanni or the sister Nicolosia Bellini and, lastly, Anna Rinversi, Jacopo's wife. An identification partly linked to somatic features, which are really the outcome of various embellishments due to restoration work over the years, such as to give dark and intriguing characteristics to Giovanni's presumed self-portrait. This may be the work of the very respectable and painstaking Paolo Fabris, painter and professor of restoration at the Accademia di Venezia, who was not as famous as his elder brother Placido Fabris, copyist of ancient fifteenth and sixteenth-century pieces in the mid-nineteenth century, but was known for specializing in the restoration of Renaissance works, with masterpieces by Bellini, Giorgione and Titian spending time in his studio. We should also not forget how, in February 1949, additional restoration work was carried out by Mauro Pelliccioli. One of these interventions was responsible for ample changes to the features of the first figure on the right – which Robertson was the first to suggest may be a self-portrait of Giovanni Bellini[15] – with his plentiful tousled locks, his intense gaze directed at the viewer and his dark curled eyebrows and lips. His features are therefore the result of subsequent additions and are totally discordant with the rest of the paint application. This is highlighted by the profound difference between this man and the only definite image we have of Giovanni, that is to say the medal by Vittore Gambello. Therefore, as things currently stand, no identification theory can be deemed to be credible.

As this work is undated and unsigned – so much so that even the attribution to Giovanni Bellini has been thrown into question for many years – art historians have racked their brains trying to pinpoint the exact relationship between the two versions of the *Presentation*, in an attempt to establish which is the original and which is the copy.

The starting point has to be the collecting history of the works and the chronology of the two paintings.

Mantegna's thin linen canvas – plausibly once mounted on two wooden panels fitted into the frame – entered the Solly collection in 1821 and can credibly be identified with the "panel picture of Our Lady who presents the Child for circumcision was by the hand of Mantegna, and is in half figures," recorded by Marcantonio Michiel,[16] in around 1525 or a little later, in the Paduan collection of Pietro Bembo. The cardinal's home then came into the possession of the Gradenigo family and the painting is described as being in this collection by Giovanni de' Lazara, in great detail, in a letter dated 9 March 1803,[17] the year the Gradenigo family sold it.

Bellini's work, cited since 1844 in the inventory of the collection of Count Giovanni Querini Stampalia – with Merkel theorizing that it could already be found in 1552 among the assets listed in the inventory of Francesco Querini[18] - was attributed to Mantegna in the early nineteenth century, following the indications of the italic writing "Andrea Mantegna" legible on the back of the panel, together with the letters "M R N S", the meaning of which is currently unknown, before being mentioned by Bonsignori in the legal inventory of 1869. The first to raise the question of its status was Giovanni Morelli,[19] initially judging the Venetian panel to be a "reproduction" of the Mantegna in Berlin, a later autograph copy painted in the last decade of the fifteenth century, before going on to deem it an original by the master and linking it to the painting recorded by Marcantonio Michiel.[20] This theory was accepted for some time – and ultimately only upheld by Anderson[21] – but Kristeller soon refuted it unequivocally, dating the Berlin canvas to around 1456 and identifying the Querini Stampalia panel as a weak later copy.[22] Berenson was the first to claim that the Berlin masterpiece "must have profoundly impressed Giovanni Bellini, for it would seem as if he made a version or it - or at least had it made under his own eye - which is still to be seen,"[23] that is to say the Querini painting. Since then, the attribution to Bellini has become almost unanimous.[24]

When exploring the chronology for Mantegna in detail, on the basis of the style of the Berlin canvas, it does not seem possible to imagine a link with his stay in Mantua but, instead, a chronology of around 1453–1455, with which most critics seem to agree today.[25] Meanwhile, the dates for Bellini fluctuate significantly, varying from c. 1455 as proposed by Coletti (1953) to the late 1470s suggested by Robertson (1968).[26] The thinking of Roberto Longhi is emblematic of the debate and assessment of the relationship between the brothers-in-law.[27] Agreeing with Fiocco regarding Bellini's date of birth before that of his brother-in-law,[28] he insinuated that the paintings were produced at around the same time in 1465 and attributed Giovanni with having come up with the idea, thereby radically changing his mind compared to his earlier opinion (1949), when he dated it to c. 1475.[29] The latter is the most appropriate date for the work, if associated with texts datable to that same period, first and foremost those regarding the Pesaro altarpiece. In it we find the same physiognomic models, from the head of the Madonna that is replicated in that of the crowned Virgin, to the young man on the right near the crowning Christ and the priest Simeon when compared to St Jerome in the altarpiece. There is also a close resemblance in the chromatic rendering and decoration of the fabrics and, particularly, on the basis of what we are able to read today beneath the paint layer, in the underdrawing that distinguishes the experimental and instinctive temperament of Giovanni Bellini, who based his very fine pictorial art on drawing. Indeed, it is in the flesh tones of the Querini Stampalia panel, now revealed by restoration work, that the naked eye can identify the graphic sign of that period: short, hard and cutting strokes, defining a diagonal and parallel hatching in the definition of faces and figures that are then softened by modulating the paint layer or describe the decoration of the cope, with streaks of gold luminescence. A plastic and structural design that shows, in certain details, a conceptual independence and research oriented towards the greatest possible empathy between the holy characters. In this sense, it is significant to note Bellini's first arrangement conceived for the mute dialogue between the Virgin and Simeon, comprised of an exchange of glances designed with a very different look from the end result: the Virgin's eyelids appeared more open, her gaze directed at the priest was mild and fully aware, and not intimately collected and humble as it appears in the painted version. The priest responded to this look with a more severe countenance, which looked more like a frown in the drawing.

Under infrared light this drawing is almost evanescent, perhaps traced out with an iron gall ink or with a highly diluted carbon component, so that it is more perceptible to the eye than to instruments. What is more, the underdrawing reveals a significant matrix, perfectly placeable within Giovanni Bellini's work between the 1460s and 1470s. While the X-ray and infrared reflectography campaigns only revealed a minor alteration regarding the outline of Simeon's head, they certainly backed up the theory that it was transferred from a cartoon via engraving, as shown in the X-ray analysis, which reveals clear traces of this in the central part. What is more, the perfectly matching composition of Bellini and Mantegna's works presupposes the use of a cartoon based on the Paduan prototype. This fact may be useful in confirming the date of the painting by Mantegna. If it was a votive painting to celebrate the birth of his first son, it may have been painted in Venice and remained in the Bellini workshop for some time, giving Giovanni time to capture the finished image in a cartoon. As the analyses conducted on the Berlin painting have revealed various alterations made during the painting process, particularly to the face of the Virgin – which is higher and with a foreshortened halo – and in Simeon – his head bare, his ear visible, and with a large collar – this emphasizes how the chromatic and compositional arrangement must have been even more accentuated by the foreshortened haloes, then eliminated following the inclusion of the two secondary figures. Meanwhile, infrared reflectography reveals the widespread and subtle brushstrokes of white lead to heighten the areas of light and shade, particularly on the faces of the Mother and Child, as well as a mark left by a thick brush, going right around various alterations, in a work in which the underdrawing appears less fine and accurate than the one that can be observed in later works by Mantegna. This use of a mechanical drawing alongside freehand sketching and shading is typical, according to analyses carried out to date, of Mantegna's work until the end of the 1470s.[30] After that, his pure outlines painted with a brush are rarely accompanied by significant variants, as demonstrated by reflectography analyses. Due to the accuracy of the lines, this often means they were transferred from paper in some way. The traces are sometimes apparent to the naked eye, particularly where they are barely concealed by thin expanses of red lacquer – as in some of the clothes of those portrayed – but transparent under infrared light, yet another symptom of the use of iron gall inks or very pale grey inks. In the case of the canvases, wear and later repainting sometimes complicate the interpretation of the analytical results.

While Giovanni Bellini made innovation and the ongoing discovery of technical solutions the common thread of an extraordinary career, by remaining iconographically steadfast in the substantial involvement of a few inventively varied subjects – Virgins and Child, Pietà, Crucifixions – Mantegna moved in the opposite direction. In fact, the creative power of his genius was exceptional, boundless and certainly unparalleled at the time, producing works calibrated to perfection right from the outset, with a technical evolution that – all summed up – changed very little over the course of his career, so that Berenson's words are still topical, even if directed at the side of practice: "Mantegna's art meets our eye from its first beginning, like Minerva, all armed. In a duration of nearly sixty years it suffered singularly little change, so little in form, contour or even type, that it requires careful and cautious scrutiny to perceive its evolution, although there was, it is true, a development in colour to warmer and warmer, ending rather hot."[31] Mantegna is therefore the skilful interpreter of a world of such descriptive precision, boundless invention, crystalline isometry and sagacious lyricism that he has enchanted artists for centuries, even acting as a model for Degas, Delaunay and Matisse, and has disconcerted exegetes, who have found it difficult to define his style. From the quarry of personal fantasy and antique archaeology, accompanied by literary suggestions, images emerge that combine sculptural rigidity and rigour with the moving fragility of infancy and maternity, and of death, all intimately participated in, with Mantegna who in his art "has only put everything he knew, but also that which he most profoundly was: a complete man, in his hardness and his sensibility, like a stone capable of shedding tears."[32] In a rarely seen combination of technique and style, scientific analysis clings to a specific redefinition of the chronology of works whose position in time has always divided critics.

Meanwhile, the development of Giovanni Bellini is the complete opposite. Studies I have carried out personally using infrared reflectography – covering around one hundred and thirty autograph works, reported on in depth in various publications together with Gianluca Poldi[33] – have made it possible to reveal the depth and the incessant research and development of his painting and, above all, the extent to which it depends on the invisible drawing, which was necessary in practical terms during the years of passage from the use of tempera bonding agent to mixed media, resulting from the introduction of oil into the mixtures. While tempera was applied with small brushstrokes, producing parallel marks whose superimposition formed tones and chiaroscuro effects, the long period of transition to the oil bonding agent, albeit never used exclusively, is marked by experimentation with a graphic technique that established a chiaroscuro sub-model. In his works from the 1460s, Giovanni faithfully followed the teachings of his father, using rigid brushstrokes and pure outlines to define the forms. Later, between the end of that decade and the mid-1480s, he applied a skin-deep design on top of the ground and any primer, using very tidy, short and diagonal lines, which played upon ranges of intensity, overlapping or otherwise, within a contour line defined by a dark, segmented line, made using a thicker brush, sometimes truncated so as to gradually recalibrate the intensity of the shapes. A ductile hatched monochrome designed to achieve the schematic partition of the planes of light and the volumes of the figures that, added to the pictorial hatching, establishes volume and shadow, particularly in the flesh tones, while also working on the basis of differentiated chromatic backgrounds. As he headed towards maturity, Bellini thinned out this contour line, thickening the graphic hatching, produced with a finer and finer brush beneath a painted surface that was now enamelled and translucent. By the 1490s, the shapes of the images had become cursive, no longer articulated in individual brushstrokes linked the one to the other, with the hand running freely over the primer so that the brush is supported by the ink; at the same time, the modular chiaroscuro hatching thins out to the point of disappearing when, towards the end of the century, firstly with a brush and then in charcoal or by means of pure engraving, only the loadbearing lines of the composition and the figurative groups are marked, now allowing his total command of colour to give life to the forms.[34] As a result, figures, architecture, landscapes and details become progressively more synthetic, with less of a chiaroscuro effect, now producing painting of pure tonalism.

This development marks out Giovanni as one of the most formidable experimenters, on a technical level, that western art has produced in its centuries-old history and also offers important markers regarding the assessment of the materials on paper variously attributed to him. Despite considering the particular statute of the underdrawing, instrumental to being covered by colour but firstly certainly admired by the patron and the workshop – significant investigations carried out on many pupils and contemporaries of Bellini, inspired to adopt his technique during the years that they attended his lessons, offer us a further element of chronological reconstruction where they have dated his paintings – as in the case of the *Lamentation over the Dead Christ* in the Uffizi,[35] which was left as an underdrawing, this makes it possible to have precise indications regarding the graphic hand of Bellini. This offers an additional critical idea to the age-old debate regarding Bellini as a draughtsman, who was so closely tied to the graphic work of Andrea Mantegna that there are still disputes regarding many works today as to whether they were produced by the Venetian or his brother-in-law, making it possible to discuss the question of graphic proofs that have been divided, merged and re-merged between the two catalogues.[36] The consideration made by Lorenzo da Pavia in 1504, when addressing Isabella d'Este, still remains highly topical today: "in invention there are none to rival Messer Andrea Mantegna who excels in this and leads the field, but Giovan Belino is excellent in colouring."[37]

In the first instance, Bellini's *Presentation of Jesus at the Temple* is an intense tribute to the Paduan lesson imparted by Donatello – at the start of his quest for the affectionate intimacy of his compositions with their deep-rooted Byzantine culture – and then to Mantegna, who is to be attributed with having come up with the original composition in his Berlin canvas. It is a striking example, in terms of textual deduction and radical transformation, of a dialogue between brothers-in-law that represented an undercurrent in their work right up to the end of their careers. This concluded dramatically with the pair of friezes commissioned from Mantegna in March 1505 by Francesco di Giorgio Corner to decorate the upper part of a room in his palace in San Polo, Venice. He wanted to celebrate the family's hypothetical descent from the *gens* Cornelia, as he was the nephew of Catherine,

Queen of Cyprus, portrayed by Gentile Bellini in the effigy now in Budapest and, together with her entourage, in the *Miracle of the Cross at the Bridge of San Lorenzo*. Upon Mantegna's death on 13 September 1506, only the frieze with the *Introduction of the Cult of Cybele at Rome* was finished and Corner contacted Giovanni Bellini between 1507 and 1508,[38] through his step-brother Nicolò, asking him to complete the work started by his brother-in-law and left unfinished, partly due to differences of opinion between the patron and the artist, according to the correspondence between Bembo and Isabella Gonzaga in 1505. Bellini decided, now that Mantegna had passed away, to compare himself with him on a secular theme, something that he had always avoided, as Michele Vianello reminds Isabella d'Este in a letter dated 25 June 1501. The years of the frieze depicting *The Continence of Scipio*[39] saw Giovanni already at work on narrative themes, involved in the creation of historic canvases for the Sala del Maggior Consiglio in the Ducal Palace and so the dialogue with Andrea, in terms of the depiction of the classical bas-relief, reached high peaks here and summed up the comparison between the *Presentations*, in the profound technical and stylistic differences between the two, with the Venetian limiting himself to re-using the faux marble background, but radically changing the figurative language. While Mantegna arranged the work with the usual graphic scrupulousness, simulating figures sculpted in Carrara stone standing out against an orange marble background and offering a viewpoint markedly from underneath in gloriously archaeological clarity, Giovanni elaborated everything pictorially, focusing everything on the chiaroscuro softness that he gives to the figures paused in space and the drapes, anticipating what he would do in the *Feast of the Gods* now at the National Gallery of Art in Washington, D.C. He then added brilliant inventions to the composition, first and foremost the knight arriving at a gallop in the distance, adding a third dimension to the space. We seem to be witnessing a competition between painting and sculpture, with the friezes ideally evoking the stunning recent inventions of Antonio Lombardo: while he played the card of updating antiquity with intangible bas-reliefs and the bright colours of inlaid marble, the same operation was carried out by his brothers-in-law with their faux white marble bas-reliefs against mixed marble and antique red breccia backgrounds.

The last brushstroke in the comparison of a life, testimony to the unquestionable legacy of the artist who was best able to interpret that desire to construct a national expressive language able to overcome local lexical specificities, was therefore made by Giovanni Bellini. A desire parallel to the national literary commitment that finds its reference figure in Pietro Bembo and then its full realization in Ariosto. It is no coincidence that both were fervent admirers of Giovanni Bellini, indeed the former was also his friend and in some cases a go-between and patron. During the early Cinquecento – what we are used to describing as the Renaissance, albeit always with the Tuscans in mind – all the various regional languages developed in the courts, cities, confraternities and religious orders seemed to converge towards a shared ideal that found a singularly balanced mediator in Bellini, as we can glean from his contemporaries, and in an operation expressed so well by the dialogue between the *Presentations* by himself and Mantegna. The first two quatrains of the fifteenth sonnet of the *Rime*, which Pietro Bembo dedicated to him, have therefore become emblematic:

> O immagine mia celeste et pura;/ Che splendi più che 'l sole a gli occhi miei,/ Et mi assembri il volto di colei,/ Che scolpita ho nel cor con maggior cura;/ Credo che 'l mio Bellin con la figura/ T'habbia dato il costume ancho di lei:/ Che m'ardi, s'io ti miro: et per te sei/ Freddo smalto, cui giunse alla ventura. [Oh!" My image celestial and pure;/ Which shines more than the sun to my eyes,/ And gathers to me the face of her,/ That I have sculpted in my heart with the greatest care;/ I believe that my Bellini with this figure/ Has given you the custom of her too:/ You that burn me, if I look at you: and for you are/ Cold enamel, reached here by chance.]

[1] Most recently, as regards the work of Mantegna – tempera on linen canvas, 69 x 86.3 cm, Berlin, Staatliche Museen, Gemäldegalerie, inv. 29 – in addition to the essay by Neville Rowley in this book, see also the entry by Catarina Schmidt Arcangeli, in Schmidt Arcangeli 2015, pp. 316–324 with her proposal regarding the commission of the painting, which she links to the Venetian patrician Bernardo Bembo. For Bellini's painting – oil on panel, 81 x 105.5 cm, c. 1475, Venice, Pinacoteca della Fondazione Scientifica Querini Stampalia, inv, 2/29 – see Babet Trevisan, in Rome 2008, pp. 176–177 and the piece by myself published herein. Regarding the relationship between the brothers-in-law, particularly in reference to recent interpretations, see Christiansen 2004a, pp. 48–74, and Bellosi 2008, pp. 103–109.

[2] Modena, Biblioteca Estense, MS Estense, III.D.22. In Lightbown 1986, p. 474.

[3] Written communication from Isabella Campagnol, to whom I would like to express my thanks.

[4] Referred to by Rothe 1992, pp. 82–83. For the technical analysis of the works, see the piece by Babette Hartwieg in this catalogue.

[5] Commissioned on 10 August 1453 by Mauro Folperti, Benedictine abbot at Santa Giustina, and now in Milan, Pinacoteca di Brera.

[6] Prinz 1962, pp. 50–54. See, more specifically, the essay by Neville Rowley in this book.

[7] To this regard see De Marchi 2104, pp. 73–82, particularly p. 79.

[8] On Squarcione's workshop and regarding a fresco from the Paduan years during the period of Mantegna's training, see Padua 1999.

[9] Neumayr 1807, p. 94.

[10] Longhi [1926] 1967, II, pp. 77–98.

[11] ASVe, *Scuola grande di San Giovanni evangelista*, vol. 72, fol. 199r.

[12] Ringbom 1965, pp. 109–110.

[13] Written communication to the Management of the Fondazione Querini Stampalia.

[14] Regarding the various hypotheses, see the different contributions in which Tempestini (1992, p. 70; 1997, pp. 34, 62, 199; 2000, pp. 27, 58, 176) refutes all the inconsistencies and contradictions of these identifications with great precision.

[15] Robertson 1968.

[16] Michiel [1525–1528] 1884.

[17] Campori 1866, pp. 351–352.

[18] Merkel 1987, pp. 133–153.

[19] Lermolieff [Morelli] 1880, p. 433.

[20] Lermolieff [Morelli] 1893.

[21] However, it should be mentioned that it was previously supported by G. Frizzoni (1870, pp. 81–112) and A. Venturi (1914, p. 477) and then taken up again by Anderson (1989, I, pp. 271–294).

[22] Kristeller 1901, pp. 143–145.

[23] Berenson 1916, p. 72.

[24] It is worth mentioning, both for the record and because of the overall importance of his writings, how L. Dussler (1935) first thought of a Venetian copyist in around 1490 and then (Dussler 1949) of a workshop piece; W. Arslan (1952, pp. 127–146) described it as a very poor copy by a mediocre sixteenth-century painter; R. Goffen (1989) imagined it to be a copy after Bellini by Mantegna, emphasizing Bellini's links with the Berlin painting, that she believed could be based on a lost original by Giovanni and, lastly, L. Syson (2009, pp. 526-535) did not accept that this was a fully autograph work.

[25] For closer chronological scrutiny, please refer to Schmidt Arcangeli 2015 (as fn. 1), pp. 318-319.

[26] Coletti 1953, p. XL and Robertson 1968 (as fn. 8), pp. 75–76. For closer chronological scrutiny see Trevisan 2008 (as fn. 1), p. 176.

[27] Longhi 1962, pp. 18, 20.

[28] Regarding the age-old question of Giovanni Bellini's date of birth, please see the last two essays, which explore the matter from opposing points of view, reiterating the difficulty of finding an archive-based solution. There are two main theories on the topic: one hypothesizing his birth in around 1425; the other putting forward the second half of the 1430s, in around 1438–1440. Very little information is available to us. The objective data that we have tells us that Giovanni was the son of Jacopo Bellini; he was not the son of Anna Rinversi, Jacopo's wife; he did not live in Jacopo's home, in the parish of San Geminiano, as he was a member of the parish of San Lio. The question is explored by W. Maze (2013, pp. 783–823) and has recently been taken up again by Gentili (2017, pp. 108–135), who, by researching Venetian laws and statutes, attempts to demonstrate that Giovanni was not the son of Jacopo Bellini, but the half-brother of the father, born between the end of 1424 and September 1428, and died in 1516, at the age of around ninety, as reported by Vasari. This theory is refuted by the publication by Brown and Pizzati (2014, pp. 148–152), on the basis of the testament of Samaritana Vendramin, aunt of a Giovanni Bellini living in Santa Marina who, on 19 January 1508 *more veneto* (or rather 1509), dictates her last will. This allows us to suppose that Bellini was born in the second half of the 1430s, towards 1440.

[29] Longhi 1949, p. 281.

[30] Regarding Mantegna's technique, see in particular: Delbourgo, Rioux, Martin 1975, pp. 25–26; Lightbown, 1986 (as fn. 2), pp. 227–233, 268; Christiansen 1992 (as fn. 3), pp. 67–77; Dunkerton 1993, pp. 26–38; Villa 2007; Menu, Ravaud 2009.

[31] Berenson 1916 (as fn. 16), pp. 63–64.

[32] Saramago 2002, p. 15.

[33] Analyses carried out from 1998 onwards, in addition to what had been published in the meantime, including: Galassi 1998; Bagarotto *et. al.* 2000 (as fn. 23), pp. 184–202; Olivari 2001, pp. 31–44; Villa 2003, pp. 73–85; Christiansen, 2004b, pp. 7–57; Dunkerton 2004 (as fn. 1), pp. 195–225; Villa 2006, pp. 308–398 and Villa 2009, pp. 9–160.

[34] A development that is clearly apparent even by simply observing the changes in the altarpieces still present on the Venetian altars, widely illustrated in the technical data in Poldi, Villa 2008.

[35] Panel, 74 x 118 cm, Florence, Galleria degli Uffizi, inv. no. 943.

[36] For a closer examination of the critical history and attribution-related reflections on the drawings of Giovanni Bellini see Villa 2008b, pp. 73–87. One could also refer to the reorganization and cleaning of the nucleus of Bellini's works as part of the Mantegna exhibition in London by David Ekserdjian, in London-New York 1992 (as fn. 3), pp. 134–137, 172–181, 192–193, and subsequently by Faietti 2006, pp. 81–89). Lastly, Goldner 2004 (as fn. 1), pp. 226–255.

[37] Barausse 2008, doc. 91, p. 350.

[38] London, The National Gallery, canvas, 73.5 x 268 cm.

[39] Washington, D.C., National Gallery of Art, canvas, 74.8 x 356.2 cm.

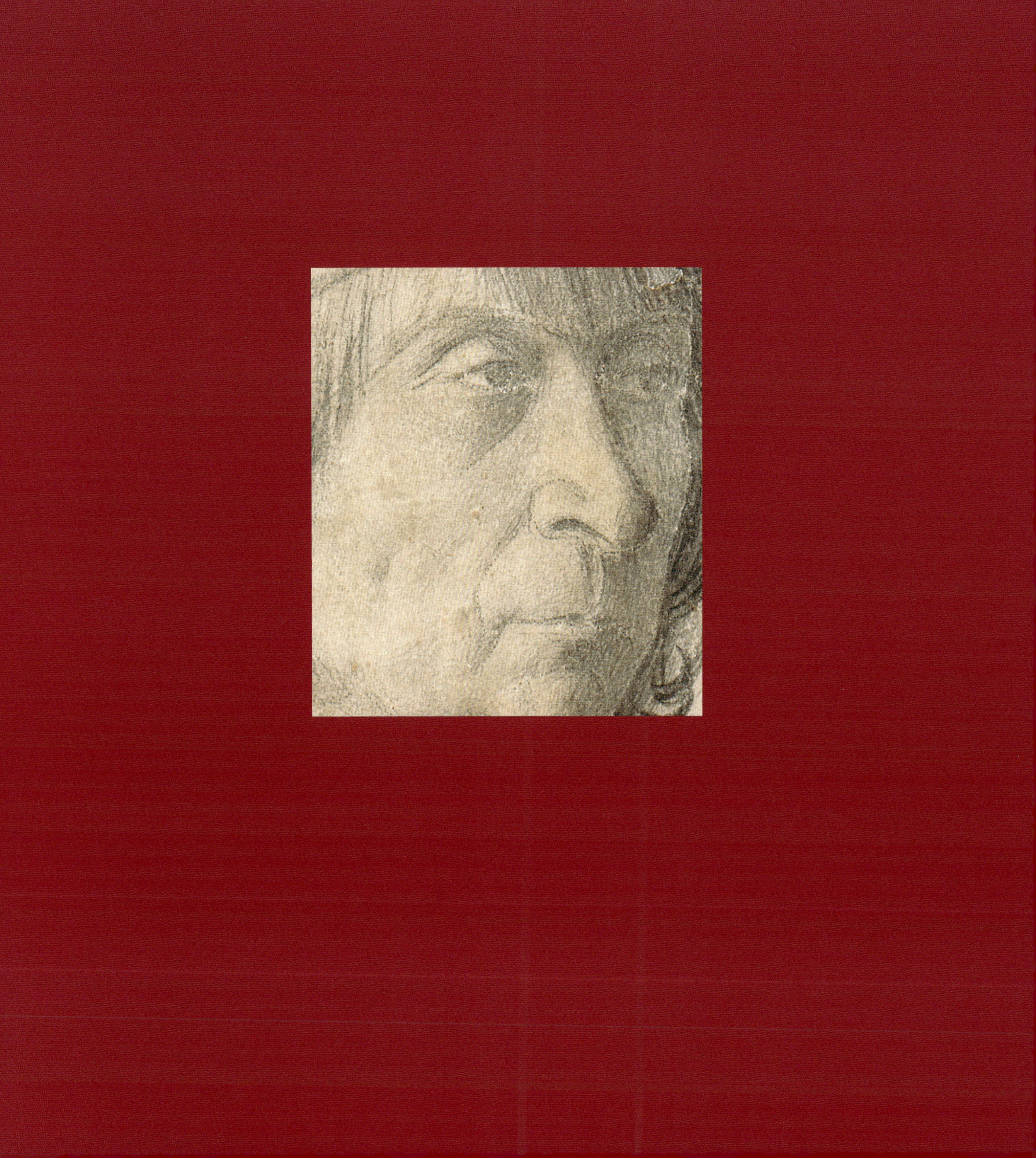

One Cartoon – Two Paintings

BRIGIT BLASS-SIMMEN

1. Pouncing for the transfer: detail by Gentile or Giovanni Bellini, *Portrait of a Man (Gentile Bellini?)*, c. 1496, black pencil on paper, 23 x 19.4 cm. Berlin, Staatliche Museen zu Berlin Kupferstichkabinett SMB (KdZ 5170)

Two paintings with an identical composition. Painted by two artists, Andrea Mantegna and Giovanni Bellini, in different places and at different times. Two brilliant works: the same and yet different.

Andrea Mantegna trained and worked in Padua during the early part of his career; Giovanni Bellini worked in Venice, his birthplace, for his entire life. Both painted a picture of the 'Presentation at the Temple', in which the compositional structure is substantially the same. Two great artists linked by family connections: in 1453, Andrea Mantegna married Giovanni Bellini's sister Nicolosia.

What leads a painter to adopt a composition used by another artist? This is exactly the question we face in the case of the two paintings by Andrea Mantegna and Giovanni Bellini: the *Presentation of Jesus at the Temple,* now respectively at the Gemäldegalerie in Berlin and the Fondazione Querini Stampalia in Venice. Which of the two works came first and thus provided the model for the other? Technical analyses of the composition of the painting by Mantegna in the Gemäldegalerie in Berlin have highlighted various changes of idea, so-called 'pentimenti'. X-rays and infrared photographs show that Mary's head has been moved down and to the right slightly in the final version (see the contribution by Hartwieg in this book, fig. 13). The changes to the head of Simeon, who originally wore a kippah, which has been transformed into headgear that covers his hair and ears, are visible to the naked eye.[1] The three-dimensional haloes have been eliminated.[2] Alterations and changes such as these during the genesis of the work are always indicative of a creative process and must certainly demonstrate the originality of the work itself.

Meanwhile, the Bellini panel in Venice shows some engravings (see the contribution by Hartwieg, fig. 22)[3] and traces of 'pouncing',[4] a technique used to transfer a scale drawing to another surface by perforating the outlines and dusting them with coal dust (fig. 1). The layout of Bellini's work has therefore been copied from a pre-existing drawing, subsequently reworked with the application of layers of colour. The central parts of the two works are identical (fig. 2). This means that Bellini must have used a 1:1 scale cartoon of Mantegna's composition as his model, with the help of which he was able to transfer the outlines of the drawing onto the panel of his painting. Research is more or less agreed regarding the date of Mantegna's *Presentation*, which has been established as just after his wedding to Nicolosia Bellini in around 1454–1455.[5] The dating of Bellini's panel is, however, more controversial and

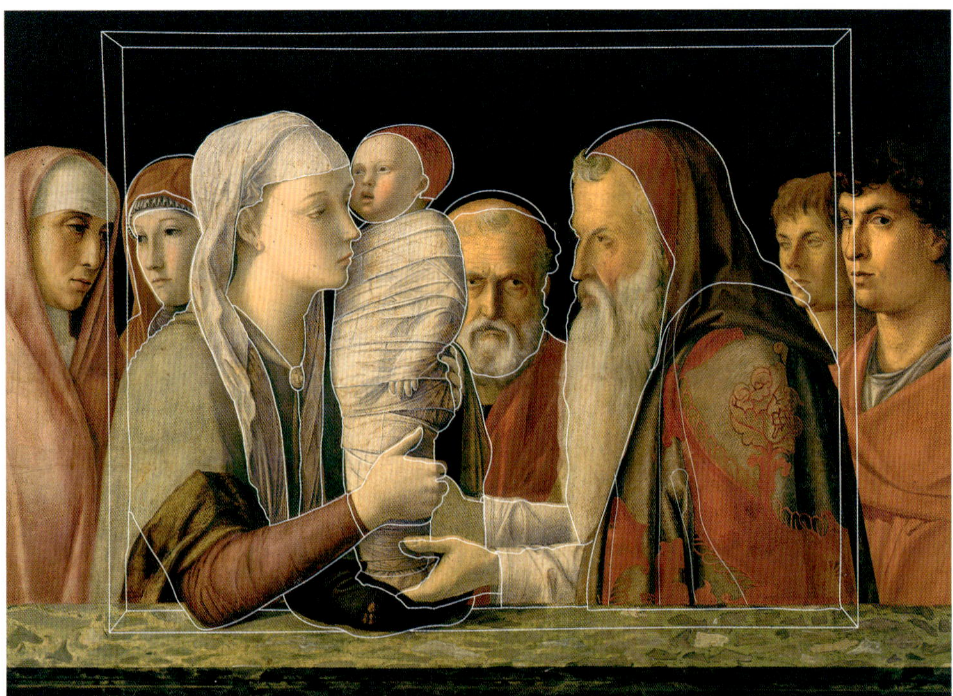

2. Outlines of Andrea Mantegna's composition over Bellini's *Presentation in the Temple* (enlarged with the help of Photoshop in 1:1 scale)

an object of debate due to uncertainty regarding the date of his birth.[6] Giovanni Villa proposes a convincing date for Bellini's *Presentation*, placing it in the years around 1470 and primarily explaining this by referring to the high-quality of the underdrawing, which extends the outlines of the model and is characterized by great sophistication typical of this period of Bellini's activity.[7]

It was common practice to use the same cartoons in the same workshop in order to satisfy clients' wishes and simplify production processes.

We know of numerous cases of scale replicas of compositions in the Bellini workshop. However, what is unusual here is the use of a single cartoon in two different workshops.[8] We know that these and other models, which represented real artistic potential, were put away and kept strictly secret and that artists even took each other to court over stolen models.[9]

Why did this exchange take place between Mantegna and Bellini? After a lapse of around twenty years, if the dates are correct? The two artists were brothers-in-law. By marrying Nicolosia, Giovanni Bellini's sister, the young Mantegna became a member of the family. The family, or rather the father and father-in-law Jacopo Bellini, who owned the most important artistic workshop in Venice, represents the link here. The family relationship between Bellini and Mantegna led to the identification of the 'secondary figures' in the two paintings. Although it is not possible to confirm their accuracy, theories regarding the identity of the characters have become commonly accepted, at least in the case of Mantegna's work. It has been suggested that Mantegna's panel contained a self-portrait of the artist on the right, behind the priest Simeon, a portrait of his wife Nicolosia Bellini on the female side behind the Virgin, and Jacopo Bellini in the centre in the role of Joseph. The year of their marriage, documented in 1453, and the idea that the work was a votive image to mark the happy birth of their firstborn son would suggest that it dates to 1454–1455, a theory also confirmed by the stylistic elements. In Bellini's panel, the addition of the extra two figures could be logically explained as portraits of Giovanni Bellini and his wife, alongside those already present of Mantegna and his wife. The interpretation of the scene as a very private family moment has inspired theories on every possible combination and variation, including one that interprets Mantegna's painting as a thank you to his father-in-law Jacopo Bellini, who enabled him to break away from the workshop of Francesco Squarcione, his adoptive father, in Padua as a result of this marriage.

Identical Features: *"It Is in Half Figures"*

Mantegna's painting was in the collection of Pietro Bembo. Marcantonio Michiel saw it there, probably in 1529, and described it as follows in his *Notizia d'opere di disegno*: "The small panel painting of Our Lady who presents the Child for circumcision was by the hand of Mantegna, and it is in half figures."[10] Michiel, who is generally quite laconic in his descriptions of artworks, must evidently have thought that the fact it was in "half figures" to be particularly noteworthy. Effectively, we are looking at a new type of representation here: the immediate half-figure image of the Byzantine icon combined with a scenic full-figure narrative, a pictorial composition that Sixten Ringborn defined as a 'close-up'.[11] A narrative compositions of half figures inserted into a frame shown in perspective had already featured in Jacopo Bellini's sketchbook (fig. 3). The scene described is a *Lamentation of Christ* with the lower half covered by the sarcophagus. The 'internal' composition, executed in very fine and barely visible silverpoint lines (fig. 4), is framed by a sophisticated pen drawing that creates the illusion of a Renaissance-style aedicule altar. Sixten Ringborn has already underscored the relationship between the depiction in the Paris sketchbook and Mantegna's *Presentation* and described the image on the first page of the book not so much as a *Lamentation* but as the image of a *Lamentation*. Degenhard/Schmitt believe it is no coincidence that this sheet is right at the start of the sketchbook: indeed, they describe it as a key image used by Jacopo as a frontispiece at the start of all his creations and date it to around 1455, more or less during the same period when Mantegna painted his panel. They see Jacopo Bellini as a brilliant innovator in Venetian art.[12] The composition inside the aed-

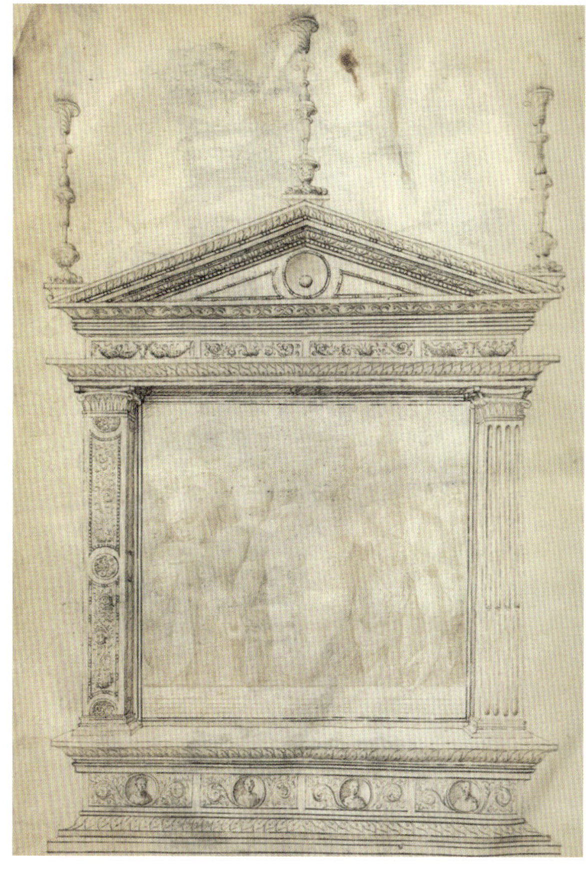

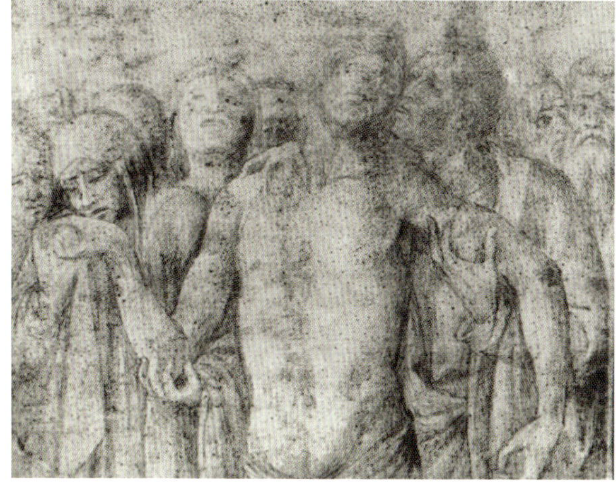

3. Sketchbook of Jacopo Bellini, fol. 7 *verso* (with the old sequence of pages fol. 1 *verso*), *Altar aedicule with a Lamentation of Christ*, pen, brush on parchment, approx. 42.8 x 29.3 cm. Paris, Louvre, Département des arts graphiques

4. Sketchbook of Jacopo Bellini, fol. 7 *verso*, detail of fig. 3, *Lamentation of Christ* (photograph in ultraviolet light)

icule reveals some analogies with our *Presentations*. The staggered arrangement of the half-figures, their distribution in two rows with the main figures, Mary and John, in the foreground, and behind them partial representations of other heads, of which the last two on the right particularly recall the heads of Joseph by Mantegna and the so-called portrait of Mantegna in the *Presentation* due to their frontal angle, or rather their unexplained sideways glances. Giovanni Bellini painted and drew around twenty extant variants of the half-figure *Pietà* in close-up.[13] In Mantegna, we once again find the half-figure composition in a frame. In the work of Giovanni Bellini they are behind a parapet, while in Jacopo Bellini's drawing we find Christ and the weeping figures behind the edge of a sarcophagus, which serves a logical purpose here.[14] The fact that a compositional arrangement is already present in the work of Jacopo Bellini and is subsequently resumed by Mantegna and Giovanni Bellini is something that is repeated frequently. The links between the Jacopo Bellini – Mantegna – Giovanni Bellini artistic triangle have still not yet been clarified definitively. The *St Jerome in the Desert* painted by the young Mantegna (São Paulo, Museu de Arte) and by Giovanni Bellini (Birmingham, Barber Institute) show similarities to the Paris sketchbook, fol. 18 *verso*, and to the London sketchbook, fol. 87 *verso*. The two paintings of the *Agony in the Garden* by Mantegna and Bellini (both at the National Gallery in London) are anticipated by Jacopo in his London sketchbook, fol. 44. The same can be said of the depictions of the *Descent into Limbo*, with various works by all three artists, all of which refer to one another: drawings, paintings and engravings.[15]

Despite the similarities between the two paintings, whose central composition is identical, there are also significant differences.

Window versus Parapet

Andrea Mantegna's composition is characterized by the fact that the scene is set in a trompe l'oeil painted marble frame that creates the illusion of a window. The strong shading of the left jamb and the architrave of the window emphasize the three-dimensional effect of this artificial frame. The compositional arrangement seems to go back over Alberti's definition of the modern image, in which the entire surface of the painting contains a coherent image of the space in perspective, within which the gaze can roam as it can from an open window: "An open window through which the sub-

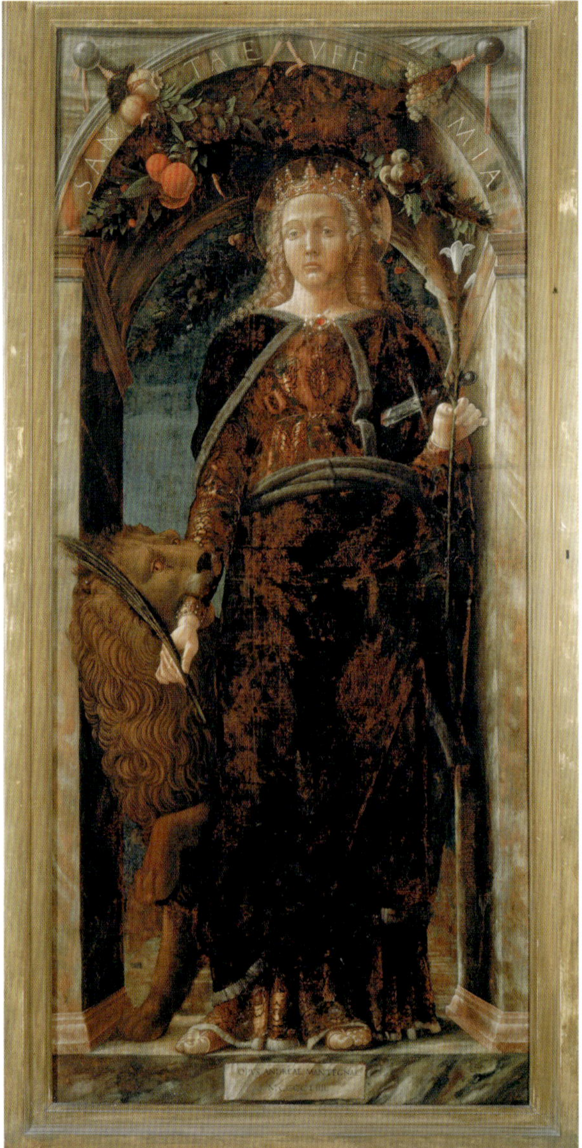

5. Andrea Mantegna, *St Euphemia*, 1454, tempera on canvas, 171 x 78 cm. Naples, Museo e Gallerie Nazionali di Capodimonte

6. Giotto, *Fortitude*, c. 1305. Padua, Scrovegni Chapel

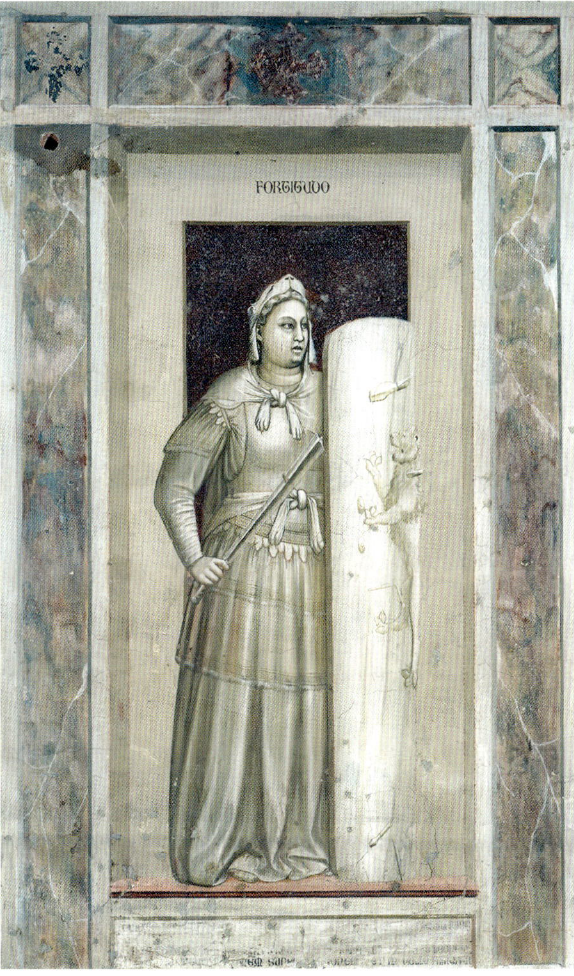

ject to be painted is seen".[16] These 'window scenes', these views framed by painted rectangular or arched windows, arches, doors or lunettes, can be found in numerous works from Mantegna's early years, such as the fresco of 1452 in the lunette on the main portal of Sant'Antonio in Padua, the *Assumption of Mary* on the central wall of the Ovetari Chapel in Padua, the *St Euphemia* of 1454 now conserved at Capodimonte in Naples (fig. 5), the *St Mark* at the Städelsches Kunstinstitut und Städtische Galerie in Frankfurt, the *Butler Madonna* surrounded by cherubim and seraphim at the Metropolitan Museum in New York and the *St George* at the Accademia in Venice.

The marble frame around Mantegna's *Presentation* recalls the painted frames in Giotto's fresco cycle in the Scrovegni Chapel in Padua. From 1448 to 1454–1457, Mantegna worked on the fresco cycle in the church of the Eremitani, immediately next to the Scrovegni Chapel, and he must therefore have been acquainted with it. The lower register of the chapel contains a grisaille painted frieze that imitates marble with depictions of the Vices and Virtues. At the viewer's head height, standing within illusory painted niches, the figures of the Vices and Virtues resemble three-dimensional sculptures, standing out against a blue background that imitates stone (fig. 6). We also find the frame as an integral part of the composition in Flemish portraits by Jan van Eyck, which bear the artist's signature on the wooden frames.[17] A further step towards imitating reality in perspective can be seen in the *Portrait of a Carthusian* by Petrus Christus, now at the Metropolitan Museum in New York. On the parapet of the painted cornice, which deceives the eye on the two-dimensional panel, immediately above the artist's signature we also find the misleading image of a fly.

A perspective 'box' arrangement with bronze frame can be found in Donatello's relief of the *Dead Christ with Two Angels* for the altar of Sant'Antonio. Donatello arrived in Padua in 1443 and worked there for over ten years. He created a large bronze cross for the main altar of the church and a series of reliefs surmounted by statues in the round.[18] Donatello's influence over the young Mantegna is apparent in the clarity and sculptural plasticity with which the figures of Mary, the Christ Child and Simeon stand out against the flat painted surface. The *Presentation* seems to allude to Donatello's relief of the *Dead Christ with Two Angels*, where the wings and feet of the angels protrude from the frame, while in Mantegna's painting the Christ Child rests on a cushion that extends out over the parapet. The Child himself, the Virgin's forearm and Simeon's hands rest on the window frame, while the other parts of the scene seem to draw back into the background on the other side of the frame. In Mantegna's *Presentation*, the comparison

with Donatello's relief is generally perceived in the representation of the parts in light and shadow and in the defined and sculpted physicality of the figures.
The clear-cut result that these almost relief figures acquire against the flat and undefined painted background could, however, also be interpreted in relation to ancient Roman funerary sculpture with a stone frame (fig. 7).[19]
The window frame creates a passage from the real world to the world of the painted image. This effect is further intensified in Mantegna's *Presentation* by an additional border that was originally nailed to the panel and painted, at least in part, as faux marble.[20] A corner of the cushion on which the swaddled Christ Child is presented seems to protrude from the frame, entering into the viewer's space.

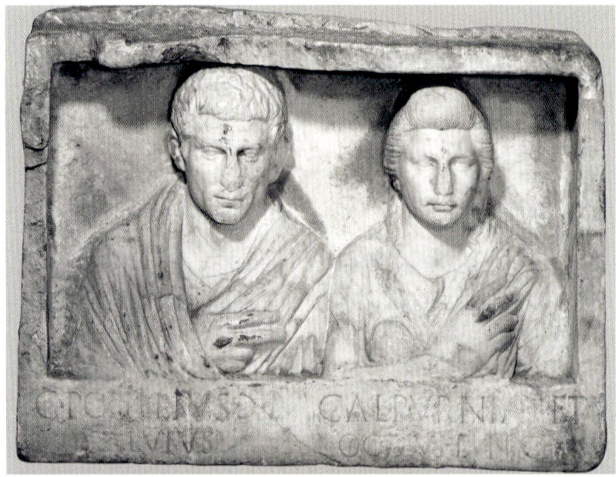

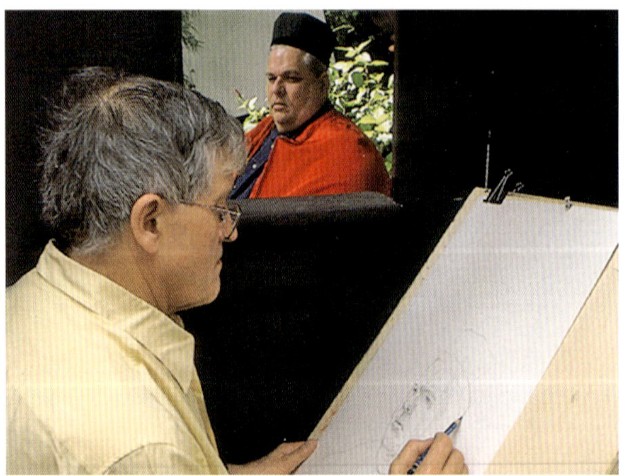

A window into the space of the Temple or *fenestra coeli*. Looking out or looking in?
A fundamental question that has to be asked – and that has also been asked by the contemporary artist David Hockney (fig. 8)[21] – in relation to these paintings framed by a window regards the involvement of the viewer. Where does the viewer stand: inside or outside? Is the viewer external to the scene and looking into an internal space from outside or, on the contrary, are they inside and looking out through the window? In the case of the *Presentation*, looking from the outside in would mean looking towards the place where the scene of the presentation itself is unfolding, that is to say inside the temple.[22] Alternatively, the viewer would be inside and looking out through the window, which would therefore become a *fenestra coeli*, in which the viewer looks out onto a transcendental celestial space.[23] The *fenestra coeli* interpretation does not sit well with the secular figures, the 'family portraits' that Mantegna painted subsequently, adding them behind the main group formed of the Virgin Mary, the Christ Child and Simeon.[24] Other decisive elements regarding whether it should be interpreted as a window looking into the temple or a *fenestra coeli* are the colour and production of the background, to which we shall return later.
In Giotto we find ourselves inside the Scrovegni Chapel, looking at an illusory painted stone niche that opens out in the background onto another space with a blue surface. It is unclear whether the blue background represents a stone surface or an indeterminate open space. In any case, the shield of *Fortitude* has a slightly oblique angle and therefore protrudes between the second frame depicted in the style of a passe-partout and the background, suggesting the idea of an open and undefined space (fig. 6). The space of the faux niches is occupied entirely by the painted figures, but the individual characters do not emerge beyond the margins of the niches themselves. The gaze therefore moves from an internal space into a further fictitious space. In Jacopo Bellini, there is no compositional link between the aedicule that acts as a frame and the

7. Roman funerary stone with busts of Papillius and Calpunia, 20–1 BCE. Pacific Palisades, Los Angeles, The J. Paul Getty Museum

8. David Hockney, *Secret Knowledge in Painting*

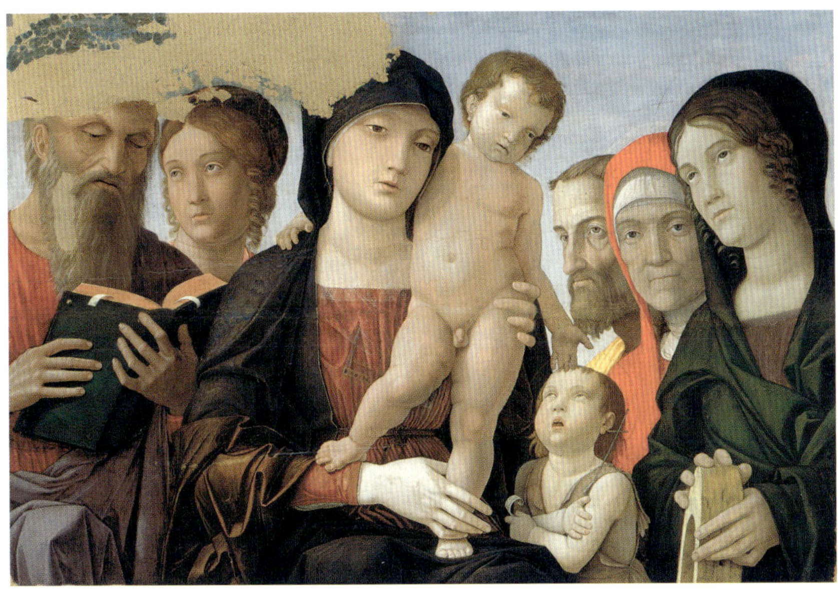

9. Andrea Mantegna, *Virgin and Child with Saints*, tempera grassa on panel, 61.5 x 87.5 cm. Turin, Galleria Sabauda

Lamentation of Christ, as if they were produced at different times. This 'fracture' between the frame and the composition that it surrounds is also highlighted by the different execution techniques and the media used for the drawings: bistre and brush for the aedicule and silverpoint for the 'internal' scene. There are no superimpositions between the composition of the figures and the frame. Jacopo's framing seems rather to be an architectural element that surrounds the scene and does not appear to serve the purpose of opening up the gaze by directing it towards another sphere.

In Mantegna, the cornice, which appears from a slightly lowered perspective, seen from below at the front, is used – as in the work by Jacopo – to delimit and establish the frame. The half figures find their logical delimitation in the painted frame. Mary's right arm, supporting the Christ Child, protrudes over the cornice and induces us to maintain that Mantegna, influenced by Donatello's relief, primarily intends to produce a three-dimensional effect in a two-dimensional panel.

The Blue Background

An analysis of Mantegna's painting under a microscope found a large number of azurite pigments in the background of the painting (to this regard, see the contribution by Hartwieg in this book),[25] which are also apparent to the naked eye. We have to imagine that the original background of the *Presentation* was blue. The same also applies to the aforementioned early works by Mantegna, in which our gaze takes us beyond an architectural structure: the backgrounds of Mantegna's lunette with Saints Anthony and Bernardine, originally painted for the main portal of the basilica of Sant'Antonio in Padua, commissioned from the painter in 1448, and the *St Mark* in the Städelsches Kunstinstitut und Städtische Galerie in Frankfurt and the *St Euphemia* dated 1454 and now in the Museo di Capodimonte in Naples (fig. 5), were originally blue.[26] We also find blue backgrounds in numerous portraits by Giovanni Bellini. The most famous example is the *Portrait of Doge Leonardo Loredan* at the National Gallery in London, although the *Portrait of Georg Fugger*, painted in 1474 and now at the Norton Simon Foundation in Los Angeles (Pasadena), should also be imagined with a background that was originally blue.[27] The same can be said for Mantegna's profile portraits at the Museo Poldi Pezzoli in Milan and the National Gallery of Art in Washington, D.C. Another extant religious half-figure composition against a blue background attributed to Mantegna is the *Virgin and Child with Saints* at the Galleria Sabauda in Turin (fig. 9). Mauro Lucco ascribes this painting to Mantegna's late period and observes that the painter resumes the use of the half-figure composition in a horizontal format in this work following a long interval, reviving the dialogue with his brother-in-law Giovanni Bellini and with his iconic close-up half-figure compositions.[28] The blue background makes evident reference to the frescoes of Giotto and the city of Padua where they were created. The paler original background of Mantegna's composition must also have enhanced the spatial effect of the painting, further emphasizing the dark parts in shadow of the frame, the architrave and the left jamb by means of added contrast. The azure base

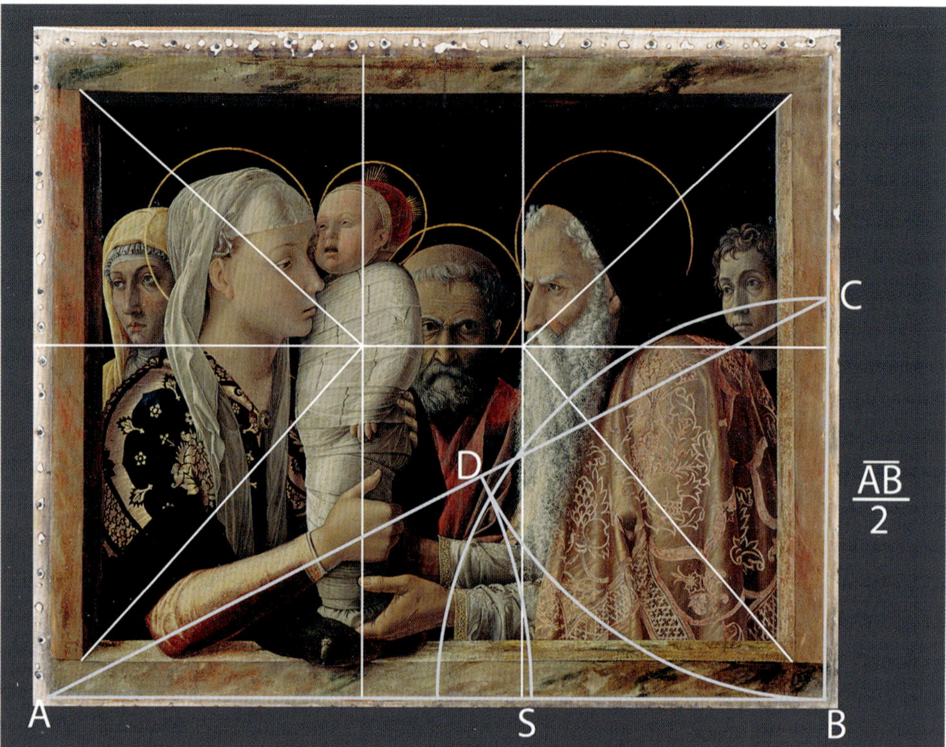

10. Andrea Mantegna, *Presentation at the Temple*, geometric construction AB/2 = BC, proportional relationship of the base line AB in *divina proportione* = S

evokes the idea of the sky and therefore opens our gaze up to a *fenestra coeli*, an imaginary and transcendental space.

Divina Proportione versus Harmony of Colours

Mantegna's *Presentation* has a strictly formal composition and the most striking aspect is the rigid vertical line formed by Simeon's forehead, beard and nose. Measurements reveal that it has the proportions defined by Luca Pacioli as *Divina proportione*, which subsequently became known as the *golden section* (fig. 10).[29] The painted frame is not constructed according to the rules of central perspective: the short vanishing lines at the corners of the frame vanish in different directions, towards two points placed on a horizontal line at the height of the Child's chest and Simeon's nostrils. If we draw a vertical line through these points, we can see that they almost comply with *Divina proportione* in relation to the horizontal surface of the image. They determine the highly visible line that delimits the forehead, nose and beard of Simeon and the axis formed by the upright Christ Child. The angle of Mary's forearm is formed by the connection between point (A) and point (C), achieved by shifting the middle of the horizontal AB line to vertical. Whether deliberate or due to the artist's instinct, this geometric construction is fundamentally what gives the composition its severity, strength and gravitas.

Thanks to the cartoon, Giovanni Bellini makes substantial use of Mantegna's structure, although, by maintaining the same composition for a larger painting, the proportional relationship of *divina proportione* is lost.[30] Bellini, who was a great master of perspective, was not interested in stringent geometric construction,[31] which is deliberately 'softened' here. The vertical line, which delimits Simeon's forehead, nose and beard in Mantegna's painting, is attenuated in Bellini's piece and Simeon's white beard extends softly towards the Virgin and Child. In Mantegna's work and in the cartoon, the forehead is curved back, while Bellini corrects and realigns it subsequently (flesh tones against a black background). Bellini lingered extensively on the line of Simeon's forehead, as demonstrated by various reworkings on the forehead and nose (fig. 11). As a result, the representation of the relationship between the figures is not shown as a confrontation, but is characterized by greater closeness and harmony. The various luminous tones of white highlight the important relationships between the figures: Simeon's face and beard, his arms that reach out to the Child wrapped in swaddling bands. The lightest points in the scene are predominantly accompanied by other pale hues of red, purple and grey. The dark background above and the shadowy balustrade at the bottom of the image cause our eyes to focus on what is taking place in the central part of the scene.

Mantegna originally combined contrasting shades of blue, red and yellow. The most striking difference is the cloak of the figure immediately behind Mary, which is a luminous yellow in Mantegna, while in Bellini it is oxblood red. The design of the brocades is also different: Bellini's fabrics are more understated and less showy and discordant than in Mantegna. The Virgin's cloak is made from a simple fabric, which is not elaborate like brocade, and the same applies to the sleeves of the high priest Simeon. The *soprarizzo* velvet of the tunic was, however, painted in such a precise manner that one can actually see the weave of the raised and lowered pile. Even today, despite abrasion, a purple coloured floral pattern can be clearly seen in the red parts of the garment, in two different shades of colour. This was a highly prized velvet woven with gold threads and only produced in Venice from around the mid-fifteenth century (fig. 12). To sum up and simplify matters, we can state that Mantegna's work presents the harmony of the golden section, while Bellini's presents harmony of colour.

The New Space

In comparison to Mantegna's painting, Bellini chose a larger format and arranged the figures – to whom he added two extra characters – standing behind a solid parapet of green marble. The painting by

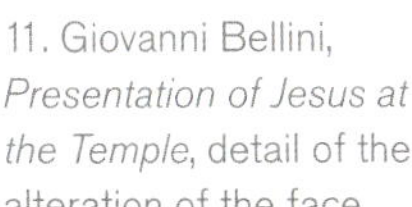

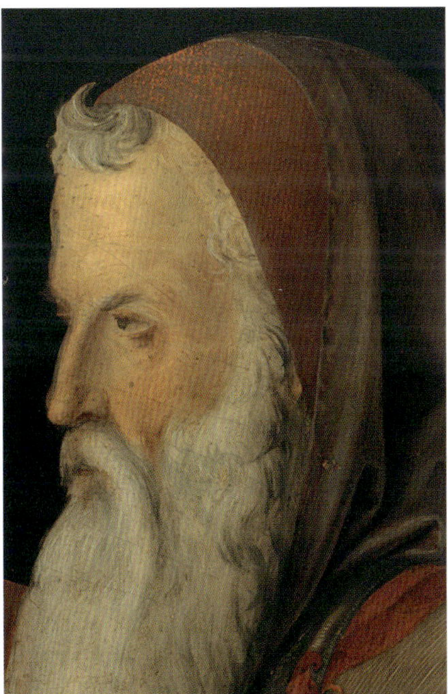

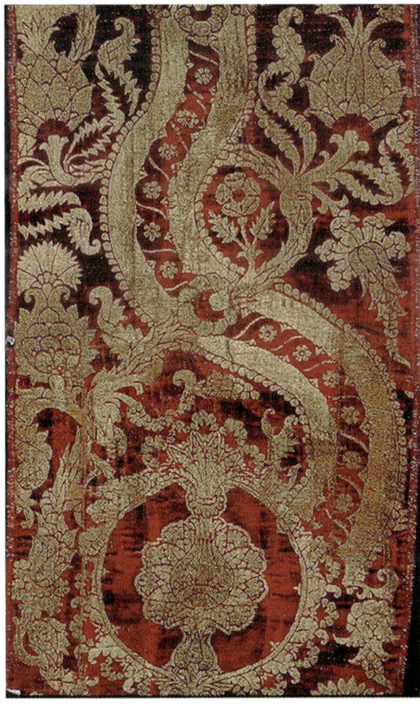

11. Giovanni Bellini, *Presentation of Jesus at the Temple*, detail of the alteration of the face

12. Report on velvet with a pile of two different heights and thread wrapped in silk and metal, second half of the fifteenth century, New York, The Metropolitan Museum of Art

Giovanni Bellini is not set within the frame of a painted window. The scene is illustrated in close-up behind a horizontal marble parapet that occupies around one fifth of the panel surface. The cushion on which the Child is presented does not protrude, as it does in Mantegna's work, from the marble parapet and does therefore not enter the viewer's space: the depth of space in Bellini is all behind the parapet. The two new added figures are larger than the two figures shown in the Mantegna: compared to Mantegna's cartoon, the figure seen from the front in the centre of the scene appears smaller, and this causes him to draw back in the space. By phasing the size of the figures in this way, Bellini achieves an effect of spatial depth.

Cartoon

While the light falls upon both paintings from the top left, there are differences in the shadows. The light in the Bellini panel is clearer, the illuminated zones are therefore richer in contrasts and the shadows projected by the Virgin's right arm and the veil on her neck are more dense. In Mantegna, partly because of the tempera technique he used, the light is created with heightening that shapes the forms with parallel brushstrokes. Bellini paints with layers of transparent colour, as in the headgear worn by Simeon, in which the shading even reveals the stitches along the hand-rolled hem.

The brocade of the garments appears similar in the two pictures, but it does not have the same pattern, suggesting that Bellini did not use the same fabric models as Mantegna.

The framing, the shadows, the colours and the decorations lead us to conclude that Bellini did not necessarily have Mantegna's painting before him, but only the cartoon, where the colours, shadows and decorations naturally did not feature. It seems likely that the cartoon did not include the parapet either and that the lower edge in the cartoon constituted the top line of the cornice upon which the Virgin's right elbow rests. On the basis of the composition layout, we can deduce that Giovanni did not have Mantegna's panel available to him, but this does not mean that he had not seen the finished painting. We have to presume that it was a cartoon of Mantegna's picture, but not the original cartoon he used in the composition of his works, as the alterations show that it is not the original version.

However, what does the fact that Giovanni Bellini used a cartoon of Mantegna's painting mean? There are various possible theories:

1. The Querini Stampalia painting is a workshop piece, perhaps by Mantegna's workshop. Rona Goffen rejects the attribution of the *Presentation* to Bellini and maintains that the Querini Stampalia painting is a copy of a lost composition by Giovanni Bellini.[32] This can be ruled out on the basis of the analysis of the underdrawing by Giovanni Villa, who clearly recognizes the hand of Giovanni Bellini.
2. Mantegna's painting belonged to Jacopo Bellini or one of his sons and Giovanni could have produced a cartoon of it.[33]
3. Due to family links, Mantegna's cartoon ended up in Jacopo or Giovanni's workshop in Venice and remained there.
4. There is a third common element. If this were the case, it could be spotted in the activity of Jacopo Bellini.
5. The two artists each had access to the other's workshop. The use of the same cartoon generally suggests a shared workshop or a close link between two workshops.

Invention versus Colour

Did Bellini want to establish a dialogue with his brother-in-law by using the same composition? Did he want to show him his concept of painting? Is this something like the competition between Jacopo Bellini and Pisanello,[34] described by Ulisse degli Aleotti and Angelo Decembrio, over which of the two was able to paint the best portrait of Leonello d'Este?

Simeon's hair and beard are not represented in

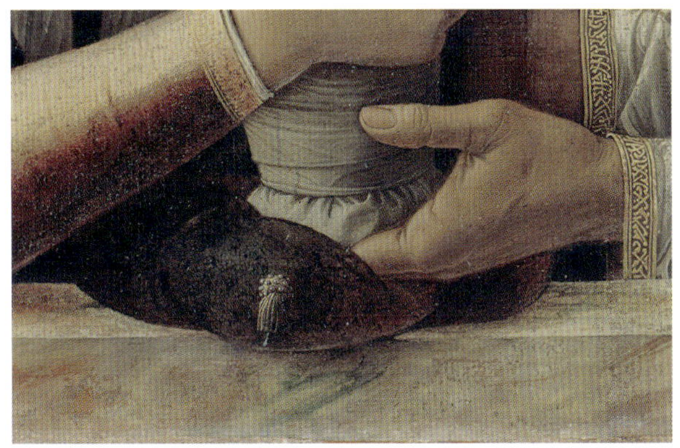

13. Andrea Mantegna, *Presentation of Jesus at the Temple*, detail of the parapet and cushion

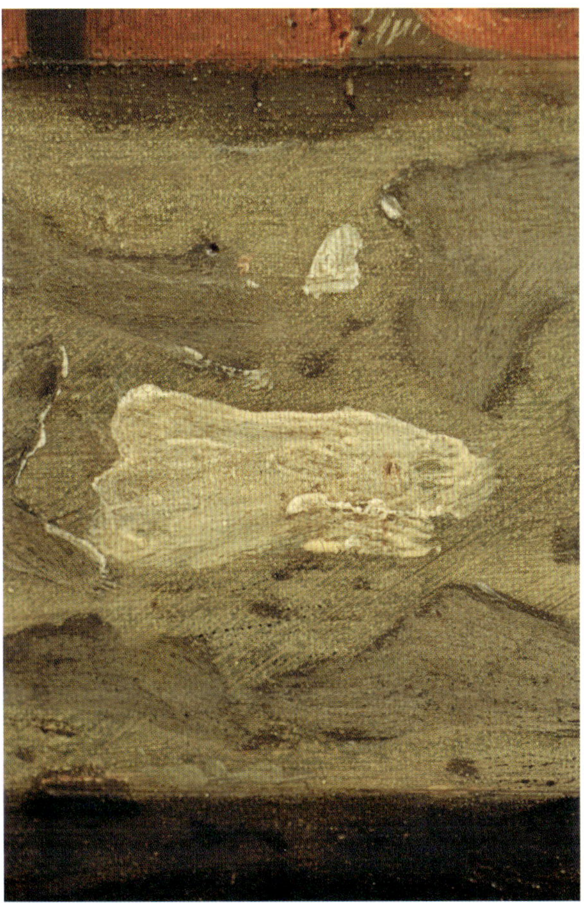

14. Giovanni Bellini, *Presentation in the Temple*, detail of the parapet

Mantegna as long wavy locks, in which each individual silvery hair can be identified. The tempera technique made it possible to give the forms a precise definition. Instead, Bellini paints with pigments bound in oil, resulting in a more painterly rendering of the material essence of things. Layers of fluid and transparent colour with heightening and darker brushstrokes in the shaded zones give the beard the effect of a soft voluminous and dishevelled mass. While in Mantegna, the lighting is handled in a similar way to sophisticated Flemish painting, for example on the pearls that embellish the cushion tassels (fig. 13), in Bellini we find a simple woven tassel. The white lines, applied with surprisingly modern freedom, using irregular and almost pasty brushstrokes, which dart over the marble parapet, should not be interpreted as veins in the marble, but reflections of light.

In Mantegna we find an intentional relief effect, a compact and compressed construction, a severe power. In Bellini, on the other hand, a deep and undefined space opens up. The lines that define the construction of the image in accordance with the rules of *divina proportione* are softened. The subtle sfumato and the harmony of the colours and densely coloured darting lines create spectacular lighting effects. In the pattern of the brocade cloak worn by Simeon and in the parapet (fig. 14) they produce an innovative textured rendering (to this regard, see the contribution by Giovanni Villa in this book).

Just as Lorenzo da Pavia wrote to Isabella d'Este in 1504, Mantegna is unbeatable when it comes to *invention* (cartoon!) and the same can be said of Bellini in the use of colour: "In invention there are none to rival Messer Andrea Mantegna who excels in this and leads the field, but Giovan Belino is excellent in colouring."[35] The Messianic narrative, the revelation of the divinity of the Christ Child at the Temple, his recognition by Simeon are depicted consciously or subconsciously by Mantegna in *divina proportione* as a glance through the *fenestra coeli*. In this, he is in every way a child of his city, Padua, a university city and a place with a passion for the classical world of Giotto and Donatello. Bellini is and remains profoundly Venetian: he observes the pattern of the reflections of light and colour on the surface of the calm or rippled water and instils this experience in his painting.

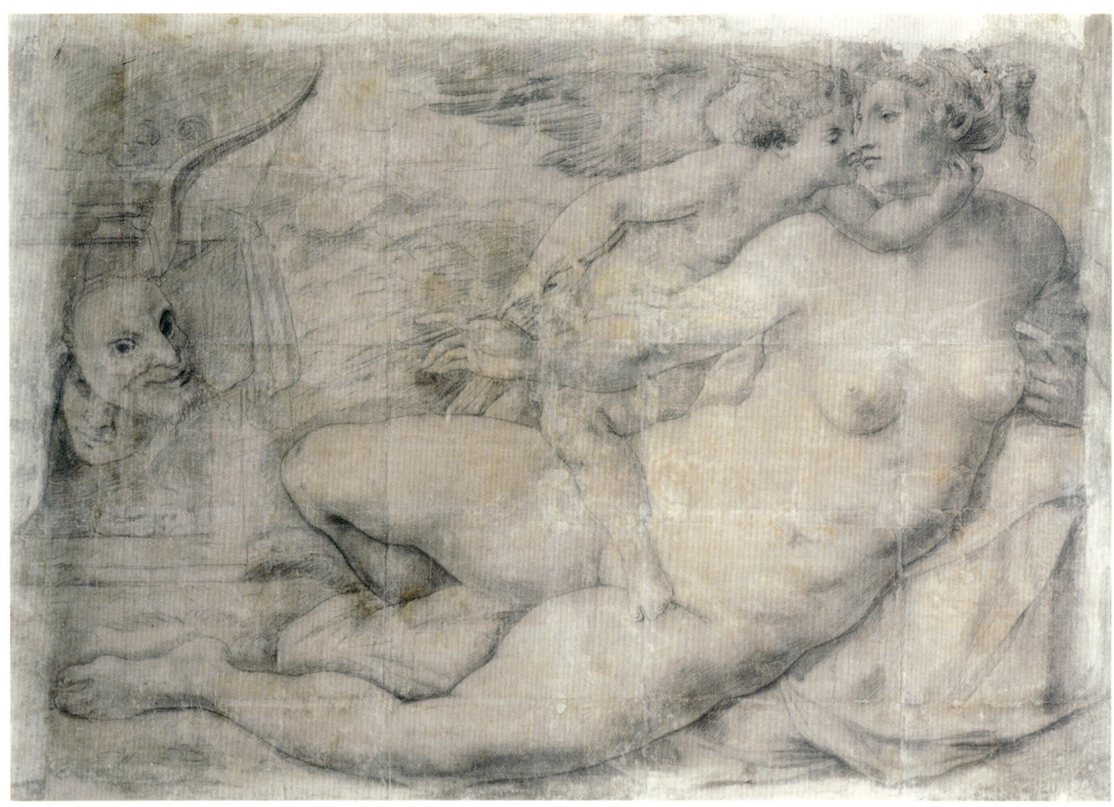

15. Michelangelo and his workshop (attributed), cartoon for *Venus and Cupid*, c. 1532–1534, charcoal on paper, 127.7 x 183.3 cm. Naples, Museo Nazionale di Capodimonte, Gabinetto disegni e stampe

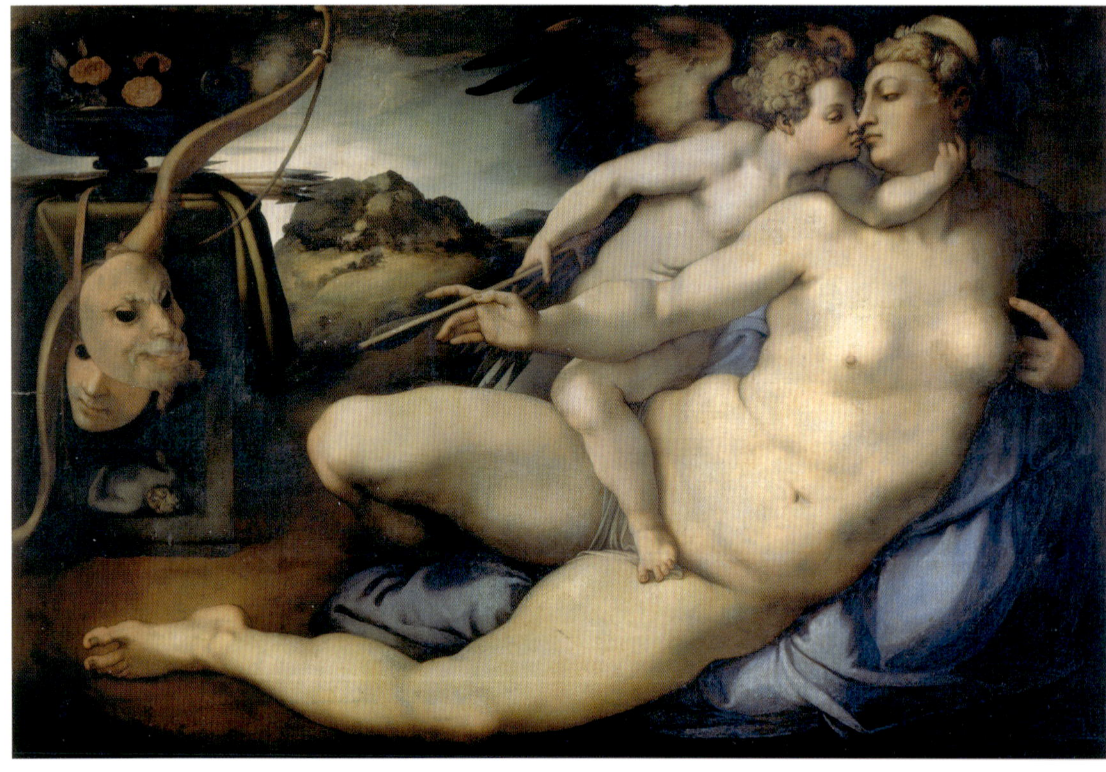

16. Jacopo da Pontormo after Michelangelo, *Venus and Cupid*, oil on panel, 128.5 x 193 cm. Florence, Galleria dell'Accademia

Epilogue

Vasari explains the use of one cartoon by two different artists with the creation of the perfect artwork. The other rare case of using a single cartoon, described by Vasari, combines the *design* (in the sense of idea and creation) of Michelangelo and the *colour* of the Venetian artist Sebastiano del Piombo.[36] Unlike our case of Mantegna and Bellini, there only the creation of the work is shared: Sebastiano's *Pietà* for San Francesco in Viterbo and the *Resurrection of Lazarus*, now at the National Gallery in London. Both paintings are based on drawings by Michelangelo.[37] Carmen Bambach views the matter in a pragmatic fashion. In her opinion, Michelangelo was well organized and supplied the cartoon to his friend and colleague in Rome while he was in Florence. According to Carmen Bambach, Michelangelo separates the idea (design) from the execution while profiting from both at the same time.[38] This theory is supported by the fact that Michelangelo established relationships of this type with various artists. For example, Vasari himself describes an analogous partnership between Michelangelo and Jacopo Pontormo.[39] According to Vasari, the military leader Alfonso d'Avalos, having received the cartoon for a *Noli me tangere* from Michelangelo, had it painted by Pontormo at Michelangelo's suggestion. We know from Vasari that the painting *Venus and Cupid* (Florence, Galleria dell'Accademia), a large extant painting, was produced on the basis of a cartoon by Michelangelo (figs. 15–16).[40]

[1] See the X-ray in Rothe 1992, pp. 82–83, fig. 4.
[2] Rothe 1992, p. 83; the flat haloes visible today are painted on top of the last layer of colour and are by a later hand, see Schmidt Arcangeli 2015, p. 317 and p. 323, note 14.
[3] Bagarotto *et al.* 2000, pp. 188–189, fig. 26, upon observing the pencil engraving lines revealed by the X-rays and the white lines that outlined the Christ Child, already thought that Bellini's *Presentation* was based on the use of a cartoon by Mantegna or a model. See Blass-Simmen 2017, pp. 16–18.
[4] Bagarotto *et al.* 2000, p. 189.
[5] To this regard see Schmidt Arcangeli 2015, p. 319.
[6] The range of dates is quite extensive, going from c. 1455 suggested by Coletti (1953) to the latter part of the 1470s as proposed by Robertson (1968). The dates and attributions are all indicated in: Caburlotto 2000; Trevisan 2008.
[7] Two extensive reflectography and X-ray campaigns have revealed a very clearly defined and high-quality underdrawing, definitely in his own hand and with a significant matrix, which can be placed perfectly within Giovanni Bellini's oeuvre from the 1460s–1470s. See Villa 2017, pp. 86–87. Ibid. in this catalogue. Christiansen 1992c, pp. 154–155, note 26, emphasized the high-quality underdrawing as an argument supporting the attribution of the Querini Stampalia painting to Bellini.
[8] Both Perugino and Raphael used cartoons to produce their works. Although Raphael was a pupil of Perugino, we know of no works that show the use of the same cartoon by both artists. To this regard, see Hiller von Gaertringen 1999, pp. 30–32, 301–311.
[9] Bambach 1999, p. 1, pp. 10–22. As regards the dispute that took place in 1398 due to motifs stolen from an artistic workshop by Jacquemart de Hesdin, which resulted in a fatality, see Blass-Simmen 1998. There was also a case regarding *unum cartonum cum quibusdam nudis Poleyoli* linked to Squarcione, who loaned it to the painter Marinello da Spalato and never received it back. See Lazzarini-Moschetti 1908 [1974], doc. LXI, pp. 41–42, pp. 169–170; Lightbown 1986, p. 19. I would like to thank Neville Rowley and Mattia Vinco.
[10] Although the painting by Mantegna is not an exact match for Michiel's description (Michiel describes a wooden panel, while the painting is on canvas), we can state with certainty that the Berlin Mantegna is the one from the Bembo collection, given that it bears the Gradenigo family seal. The Gradenigo family were the direct heirs of Elena Bembo, the daughter of Pietro Bembo, who married Pietro Gradenigo. See most recently Lauber 2013, pp. 461–462.
[11] The term close-up was used in the 1960s by Ringbom 1965 – certainly also in connection with zoom, which was now technically possible in photography and film – to indicate the half-figure image seen from close up. This definition intends to indicate the link between figures presented as in Byzantine icons, where only the head and trunk are seen, and the scenic *historia* (Ringbom 1965, pp. 109–110).
[12] Ringbom 1965; Degenhart-Schmitt 1990, vol. 6, p. 303.
[13] In Venice, *quasi alterum Byzantium*, to cite the Greek cardinal Bessarione, people were more familiar than in other parts of Italy with the sanctity of the eastern icon, and it is therefore entirely logical that the link between the icon and the history of the Renaissance was forged here. See Goffen 1989, pp. 26–28.
[14] Jacopo Bellini painted almost all his Madonnas as half figures behind a parapet. See Goffen 1975. Rona Goffen sees the half figure as an element that revives the Byzantine icon, the parapet as a reference to the tomb of Christ and the altar table. A Eucharistic reading of the sarcophagus seems likely. Even the parapet in the *Presentation* can be interpreted as an altar table, on which the Christ Child, like the *Corpus Cristi*, is displayed by Mary. The red velvet cushion on which Christ is resting closely resembles the liturgical cushion (*plumacium*) on which the host is displayed or the Eucharist chalice is presented and therefore suggests a Eucharistic reference to the sacrifice on the altar (p. 500) Regarding the parapet in particular see pp. 499–505; Krüger 2001, p. 69; Schmidt Arcangeli 2015, p. 323, note 6.
[15] See London-New York 1992, pp. 258–272. The *Descent into Limbo* is shown in numerous engravings by Mantegna and his school and also on a small wooden panel (formerly in the Barbara Piasecka Johnson Collection). All the versions show Christ from an unusual perspective seen from below and from behind, bent forward in the act of entering Hell. The air emerging from Limbo causes Christ's robes to billow out, adding a dramatic touch to the scene. Bellini uses the composition again in a work on parchment now conserved at the Bristol Museum and Art Gallery. It is interesting to note that once again there is a composition by Jacopo Bellini that already features the motif of the gate of Hell lying destroyed on the ground and the male nude holding the cross. The small panel in the Museo Civico in Padua was first cited by Colin Eisler in relation to the altarpiece for the Gattamelata Chapel at Sant'Antonio in Padua, mentioned in documents with an inscription by Jacopo, Gentile and Giovanni Bellini and believed to be lost (See Eisler 1985 [1986]). See also the sketchbook of Jacopo Bellini, Paris, fol. 21 *verso*.
[16] Alberti [1435–1436] 1975, §19.
[17] See Lucco 2013, pp. 58–63.
[18] Ringbom 1965, pp. 72–77 has already emphasized the relationship between Donatello and Mantegna, referring to the *Madonna Pazzi* now in the Bode Museum in Berlin.
[19] Ringbom 1965, p. 76.
[20] Rothe 1992, pp. 82–83. Some shards of wood in the edges of the canvas come from the wooden frame that has since been lost. The layer of brown colouring in the faux frame can also be seen on these shards, leading us to suppose that the actual frame formed a spatial continuation of the faux frame.
[21] Hockney 2001; Hockney-Grayford 2016, pp. 94–107.
[22] Ringbom 1965, p. 76: *fenestra templi*.
[23] Schmidt Arcangeli 2015, p. 317 interprets the composition as a *fenestra coeli*.
[24] Regarding the subsequent addition of the 'lateral' figures, see Villa 2017, p. 88. As confirmed in numerous interviews, Babette Hartwieg, director of the department of restoration and conservation at the Gemäldegalerie in Berlin, the paint layer of the lateral figures on right and left is higher than that of the main figures, which were painted earlier.
[25] Dunkerton 2004, p. 197, p. 311, note 8 states that the chemical transformation of the egg used to bind the azurite pigments may also cause the colour to blacken. The azurite pigments also appear in the cloak of the Madonna, which appears black and gold today, but originally had a blue and gold design. Schmidt Arcangeli 2015, p. 323 mentions a layer – possibly additional – of opaque brown. See also the fundamental and comprehensive study by Rothe 1992, pp. 80–88, particularly p. 82.
[26] Regarding the changes to the background of the *St Mark* see Christiansen 1992b, pp. 119–121 and Sander 2004, pp. 29–46, p. 40, note 39.
[27] Currently undergoing restoration at the Getty Museum. I would

like to thank Yvonne Szafran, chief restorer at the J. P. Getty Museum in Los Angeles. Here we can imagine a work similar to the copy of the portrait with the blue background, auctioned by Christie, Manson & Woods 1978, Lot 121. I would like to thank Carolyn Wilson for this information. See also Pilo 2008.

[28] Lucco 2013, pp. 299–301. See also the other half-figure compositions from the late period at the Brera in Milan, the Fort Worth Kimbell Art Museum, the Kunstsammlungen Alte Meister Gemäldegalerie in Dresden, and the Mantegna Funerary Chapel in Mantua. Another late half-figure painting is the *Adoration of the Magi* at the J. P. Getty Museum in Los Angeles. Yvonne Szafran, chief restorer at the J. Paul Getty Museum, confirmed on 15/1/2018 that the painting on canvas was framed by a painted window, no longer visible today, like the *Presentation*.

[29] The mathematical principles of the golden section have been known since antiquity. The earliest descriptions that have reached us are found in Euclid's *Elements*. Leon Battista Alberti, in his treatise *Della Pittura* from 1435–36 (including § 2–7), established the requirement for painting to be based on the fundamental principles of geometry and optics, referring to Euclid's *Elements*. Luca Pacioli, who had published Euclid's work, dealt intensely with the golden section and called it 'Divina proportione', giving the name to his treatise *De divina proporzione* published in Venice in 1509.

[30] The painting by Giovanni was later cut at the corners. See the contribution by Hartwieg in this book.

[31] See most recently: Godla, Allen 2015.

[32] Goffen 1989, pp. 281–285, the question of attribution is summed up by Caburlotto 2000 and Trevisan 2008, p. 176.

[33] Marinelli 2011, pp. 467–468 supports the theory according to which Mantegna's painting originally belonged to Jacopo Bellini, who left it to Gentile, after which it passed into the Giovanni's hands. Through the mediation of Isabella d'Este, it entered – together with the portrait by Jacopo of his teacher Gentile da Fabriano, also described by Michiel and since lost – the collection of Pietro Bembo. Schmidt Arcangeli 2015, pp. 321–322 finds it unlikely that such an important painting was sold by the heirs and supposes that Mantegna's painting was commissioned by Pietro's father, Bernardo Bembo.

[34] Cordellier 1995, doc. 38, pp. 96–100, doc. 52, pp. 120–122.

[35] Barausse 2008, doc. 91, p. 350.

[36] Vasari [1550–1568] 1967–1987, vol. 5 p. 89. He also discusses the rivalry with Raphael.

[37] The subject is covered extensively in London 2017, pp. 117–123, 142-151. See Dunkerton-Billinge-Wivel (in press). I would like to thank Jill Dunkerton for allowing me to consult the draft.

[38] New York 2017, pp. 142–146, 164–168. Interview with Carmen Bambach https://www.metmuseum.org/blogs/now-at-the-met/2017/carmen-bambach-interview-michelangelo-catalogue?utm_source=homepage&utm_medium=banner

[39] Vasari [1550-1568] 1967–1987, vol. 5 p. 326.

[40] Frankfurt 2016, cat. 79, pp. 190–191. According to Carmen Bambach there are still thirty-two copies in existence today.

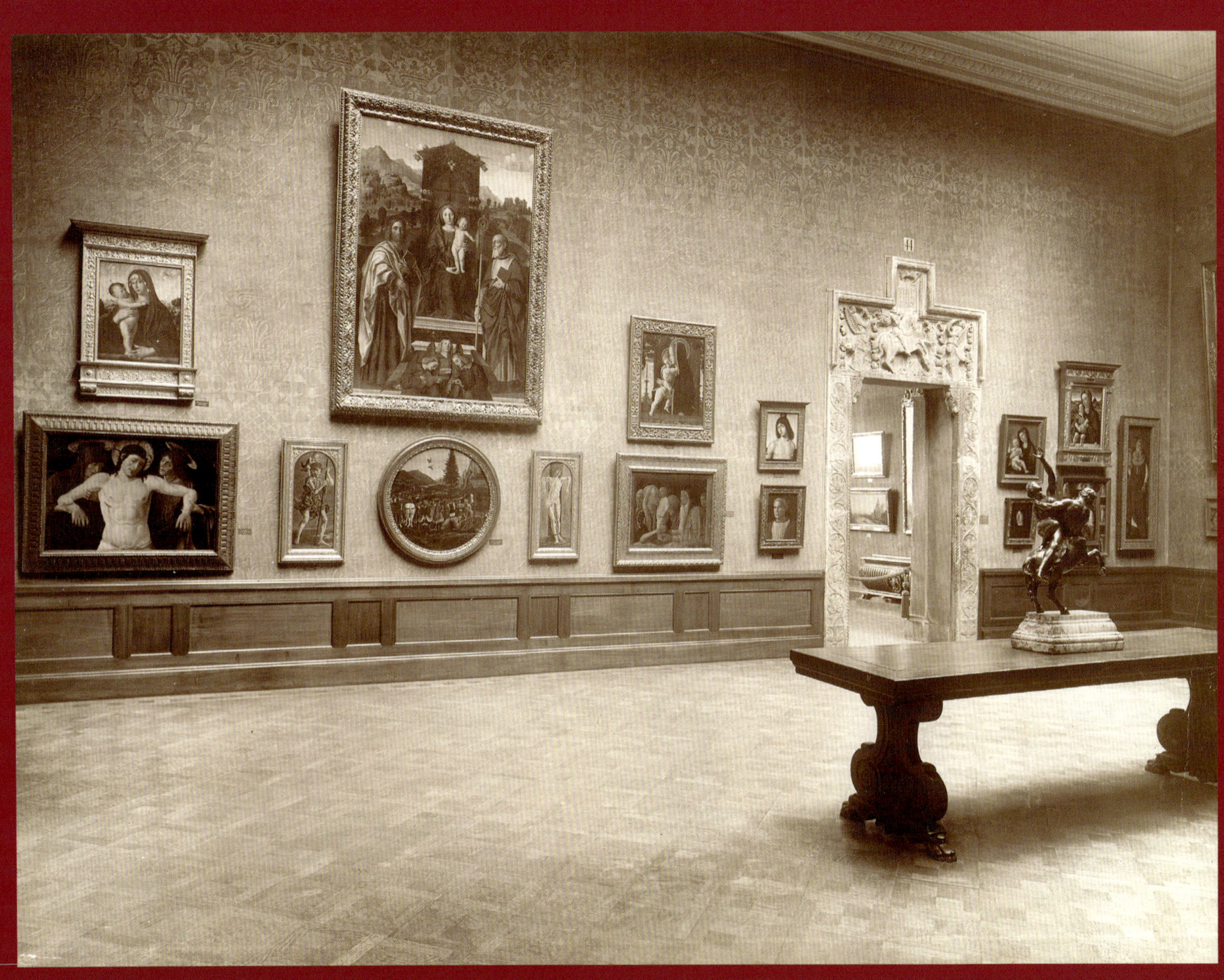

Critical Fortunes and Worldly Vicissitudes of Andrea Mantegna's *Presentation of Jesus at the Temple*, Now at the Gemäldegalerie in Berlin

NEVILLE ROWLEY

1. Berlin, Kaiser-Friedrich-Museum, 1926

Two Early 19th-Century Descriptions

The first reference in print to Andrea Mantegna's *Presentation of Jesus at the Temple*, now conserved at the Gemäldegalerie in Berlin, dates back to 1800, when Abbot Iacopo Morelli, custodian of the Marciana Library in Venice, published a previously unknown, anonymous early 16th-century manuscript that listed numerous works of art to be found in the Lombardy and Veneto regions. Among them was the following entry, "in the home of M. Pietro Bembo" in Padua: "The little painting on panel, which shows Our Lady presenting the child for circumcision, comes from the hand of Mantegna, and is executed in half figures".[1]

When Morelli published this manuscript – which would turn out to have been penned by a friend of Bembo's, the Venetian noble Marcantonio Michiel – he had no knowledge of the fact that the work described had remained in Padua, in the very same palace which in the mid-16th century had come into the possession of the Gradenigo family.[2] A letter of March 9, 1803 from scholar Giovanni de Lazara to his collector friend Giovanni Maria Sasso clarifies this fact with a wealth of detail:

> Moving now from the prints to the paintings I will tell you that in recent days I saw once more with great and renewed pleasure the surprising St Sebastian of our unrivaled *Mantegna* in the Gradenigo palace, where I also saw his other painting of the Circumcision that is also cited by the anonymous source published by the erudite Abbot Morelli, and since I'm pleased to think that you might take some delight in being reminded of it, I shall describe it for you.
>
> The Virgin Mary is portrayed in a half figure in profile and looking to the right of the person observing the painting, with the child wearing a bonnet on his head, fully swathed, held erect by her on a pillow placed on a marble window, and presented for Circumcision to the Priest with a long white beard, also portrayed in a half figure, who prepares to receive him in his arms with a most devout expression. Between the Madonna and the Priest only the head of St Joseph is visible, and behind on the sides, that of a woman, and a young man who bears some resemblance to [Mantegna's] portrait painted next to that of his mentor *Squarcione* in the St Christopher section of the Eremitani Chapel. The painting is in tempera, and is neither as beautiful nor as well preserved as the other of St Sebastian. I believe it to be of his earlier works, done around the time when he was painting the abovementioned Eremitani Chapel: on the Virgin's sleeves appear the same figures or letters as in the prints, and in many of his paintings [...].[3]

The identification of the work described in the letter with the painting in Berlin is demonstrated not only by the latter's perfect correspondence with de Lazara's description, but also by a detail hidden behind the Berlin painting: the seal of the Gradenigo family (see the contribution by Babette Hartwieg in this book, fig. 4).

The work likely left the palace that very same year, subsequently becoming the property of English banker and collector Edward Solly at an unspecified moment.[4] In 1821, Solly's collection was purchased by the King of Prussia and formed the core of the future Royal Museum in Berlin – a story that can also be followed by tracking the various seals and labels on the back of the painting, as Babette Hartwieg has carefully done in the present volume.[5] In Berlin, memory of the work's Paduan origins may have been lost, but the same could not be said of the name of Mantegna, which was mentioned in every inventory and catalogue of the nascent Berlin museum, aside from Aloys Hirt's hasty attribution to Gentile Bellini in the 1820s.[6]

In 1866 Marquis Giuseppe Campori published in Genoa his *Lettere artistiche inedite*, which included Giovanni de Lazara's long description of Mantegna's *Presentation of Jesus at the Temple* seen in the Gradenigo palace. Art history could have benefitted greatly from a prompt acceptance of de Lazara's observations: the dating of the painting to Mantegna's early years, the connection to the painting mentioned in the Bembo palace "by the anonymous source published by the erudite Abbot Morelli," but also the identification of far right-hand figure with the painter's self-portrait, are all aspects on which contemporary scholars agree. Yet quite the opposite occurred: the dating was quickly contested, then the provenance, and, shortly thereafter, even the very attribution to Mantegna. No further mention was made of the presumed self-portrait or, when it did occur, was quickly forgotten. This singular fate is revealing of the empirical method by which art history is constructed, with sporadic steps forward as well as backward. Let's examine it in detail.

The Morelli Controversy

The protagonist of the *Presentation*'s "critical confusion" had no connection to the abbot-editor of the Michiel manuscript, despite sharing his last name. Today Giovanni Morelli is recognized as one of the most important art connoisseurs of the second half of the 19th century, inventor of an experimental method for identifying a painting's authorship through the analysis of features that painters tended to execute mechanically, almost without thinking, such as ears or fingernails.[7] On this basis, Morelli boasted of having corrected a whole series of erroneous attributions he claimed had been made for paintings in many famous Italian and German collections, from the Borghese and Doria-Pamphilj galleries in Rome to the Gemäldegalerie in Munich, Dresden and Berlin. And it was in a volume that Morelli dedicated to German museums, published in 1880, that Mantegna's *Presentation* began to lose its luster. The painting's canvas support not only moved the author to propose a later dating, in the last decade of the fifteenth century (unlike what had been argued a decade earlier by Joseph Arthur Crowe and Giovan Battista Cavalcaselle, who had underlined the connection with the Michiel and de Lazara descriptions), but this support contradicted the sixteenth-century description of the painting in the Bembo home, where it was called a "painting on panel."[8] In Morelli's view, that painting could not be the Berlin canvas; it had to be the panel painting in the Querini Stampalia collection in Venice that portrayed the same subject with an extra figure on each side.

Giovanni Morelli died in 1891, but his fame only grew in the years to come. Two years later, his close collaborator Gustavo Frizzoni undertook to publish a new edition of his essay on the Berlin gallery, which Morelli had managed to revise before his death. The *Presentation of Jesus at the Temple* is described as "in ruins," no longer to be considered an original Mantegna, as had previously been the case, but rather a copy of the Mantegna original in the Querini Stampalia collection. In a classic example of

Morelli's analysis, he corroborated this assessment by saying that all one had to do was look carefully at the ears of Christ and the Madonna to be convinced that "it was not like Mantegna to draw so weakly. In the execution of his works he remains the impeccable model."[9] This disdainful judgment could make us question if Morelli's gifts of connoisseurship – which he certainly did possess – were his critical conclusions not conditioned by a very specific cultural attitude: as a senator of the Italian Republic, fervently committed to preventing foreign museums from laying their hands on Italian art, Morelli had developed a preference for any works had remained in Italy over any that had left. And it was no coincidence that this stance was followed several years later by another senator committed to defending the national heritage, Adolfo Venturi, in the pages of his monumental *Storia dell'arte italiana*.[10]

But Morelli's thesis did not convince everyone. In his extensive monograph on Mantegna, published in English in 1901 and in German the following year, Paul Kristeller argued strongly both for the attribution of the Berlin painting to Mantegna, as well as its early dating. Kristeller also rejected Morelli's identification of the "painting on panel" seen by Michiel in the Bembo palace with the version in the Querini Stampalia collection: after all, the next work in Michiel's list, Raphael's *Portrait of Andrea Navagero and Agostino Beazzano*, is also indicated as being on wood, while the painting in the Galleria Doria-Pamphilj in Rome is "on canvas, as everyone knows."[11] For Kristeller, however, the most decisive argument was the mediocrity of the Venetian work, "a poor, later copy in oil." Just as Morelli had needed to degrade the Berlin exemplar in order to exalt the one in Venice, which he was introducing into the scholarly debate, the reevaluation of the Berlin work occurred through the debasement of its Venetian "relative." These positions were perpetuated for several years. Morelli's most brilliant student, Bernard Berenson, defended his mentor's theses, though he quietly corroborated the Berlin painting's attribution to Mantegna. As for the Berlin museum's curator, Wilhelm Bode, he would strenuously defend the importance of 'his' version.

Bode's attitude can also be chalked up to personal enmity: he had crossed paths with Morelli, who had blatantly ridiculed him in his writings, and done his best to prevent Bode's museum from acquiring important works, including Giorgione's *The Tempest*, which remained in Venice thanks to Morelli's guile.[12] Bode's rivalry with Berenson was also linked to the market, the competition coming this time from the numerous acquisitions by American collectors.[13] As a polemicist, Bode knew no limits: just as he had not hesitated to ridicule Morelli's methods immediately after his death, an attitude many viewed as shocking, he also used the good part of a review of Kristeller's volume to attack another article on the book, written by Mary Logan in the *Gazette des Beaux-Arts*, guilty, in his eyes, of being too favorable to Morelli and Berenson's theories.[14] But rather than make a scholarly argument, Bode preferred to insist on the fact that Mary Logan also happened to be… Mrs. Berenson![15]

Good manners may not have been one of Bode's strong suits, but he was nevertheless correct to defend the Berlin painting's attribution to Mantegna, as well as its early placement in the artist's career. The German art historian was also the first to support Giovanni de Lazara's thesis regarding the likely presence of the painter's self-portrait in the figure on the far right-hand side of the painting, and extend this reasoning to the woman on the far left, who, in Bode's view, could be none other than Nicolosia Bellini, Jacopo's daughter and Mantegna's wife.[16] Yet this quite sensible proposal did not make headway in the art world and was often forgotten until after World War II, when this identification finally won a consensus. Ultimately, the only scholarly criticism one might make against Bode concerns his harsh treatment of the Querini Stampalia *Presentation*, guilty only of not being by Mantegna and – most of all – of being too highly praised by Morelli and

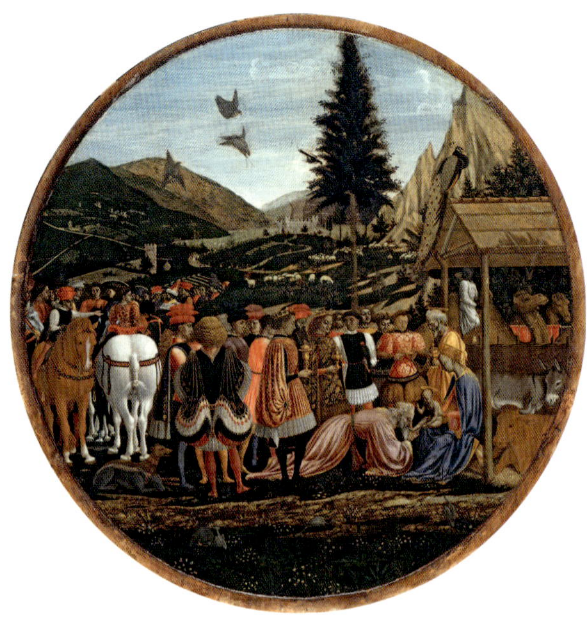

Berenson. It would fall to the latter, in 1916, to connect the painting to its true author: Giovanni Bellini.[17]

Peregrinations in Dark Times

Two photographs exist to document the presence of Mantegna's *Presentation of Jesus at the Temple* in Berlin before World War II. Both were taken at the Kaiser-Friedrich-Museum, a museum that Bode had championed to house the Renaissance painting and sculpture collections and that opened in 1904 (in 1956, it would be renamed the Bode-Museum). The first photo dates to 1926 (fig. 1). In it we can glimpse some of the then 80-year-old Bode's museological choices, starting with the dialogue between painting and sculpture (the latter represented by the late-15th-century Genoese portal, which dialogues more effectively with the paintings than Giambologna's *Abduction of Deianira* displayed on the table). In the arrangement of the paintings it's symmetry that defines the artistic hierarchies: thus the most important work is surely the *Adoration of the Magi* tondo (fig. 2), which Bode positioned among the Verona, Padua and Venice schools because he believed it to be a masterpiece by Pisanello (in 1925, Roberto Longhi had just linked it to Domenico Veneziano and the Florentine school).[18] The *Presentation of Jesus at the Temple* also garners an important placement, beneath the *Madonna and Child* by Mantegna's mentor and adoptive father, Francesco Squarcione (fig. 3), a work previously owned by Giovanni Maria Sasso, addressee of the letter mentioned at the beginning of this essay, and beside the *Portrait of Cardinal Ludovico Trevisan* (fig. 4), whose attribution to Mantegna was never questioned, even by Morelli.[19] In the photo, a third presumed Mantegna is concealed by Giambologna's small bronze: a *Madonna and Child* (fig. 5) framed by putti carrying the instruments of the Passion, which Bode came to believe, after some initial uncertainty, was an early Mantegna.[20]

The second photograph was taken just seven years later (fig. 6), but everything had changed: the vast room, multi-level presentation, and contextual choice have been replaced by an austere ambience and a more strictly monographic approach. Squarcione's

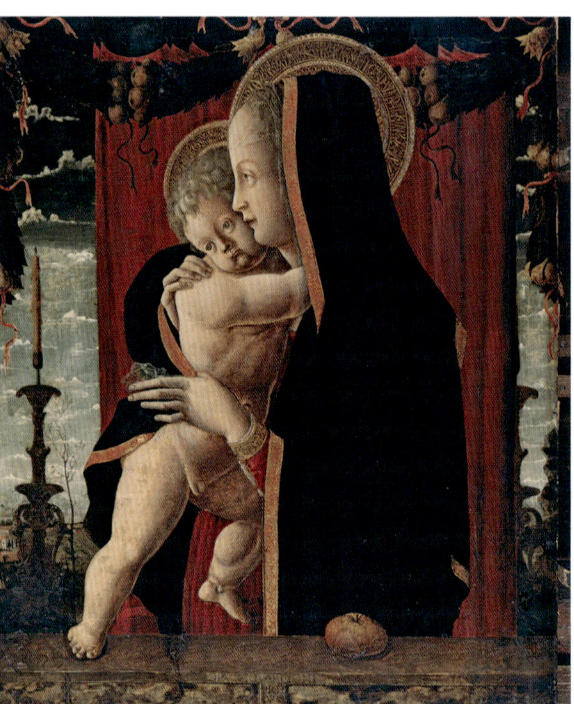

2. Domenico Veneziano, *Adoration of the Magi*. Berlin, Staatliche Museen, Gemäldegalerie

3. Francesco Squarcione, *Madonna and Child*. Berlin, Staatliche Museen, Gemäldegalerie

4. Andrea Mantegna, *Portrait of Cardinal Ludovico Trevisan*. Berlin, Staatliche Museen, Gemäldegalerie

5. Lazzaro Bastiani, *Madonna and Child*. Berlin, Staatliche Museen, Gemäldegalerie

6. Berlin, Kaiser-Friedrich-Museum, 1933

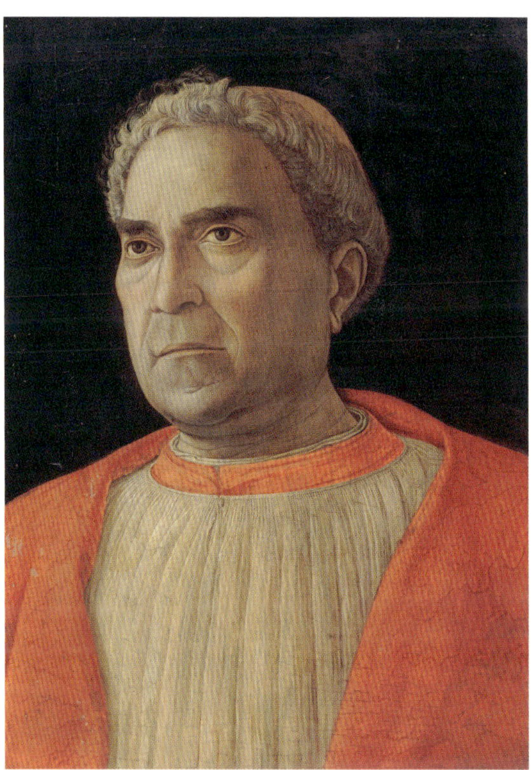

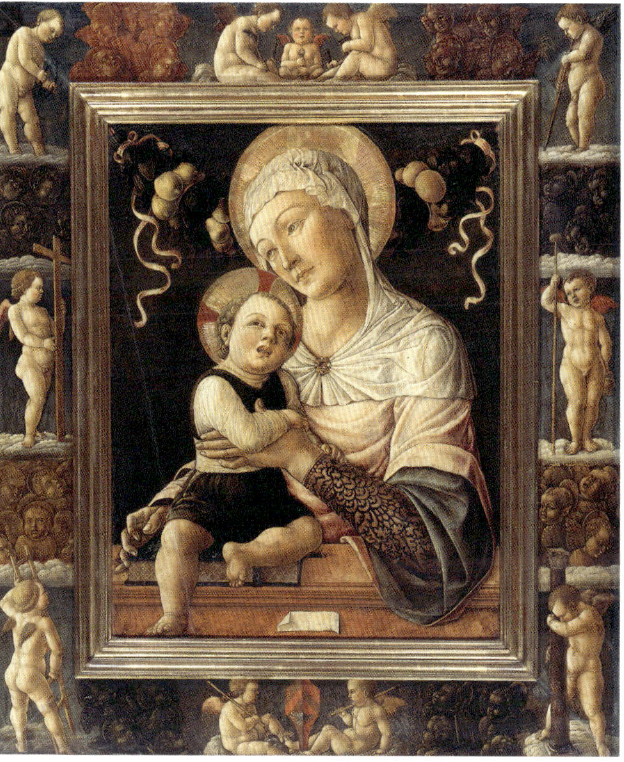

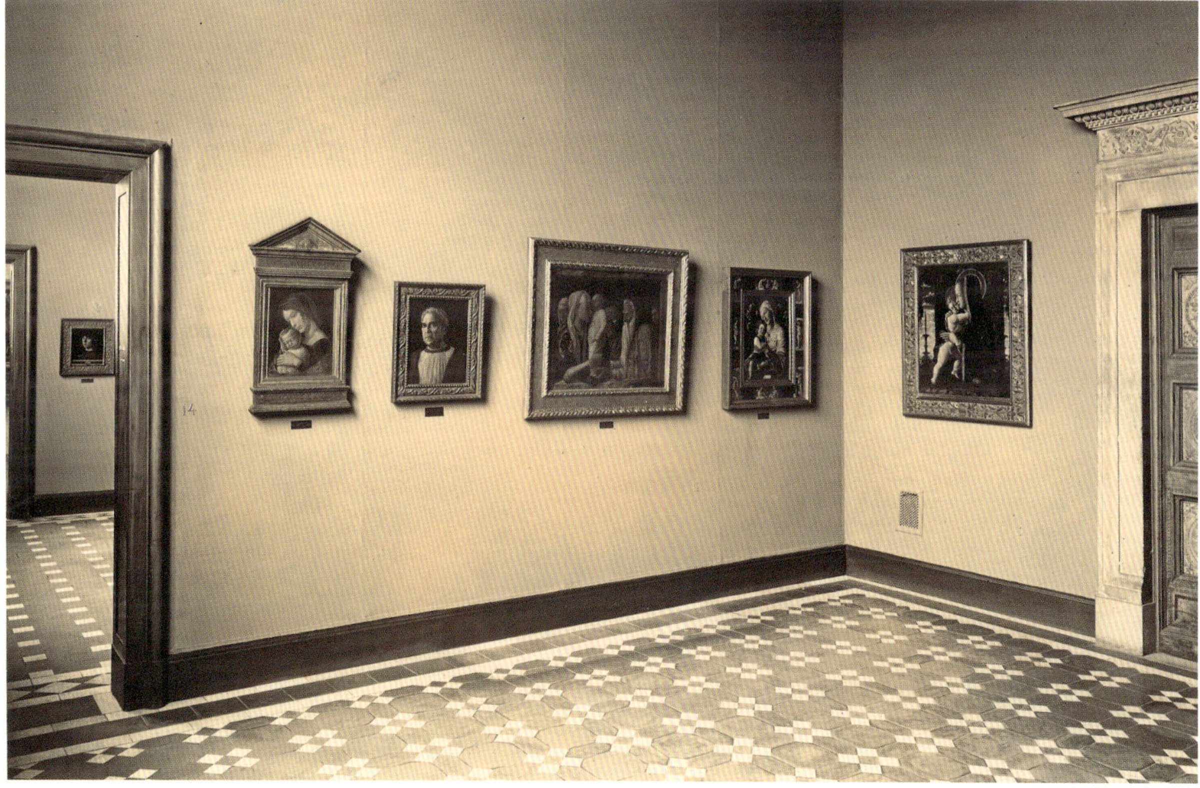

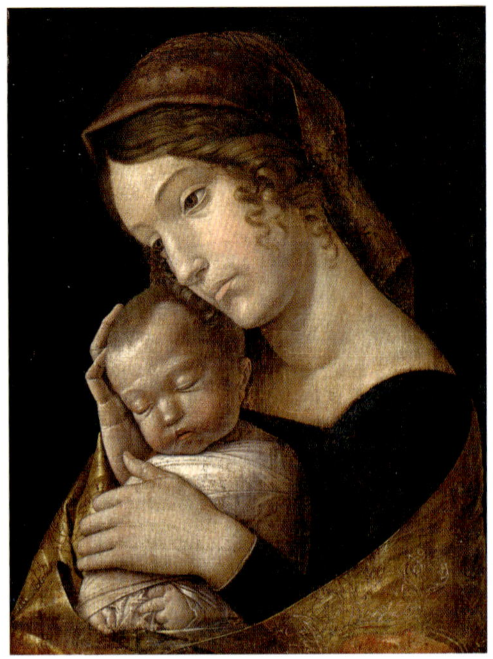

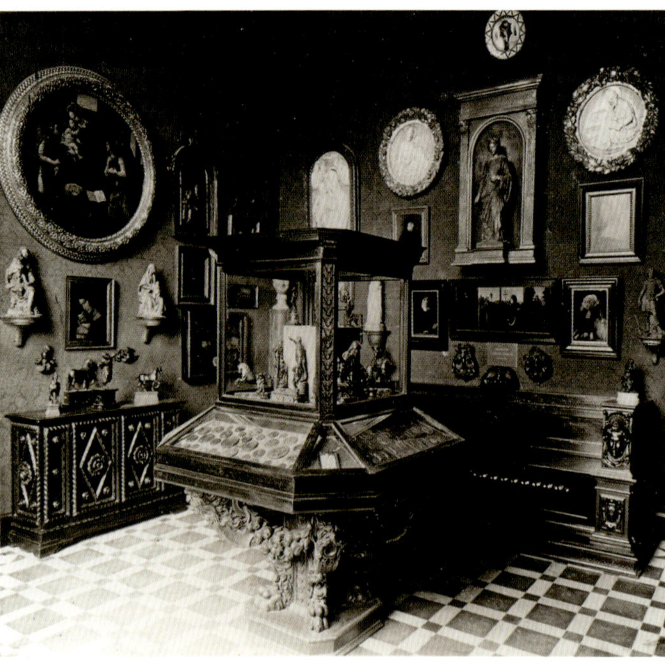

7. Andrea Mantegna, *Madonna and Child*, or *Simon Madonna*, Berlin, Staatliche Museen, Gemäldegalerie

8. Berlin, Kaiser-Friedrich-Museum, . c. 1909: the "Simon Cabinet"

Madonna occupies the wall to the right, while the three presumed Mantegnas are on the adjoining wall, with a fourth painting, a *Madonna* also by Mantegna (fig. 7), that was part of the James Simon donation and had been displayed in a different part of the Kaiser-Friedrich-Museum upon its opening in 1904. The "Simon Cabinet" (fig. 8) ought to have remained untouched for a century; but starting in 1933 the prominent presence of the name of a Jewish donor was no longer compatible with the tastes of the Nazi regime, which gradually eliminated all references to the room just as it was removing the most relevant works from the museum's permanent collections, beginning with Mantegna's *Madonna*. The room would be completely dismantled in the second half of August 1939, just days before the German invasion of Poland and the beginning of World War II in Europe.[21] Night had fallen on Berlin.

With the war, Berlin's museums closed and their art was stored in a depot beneath the Pergamon Museum, close to the Kaiser-Friedrich and judged more resistant to air attacks. In 1942, however, even this location was thought to be too exposed to risk; the Berlin paintings were transferred to a newly-constructed anti-aircraft bunker in Friedrichshain Park. In March 1945, with the Red Army at the gates of Berlin, Hitler himself decided to transfer at least the most important paintings (at least those that could be moved) to salt mines in Thuringia: Mantegna's *Presentation of Jesus at the Temple* was among them. This voyage certainly put these works in grave danger, but it ended up being their salvation: in May 1945, two mysterious fires struck the Friedrichshain bunker and consigned to the flames the paintings that had remained there, among them works by Signorelli, Caravaggio, and Botticelli, as well as the *Pietà* with the black background visible in the 1926 photo, which at the time was attributed to Jacopo Bellini (fig. 9).[22] Many frames of the evacuated paintings had remained in the bunker; the one belonging to the *Presentation* (fig. 10) was lost forever.[23]

Along with the other works of art discovered by the Allies in Germany, Mantegna's *Presentation* came to the Central Collecting Point in Wiesbaden. But it didn't stay for long: in December 1945 it was taken to Washington and inserted in the collections

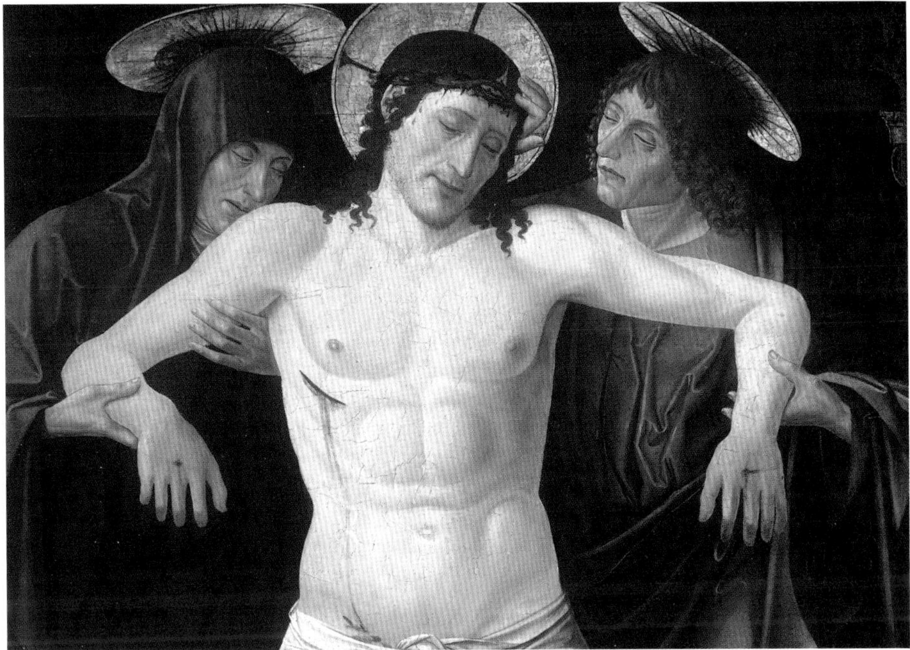

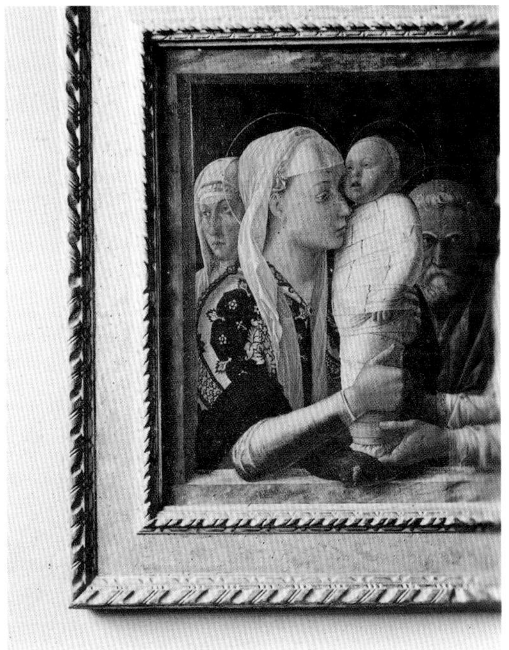

9. Anonymous Venetian, *Dead Christ between the Virgin and St John*. Previously in Berlin, Kaiser-Friedrich-Museum (disappeared in 1945)

10. Andrea Mantegna, *Presentation of Jesus at the Temple*, detail of the painting's frame before 1945

of the recently founded National Gallery, along with two hundred other masterpieces from the Gemäldegalerie (among them, Mantegna's *Portrait of Cardinal Ludovico Trevisan*). This secret attempt at plunder was foiled by American Captain Walter Farmer, director of the Central Collecting Point, who wrote a manifesto protesting against an act that violated every international agreement then in force.[24] Soon, the failed theft was transformed into propaganda: the two hundred paintings from Berlin were displayed in Washington in 1948 in an incredibly successful exhibition, followed shortly thereafter by a series of thirteen other shows around America. The most fragile paintings weren't taken on tour but returned to Wiesbaden; such was the case of our *Presentation*, but it only returned to Berlin in the mid-1950s, thanks to the efforts of the friends of the museum, the Kaiser-Friedrich-Museumsverein. The works were installed in the American sector of Dahlem, located in what was the the western part of the city.[25] In 1961, the painting was lent out for the great Mantegna retrospective organized at the Ducal Palace in Mantua, for which it was labelled as belonging to the "old National Museums" (*Ehemals Staatliche Museen*), as if the now-split Berlin museums were no longer even sure of their own name.[26] The work has never moved since, aside from its 1998 trip across town to the Gemäldegalerie's new location next to the Tiergarten, in a reunified Berlin.

New Exegeses

The 1961 Mantua exhibition's catalogue entry for the *Presentation* bears witness to a degree of continuity with early 20th-century studies: Giovanni Paccagnini grapples with the whole Morelli controversy, but sides with Bode. Yet the author fails to mention the German art historian's argument for identifying the couple at the sides of the painting with the painter and his wife. This absence would have a direct consequence: the following year, Wolfram Prinz felt legitimated to claim this identification as his own, as if no one had ever thought of it before – a careless judgment which would unfortunately mislead even the foremost Mantegna scholars for several decades.[27] Prinz, however, did base his claim on a new argument, the association of the painting's presumed self-portrait with the monumental grisaille head painted on the wall of the Ovetari Chapel (fig. 11), which Giuseppe Fiocco had identified a few years earlier as a potential self-portrait of Mantegna.[28] The identification of the woman on the left with Nicolosia Bellini also made it possible to settle the still-open question of the work's dating, placing it around the time of Mantegna's marriage to Nicolosia in 1453, or perhaps a few months later: the theme of Christ's presentation at the temple would have been particularly well-suited to the birth of a first son.[29] Now the entire painting came to be interpreted as a symbolic act, a declaration of Mantegna's emancipation from his adoptive father, Squarcione, at the very moment he had found a surrogate, his father-in-law Jacopo Bellini.[30] Scholars also asked themselves what the two newlyweds might be gazing at so intensely in the left part of the painting: a church altar, or perhaps the painting's light source, thus suffusing the work with a symbolism linked to the mysticism of light, associated with the Feast of the Purification of the Virgin in the Temple?[31] By nature, those questions remained unanswered.

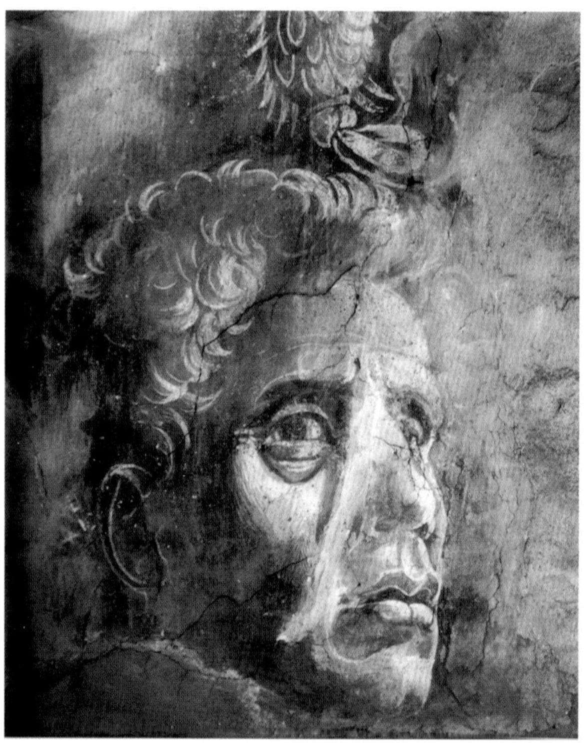

11. Andrea Mantegna, *Self-Portrait*. Previously in Padua, Church of the Eremitani, Ovetari Chapel (destroyed in 1944).

But the Berlin *Presentation*'s most striking feature for post-World War II scholars would be the fact that its protagonists are cut "in half figures," as Marcantonio Michiel had already noted in the sixteenth century. The first to realize the historical importance of Mantegna's approach was Erwin Panofsky, in the pages of his vast monograph on Albrecht Dürer.[32] A few years later, Millard Meiss took this insight a step further, calling Mantegna's *Presentation* "the first 'close-up' of a religious narrative that we know in Italian or indeed Northern painting."[33] This designation soon turned into an analytical category thanks to Finnish art historian Sixten Ringbom's *Icon to Narrative. The Rise of the Dramatic Close-Up in Fifteenth-Century Devotional Painting*, published in 1965 to relative obscurity but which over the years has been transformed into a classic. For Ringbom, one of Mantegna's potential sources was Donatello's *Pazzi Madonna* (fig. 12), also conserved in Berlin, at the Bode-Museum (and which was also in West Berlin during the Cold War).[34] If Wilhelm Bode, who acquired the *Madonna* for the Berlin museums, never made this connection because he rightly judged the work to date from Donatello's Florentine years and not his decade in Padua, we must nevertheless underscore the potency of this association: the two "marble windows" (to use Giovanni de Lazara's perfect formulation) seem to communicate with one another, making Mantegna's *Presentation of Jesus at the Temple* a work that straddles the genres of icon and narrative scene. After Ringbom, many other art historians have insisted on this crucial point.[35]

So much analysis has unfortunately managed to explain for which patron and which location Mantegna created such an innovative painting. The most recent study of the painting suggests Pietro Bembo's father, Bernardo, as the work's possible patron, which would explain its presence in the family palace at the beginning of the sixteenth

12. Donatello, *Madonna and Child* a.k.a *Pazzi Madonna*. Berlin, Staatliche Museen, Bode-Museum

13. Jacopo da Valenza (attributed), *Portrait of a Young Man*. Bergamo, Accademia Carrara

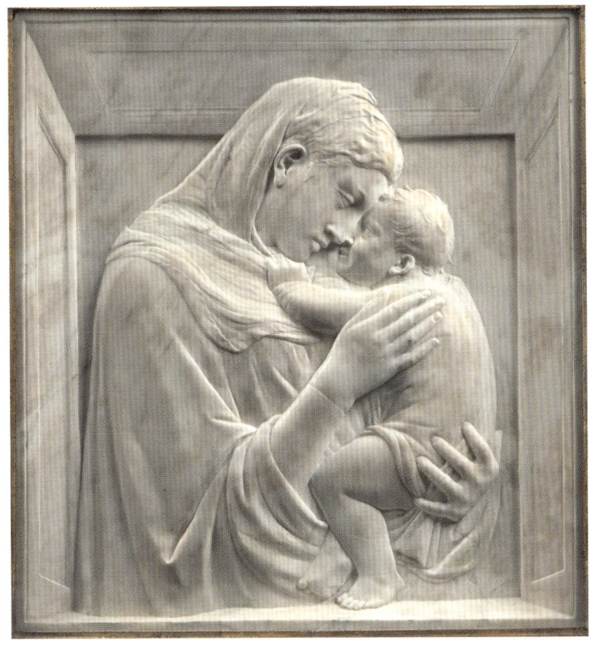

century.[36] But why would Mantegna have inserted (in a second moment) his own portrait, and that of his wife, in a painting destined to leave the family circle? And why would Giovanni Bellini have had the opportunity (and desire) to copy it in the early 1470s, making use of a cartoon that was not drawn freehand but rather traced directly from his brother-in-law's finished work? That Mantegna's painting was destined for his father-in-law, Jacopo Bellini, seems a far more fitting interpretation.[37] What's more, the dating of Giovanni Bellini's 'copy' corresponds with the moment of Jacopo's death: one can thus imagine its creation in the context of the patriarchal succession, when the sketchbooks passed into the hands of the brother, Gentile. In duplicating this family portrait, Giovanni also doubled the number of portraits; the key to the riddle must be sought in their as-yet-unresolved identification, but which must surely be connected to the *Portrait of a Young Man* conserved at the Accademia Carrara in Bergamo (fig. 13), extraordinarily similar to the figure on the right of the Venetian painting.[38] These limits to our knowledge do not mean, however, that progress has not been made on other fronts, from technical analyses, developed by a pioneering essay by Andrea Rothe investigating Mantegna's pictorial techniques, to the fundamental observations proposed in this catalogue, which invite us to look at the Berlin *Presentation of Jesus at the Temple* with an eye to the creative process and the alteration of the pigments, and view the Venice version as literally "traced" from Mantegna's.[39]

But let's take one last look at Giovanni de Lazara's 1803 letter that we quoted at the beginning of this essay, a description of significant historical value that, as we've seen, also contains an important technical dimension: in his comparison with the *St Sebastian*, a later work of Mantegna's which at the time was also in the Gradenigo palace and is now at the Ca d'Oro in Venice (fig. 14), de Lazara writes that the *Presentation of Jesus at the Temple* was not "as well conserved as the other," proof that its once luminous colors had already been compromised by a careless restauration. When the author adds that the work "is not [...] as beautiful" as the *St Sebastian*, however, we

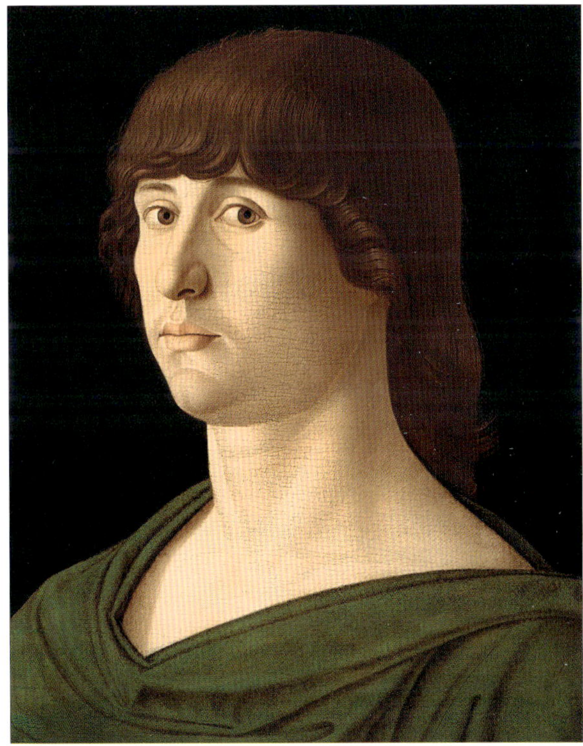

must disagree. The *St Sebastian* (fig. 14) is a mature masterpiece which remained in Mantegna's workshop until his death, his last meditation on a theme he'd already explored and on the visual device of the "marble window" he had experimented in his youth, particularly in the *Presentation of Jesus at the Temple*. The latter is a work of disconcerting modernity, paving the way for half-length narrative composition thanks to the mediation of Giovanni Bellini. The fact that Mantegna's *Presentation* is now on loan at the Fondazione Querini Stampalia in Venice, displayed side by side with his brother-in-law's version, is thus far more than an event – it's an epiphany. We're confident that, unlike what has often happened in the past, visitors to the exhibition will be able to admire both versions, without feeling the need to disparage either. For once, why not try putting Mantegna and Bellini on the same level – the highest possible?[40]

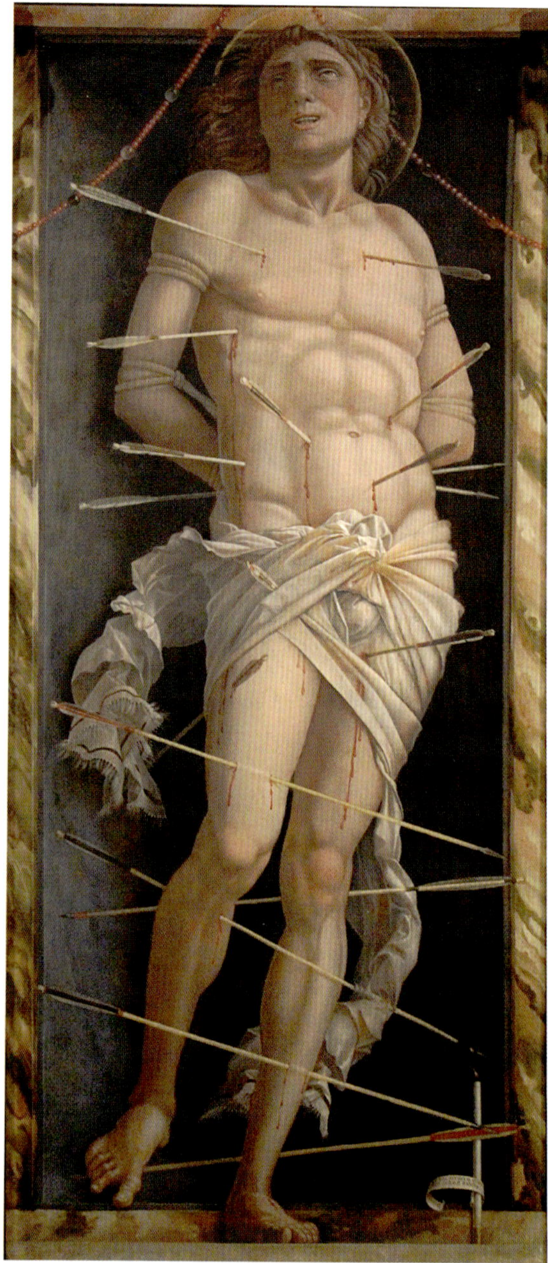

14. Andrea Mantegna, *St Sebastian*. Venice, Galleria Giorgio Franchetti at the Ca' d'Oro

Thanks to Christine Exler, Babette Hartwieg, Daniela Ranzi, Brigit Blass-Simmen, Robert Skwirblies, Maria Stein, Giovanni C.F. Villa and Mattia Vinco.

[1] Michiel [1525–1528] 1800, pp. 17–18.
[2] On the palace's change of ownership through the marriage of Pietro Bembo's daughter, see Beltramini 2013, p. 379. The dating of Michiel's manuscript to between 1525 and 1528 comes from Schmitter 2003, p. 571.
[3] Campori 1866, pp. 351–352. On the artistic taste of Giovanni de Lazara, see Caburlotto 2001, especially p. 160.
[4] Pietro Selvatico in Vasari [1550–1568] 1849, p. 190, indicates that the painting was sold by the Gradenigo family in 1803, without specifying the buyer.
[5] See pp. 76–78 in this volume.
[6] Skwirblies 2008, p. LII, no. 340. Concerning Hirt's tendency to "misattribute" Mantegna's works, see Friedrich Bury's interesting letter of November 11, 1790 to Goethe (quoted in Zimmer 2014, p. 19).
[7] On Morelli, see Anderson 1991.
[8] Lermolieff [Morelli] 1880, pp. 433–434. Crowe, Cavalcaselle 1871, I, pp. 386–387, note 3. The connection with Michiel's description had already been made by Pietro Selvatico in Vasari [1550–1568] 1849, p. 190.
[9] Lermolieff [Morelli] 1893, p. 98.
[10] Venturi 1914, p. 204.
[11] Kristeller 1902, p. 154, note 1. The author also underlines how Gustavo Frizzoni – a close associate of Morelli's, as we've seen – had forgotten the adjective "small" in his transcription of Michiel's passage concerning the "painting on panel" (cf. Michiel [1525–1528] 1884, p. 44).
[12] On the relations between Bode and Morelli, see Anderson 1996.
[13] See Brown 1996.
[14] On the negative reactions to Bode's obituary-like article, see Anderson 1996, p. 118. The article in the *Gazette des Beaux-Arts* is Logan 1902, pp. 258–261 (it discusses the Querini Stampalia *Presentation* on p. 260, claiming Paul Kristeller had unjustly left it out of his catalogue of Mantegna's works).
[15] Bode 1903–1904, pp. 134–135.
[16] See Bode 1889b, p. 116; but also Bode 1903–1904, p. 132 note 1; and Bode *et al.* 1888–1909, pp. 4–5. Bode no longer based himself on the presumed portrait of Mantegna next to that of Squarcione in the scene of the *Martyrdom of St James* in the Ovetari Chapel (as argued by Giovanni de Lazara, developing a tradition going back to Vasari), but on the bronze bust placed in the painter's funerary chapel, in the Church of Sant'Andrea in Mantua, which Bode attributed to Gian Marco Cavalli, as he did another bronze portraying the poet Battista Spagnoli (see Bode 1889a). This latter bust was at the Kaiser-Friedrich-Museum before the Second World War; for decades it was thought to have been destroyed, but has actually conserved at the Pushkin Museum in Moscow. An analysis of its current state will soon be published by Vasily Rastorguev and myself.
[17] On the critical reception of Bellini's painting in the Fondazione Querini Stampalia, see the essay by Babet Trevisan in this volume.
[18] Regarding this affair, see Rowley 2017.
[19] On these two works, as well as all those in Berlin's Gemäldegalerie mentioned in this essay, see Schmidt Arcangeli 2015.
[20] In the 1891 guide to the Gemäldegalerie, there is some question as to whether to attribute the work to a young Giovanni Bellini (*Beschreibendes Verzeichnis* 1891, p. 159). The attribution to Lazzaro Bastiani, now unanimously accepted, would be proposed by Collobi 1939–1940, p. 38.
[21] See Grabowski 2013, pp. 48–50.
[22] On the history of the paintings and sculpture in Berlin during the war, see Berlin 2015.
[23] The current frame dates to 1970.
[24] Farmer 2000; Winter 2015.
[25] On the unanswered questions in this regard, see Babette Hartwieg's essay in this catalogue. On the role of the Kaiser-Friedrich-Museumsverein in this affair, cf. Knopp 2006, pp. 15–16.
[26] Mantua 1961, p. 29. On the exhibition, see Agosti 2006.
[27] Prinz 1962; Lightbown 1986, p. 405; Lucco 2013, p. 134.
[28] See Fiocco 1937, p. 24 (The identification is erroneously mentioned at fig. 18, but the author's subsequent publications corrected this misunderstanding).
[29] Lightbown 1986, p. 405.
[30] Walter 1989. Mantegna had already legally freed himself from Squarcione's tutorship in January 1448, making this interpretation appear slightly forced.
[31] The first thesis was argued by Lightbown 1986, p. 405; and then again by Arasse (1997) 2015, p. 64. The second was advanced by Krüger 2001, pp. 62–70. Strehlke 2004, p. 196 later proposes a similar interpretation in for the case of Benozzo Gozzoli's *Purification Altarpiece*, a thesis that seems far more convincing given its contextualization in the Florentine "painting of light" (see Rowley 2010, I, p. 135). Recently, scholars have also suggested that the most important expression in Mantegna's painting is Simeon's "mortifying" gaze, whose "*occhi grifagni*" invite the spectator to identify with him (Hauser 2015, p. 145), a thesis that can be grouped with that of Cassegrain 2015, p. 81, who talks at length about the supposed symbolism of the intertwining haloes of Joseph and Christ – when both features are in fact the result of later repainting.
[32] Panofsky [1943] 1948, I, pp. 144–115.
[33] Meiss 1957, pp. 27–28.
[34] Ringbom 1965, p. 74.
[35] See particularly Belting 1981, p. 83, and Nova 2008, as well as the essay by Brigit Blass-Simmen in this catalogue. On the iconographic ambiguity between the *Presentation of Jesus at the Temple*, the *Circumcision*, and the *Purification of the Virgin*, see Greenstein 1992.
[36] Schmidt Arcangeli 2015, pp. 321–322.
[37] See recently Marinelli 2013, pp. 467–468; Gasparotto 2013, p. 55.
[38] It seems to me that the attribution to Jacopo da Valenza proposed by Gustavo Frizzoni is not to be discarded, rather than the name of Giovanni Bellini, advanced for the first time by Georg Gronau and strongly supported by Roberto Longhi (see G. Valagussa's entry in Rome 2010–2011, pp. 48–49).
[39] Rothe 1992, p. 83; See the essays by Brigit Blass-Simmen and Babette Hartwieg in this catalogue. A fundamental step in the x-ray analysis of the Berlin painting was provided by Poldi and Villa 2006, p. 56; and Villa 2007, p. 53.
[40] This is the intent of the exhibition *Mantegna and Bellini* that will open at the National Gallery in London in fall 2018 and at the Gemäldegalerie in Berlin in spring 2019, which I'm organizing with Caroline Campbell, Dagmar Korbacher and Sarah Vowles, and with the scholarly collaboration of Katharina Weick-Joch.

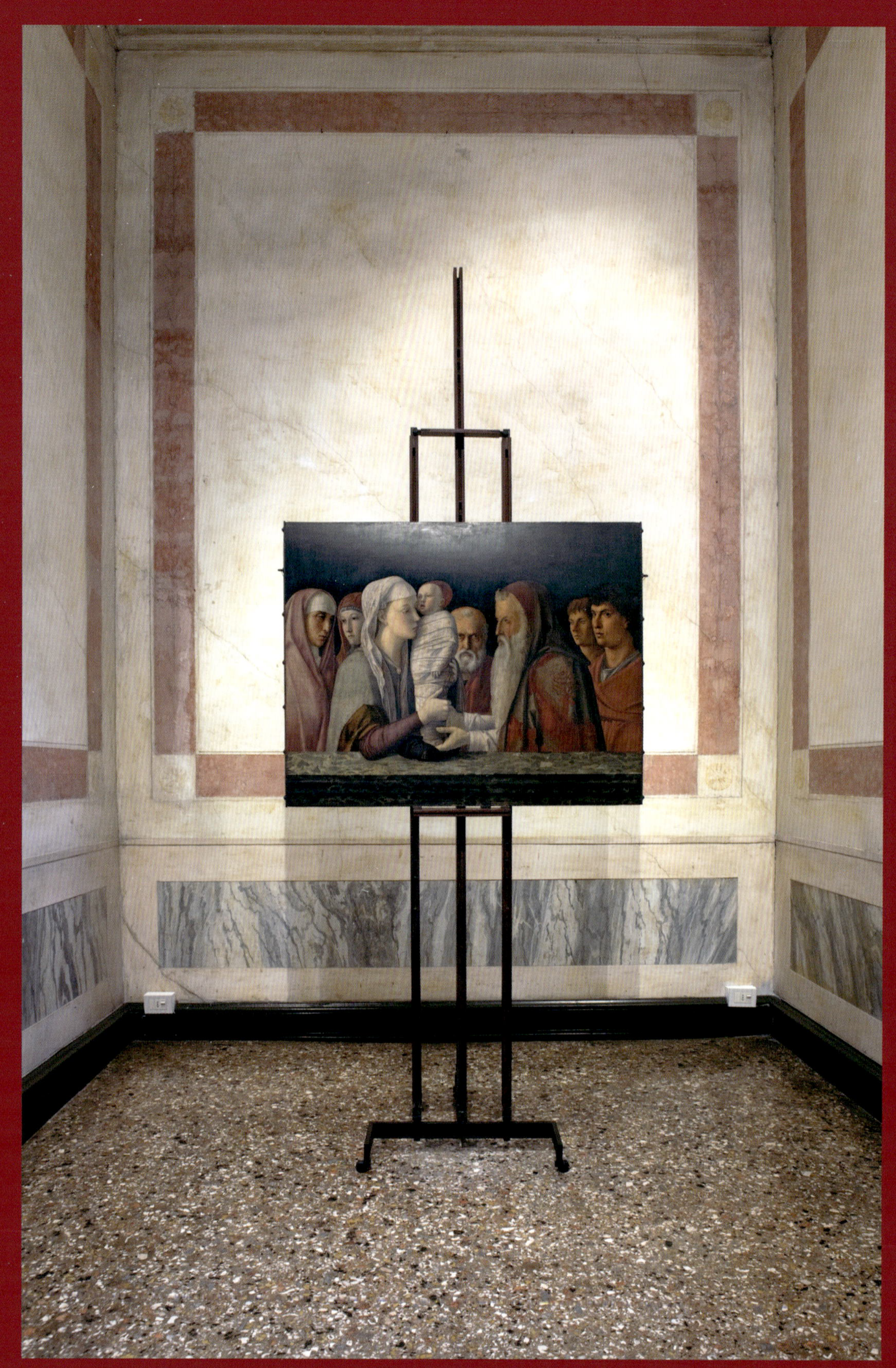

Presentation of Jesus at the Temple by Giovanni Bellini: A Family Painting at the Fondazione Querini Stampalia

BABET TREVISAN

1. *Presentation of Jesus at the Temple* by Giovanni Bellini in the Museum of the Fondazione Querini Stampalia, Venice. Present set-up

Palazzo Querini Stampalia, the ancient residence of one of Venice's wealthiest families, now home to the foundation of the same name, houses one of the masterpieces from the collection in its museum: the *Presentation of Jesus at the Temple* by Giovanni Bellini.

A small room with eighteenth-century stuccowork and soft lighting plays host to this panel by the great Venetian master, in an intimate atmosphere of holiness and meditation, where the glances and gestures depicted in the work play the principal role (fig. 1). Although the Virgin is about to hand her son to Simeon, the elderly High Priest at the Temple of Jerusalem, she seems to hold him back as if she has a foreboding about what is to come. The subject of the panel is not so much the actual ceremony of the presentation of Jesus at the temple, but the moment immediately prior to it. This is the kind of religious scene, shot through with emotion, that the Querini Stampalia family seemed to like; so much so that they owned two works with the same subject matter – one by Giovanni Bellini and the other by Sante Zago.[1]

When did these paintings enter the family collection? Were they commissioned, purchased or inherited? There are numerous questions to be answered. Unfortunately, archive documents rarely provide information on the historical sequence of events associated with assets such as these. It is only by reconstructing the family's taste as collectors that we can perhaps begin to theorise about how and when the works first came to the palazzo.[2]

This is why it is appropriate to digress somewhat and explore the commissions and purchases that led to the birth of the Querini art collection, still to this day conserved in the Querini Stampalia building.

As was the case for much of the Venetian nobility, the Querini collection also began life in the sixteenth century, but it was not until the seventeenth and eighteenth centuries that it really developed. Francesco and his wife Paola Priuli can be considered the first real collectors in the family.[3] The husband and wife favoured artists such as Bonifacio de' Pitati, Girolamo da Santacroce, Francesco Rizzo, Giovanni da Asola, Bernardino Licinio and, particularly, Palma Vecchio, whom Francesco commissioned to paint his portrait. The list of works by the painter, drawn up after his death in 1529, records that the artist's studio contained five paintings commissioned by "messere Francesco Querini."[4] They are the *Portrait of Francesco Querini*,[5] together with two unfinished *sacre conversazioni* entitled the *Virgin with Two Saints, St Francis and St Peter*[6] and the *Virgin and Child, with St John the Baptist, St Catherine and St Nicholas*,[7] and two as yet unpainted canvases.

Between 1515 and 1528, Francesco carried out maintenance and improvement work on the palazzo in Santa Maria Formosa and his *book of expenses*[8] reveals that the family had ongoing links with Palma Vecchio, and then with his workshop after his death, particularly with Bonifacio de' Pitati.

In the sixteenth and seventeenth centuries, as was customary in Venice, the Querini Stampalia often commissioned famous artists to paint portraits of important family members or to commemorate key public occasions. In the late sixteenth century, Marco Vecellio was asked to immortalise the Querini family in a series of portraits 'in memoriam' of figures who had lived two centuries earlier,[9] while Tiberio Tinelli painted *Portrait of a Boy* and *Portrait of Francesco Querini*, now conserved in Hanover (Hood Museum of Art, Dartmouth College).[10]

In the second half of the seventeenth century, the Querini family also commissioned portraits of themselves in elegant, formal attire and poses to illustrate their social status. Polo Querini asked Sebastiano Bombelli from Udine, a quintessential portrait specialist working in Venice, to immortalise his image. As well as the large full-figure *Portrait of Polo Querini* dressed as a prosecutor,[11] Bombelli also painted the *Portrait of Gerolamo Querini*, his brother.[12]

A number of unpublished letters from Bernardo Pecori, Flaminio Giberti, Giuseppe Santini, Alessandro Del Móro and Giorgio Pagani to Polo Querini, tell us about his decisive role in adding to the art collection and in fostering the wish to establish a gallery.[13] Indeed, it was during this period that the Querini family became interested in founding a family art gallery. In a letter dated 7 April 1708, Giorgio Pagani suggested to Polo that he build a chapel in his palazzo for hearing Mass and an art gallery to house the numerous paintings, engravings, relics, books and medals that he had recently acquired on the antiquarian market, often with the assistance of his son Angelo Maria Querini,[14] who a few years later would go on to become an important and learned clergyman. This unpublished correspondence enables us to link a number of works still recognisable in the museum collections today with pieces commissioned by Polo. In fact, we find that in 1688–90, Flaminio Giberti sent him some paintings by Liberi and Ruschi.[15]

Meanwhile, a number of letters from Bernardo Pecori to Polo Querini, written in 1696–1697, tell us that the prosecutor contacted Giovan Battista Foggini, court sculptor to the Medici, for a marble bust. He had to send the artist a "portrait in the clothing to be worn by the figure, and a drawing in profile for the relief."[16] The sculpture commissioned as a "head with bust without arms in fine white marble, with its pedestal in fine coloured marble" can be identified, according to Guerriero, as the marble bust displayed in the museum entrance hall and for years considered to be the portrait of Cardinal Angelo Maria Querini by Giacomo Cassetti (fig. 2).[17]

Polo's will documents his passion for art and his wish for the collection and the gallery to be kept together over the years to come.[18] In the 1670s, the family commissioned Michele Fabris, called Ongaro, to produce seven marble busts portraying five *Philosophers*, two *Saints* and one *Young Boy*.[19] It is very likely that these busts can be associated with Girolamo and Polo Querini and the Accademia dei Paragonisti, founded in the second half of the seventeenth century in Palazzo Querini Stampalia under the protection of the two brothers, both future prosecutors, and a place where noble and erudite matters were discussed. In fact, these busts should also be associated with the portraits of philosophers painted by Luca Giordano a couple of decades earlier and also present in the collection: works that testify to clear-cut collecting decisions, both in terms of style and content.[20]

In 1694, Nicolò Cassana was appointed to immortalise the ascent to the ducal throne of Silvestro Valier and the coronation of his wife Elisabetta Querini in two small pendant works.[21] However, the eighteenth century marked the height of cultural and artistic splendour as regards the enrichment of

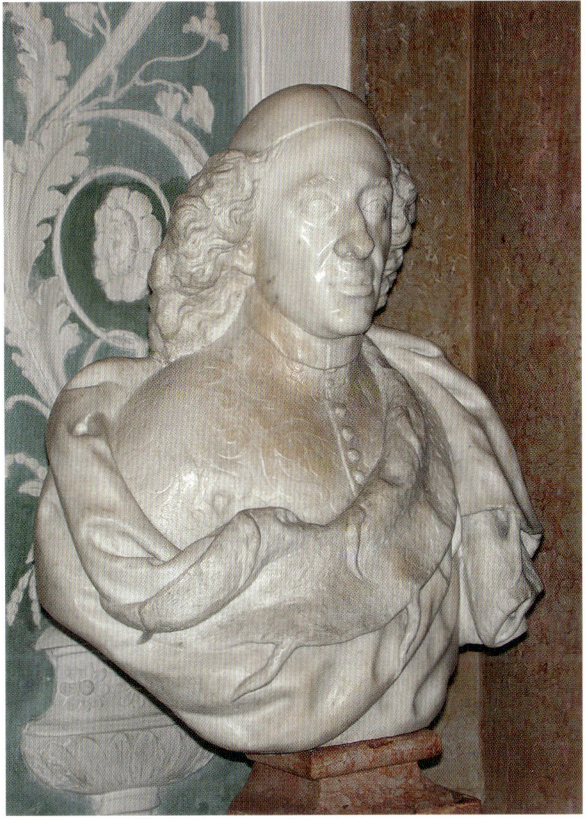

2. Giovanni Battista Foggini, *Portrait of Polo Querini*. Venice, Fondazione Querini Stampalia

the family collections. For the nuptial apartment of Zuanne Carlo Querini (1681–1763), Sebastiano Ricci painted the *Allegory of Day*, three ceiling 'canvases' depicting *Dawn*, *Afternoon* and *Evening*. Under Angelo Maria, an excellent man of the Church (1680–1755), and Andrea Domenico (1710–1795), the palazzo became a place of culture and a meeting point for scholars, poets, philosophers, artists and collectors. Numerous portraits were produced of the cardinal: two full-figure images by Bartolomeo Nazari and Fortunato Pasquetti, a series of medals and numerous engravings.[22]

His nephew Andrea, a dynamic statesman, senator, chamberlain and inquisitor, was particularly interested in studying science and the liberal arts, further adding to the family collections. A lover of art, poetry and literature, he frequented artists and scholars, forging fond friendships with them. Carlo Goldoni was a regular visitor to his home, dedicating his comedy entitled *The Prudent Man* to him in 1748. Another visitor was Pietro Longhi, who painted numerous small canvases for him: the *Geography Lesson* and the *Seven Sacraments*, both for the bedroom, the *Venetian Friary*, an ironic depiction of clergymen of the time, and the *Lion's Cage*.[23] In 1792, Andrea inherited the assets left in trust by Gerolamo Ascanio Giustinian, which included numerous paintings by Gabriel Bella depicting scenes of public and private life, Republican ceremonies and popular festivals. The canvases were initially housed in a villa in Treviso. However, after it was sold, seventy-seven works were transferred to the Venetian palazzo.[24]

The inventory drawn up on Andrea's death in 1796 provides some useful information about his collections and their location within the apartment: the "gallery chamber" contained "71 assorted paintings [...] 3 on the painted ceiling [...] 8 half busts in bare stone," which we can recognise as the three canvases by Ricci and the busts by Ongaro. The "print chamber above the river" housed "126 assorted paintings", while the bedroom had "7 paintings [...] depicting the Seven Sacraments" by Pietro Longhi. There is still no reference to the panel with the *Presentation of Jesus at the Temple* by Giovanni Bellini.

Andrea picked Alvise (1758–1834), his favourite nephew and father of Count Giovanni, as his successor. In 1790, Alvise married Maria Teresa Lippomano and the apartment on the second floor, which houses the museum today, was renovated, restored and frescoed by the Guarana brothers for the occasion. During his role as Venetian ambassador in Paris, Alvise purchased a Sèvres porcelain table service comprised of 244 items and accompanied by *biscuit* groups and figurines.[25] Alvise placed his hopes for an heir in his son Giovanni who, despite his father's pressing demands, never married, had no children and decided to leave his entire estate to a foundation that would make the family library and art gallery available to the public: "[...] after my death, my Library, Gallery, Medal Collection and

Artworks housed in my Palace in San Zaccaria shall be made available for public use [...]."[26]

The generosity and foresight of Count Giovanni allowed the city of Venice to enjoy this priceless artistic and cultural heritage: manuscripts, incunabula, sixteenth-century books, maps and geographical charts, paintings, sculptures, glassware and porcelain could thus be seen, consulted and studied in Palazzo Querini Stampalia. The museum was established on the second floor of the building in 1872 with the objective of faithfully recreating the atmosphere of the home and showcasing the rich family collection that had been built up over the previous four centuries. Indeed, during the course of more than 400 years of history, the Querini Stampalia family had collected paintings of all kinds, including religious and mythical subjects, portraits, landscapes, genre scenes and works associated with Venetian festivals, habits and customs.

However, there is a lack of archive documents able to provide an account of the history of most of the works conserved by the foundation today. This is also the case of the panel by Giovanni Bellini, which is only mentioned for the first time in the 1809 inventory.[27]

The *Presentation of Jesus at the Temple* was attributed to Andrea Mantegna and valued at 300 Austrian lire, and was mentioned as being present, together with around eighty other paintings, in the apartment on the first floor of the palazzo (now the library), in the book room (last room, overlooking the canal). The gallery chamber, also on the first floor and adjacent to the garden (current Sala delle Signorine), is noted as housing a painting with a similar subject by Sante Zago, valued at 300 Austrian lire, with a pencil note by Giovanni Querini from 1844 stating "no longer owned."

By comparing the hands in which they were written, we can establish that the 1809 inventory was drafted by Pietro Brandolese (1754–1809),[28] a bookseller by profession at Palazzo Bo in Padua, but even better known in the scholarly Venetian Republic for his great passion for studying art and books. Brandolese frequented the best salons in Padua and Venice and forged close friendships with renowned men of culture, including Giovanni de' Lazara, Francesco Bartoli, Giannantonio Moschini, Don Daniele Francesconi, Don Jacopo Morelli (the highly erudite future custodian of the Marciana library) and the Olivetan priest Antonio Maria Griffi.

Starting in 1808, Brandolese devoted himself to an extremely important bibliographical undertaking: indexing the private library of the noble Querini family in Santa Maria Formosa, where he died suddenly on 2 January 1809 at the age of just fifty-five. The early attribution to Mantegna can therefore doubtlessly be traced back to Brandolese, who had recently published *Testimonianze intorno alla Patavinità di Andrea Mantegna raccolte* and was certainly acquainted with the Berlin *Presentation of Jesus at the Temple*, then in Padua in the home of the Gradenigo family. His premature death probably prevented him from studying and comparing these two very similar works in an essay. Twenty-one years later, in the inventory of the tangible and intangible assets of Gerolamo Querini,[29] drawn up in 1830, the panel with the *Presentation of Jesus at the Temple* is no longer attributed to Andrea Mantegna, but described as being a work by his school and valued at 120 Austrian lire. It is still described as being in the apartment on the first floor, in a room next to the canal that contains paintings only, while the work with the same subject matter by Sante Zago is conserved in a room nearby.

The inventories of the tangible assets held by Count Giovanni Querini Stampalia, drawn up in 1884,[30] describe how the "large chamber used as a Picture Gallery" houses the *Seven Sacraments* by Longhi, the *Coronation of the Virgin* by Catarino and other "various oil paintings with gilded frames," together with both works depicting the *Presentation of Jesus at the Temple*: the one by Sante Zago, valued at 300 Austrian lire (with a pencil note "no longer owned"), and the one by Andrea Mantegna, valued at 1000 Austrian lire, which, together with the *Sacra*

3-4. *Presentation in the Temple* by Giovanni Bellini in the Museum of the Fondazione Querini Stampalia, Venice (green room). Set-up between 1925 and 1934

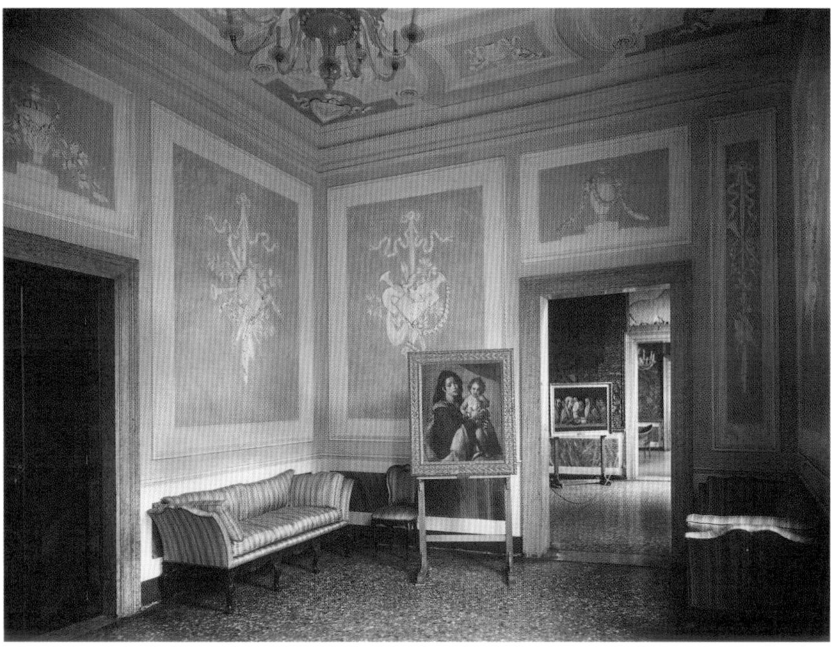

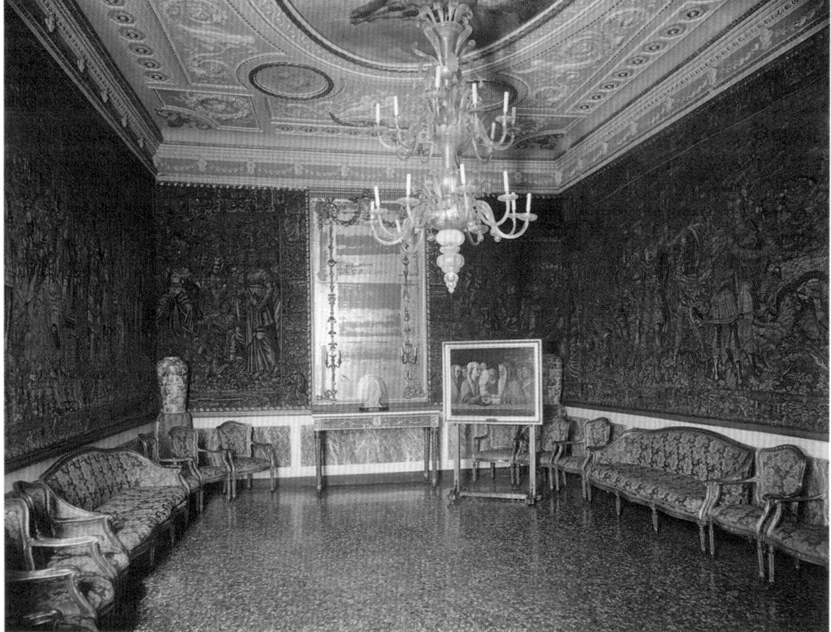

Conversazione by Palma Vecchio,[31] is the most highly valued painting that year. In the legal inventory of 1869,[32] drawn up on the death of Count Giovanni Querini, the panel attributed to Andrea Mantegna and estimated as being worth 4,000 Italian lire is still in the apartment on the first floor, in the library room, and is documented for the first time as having a gilded frame. The *Presentation of Jesus at the Temple* by Sante Zago instead disappears forever, unfortunately leaving no trace.

Following the death of Giovanni and the establishment of the foundation, the *museo d'ambiente* was created on the second floor of the palazzo. In 1872, the work by Giovanni Bellini, still attributed to Andrea Mantegna, was documented as being in the small room overlooking the canal (corresponding to the current room), together with around forty works featuring different subjects: religious themes, portraits, musicians, drinkers and heads of old men,[33] while a guide written in 1881 describes the room as containing a smaller number of works (twelve).[34]

In 1907, Arnaldo Segarizzi, director of the foundation, spoke to the board about his wish to reorganise the art gallery, mentioning the painting by Bellini as being one of the most important works therein, deserving of being displayed properly. The gallery was closed and dismantled during the First World War and numerous works, probably including the panel by Bellini, were stored down on the ground floor in galvanized iron cases. Over the following years, bearing in mind the museographic tastes of the curators of the time, Bellini's work was displayed in different rooms. In 1925,[35] described as "A copy by Bellini of the famous Mantegna at the museum in Berlin", it was displayed by Giovanni Bordiga and Angelo Alessandri in the green room, then lined with tapestries (figs. 3–4), probably on an easel together with the *Madonna and Child with Saints* by Bonifacio De' Pitati and the *Judith* by Catena, while in 1932,[36] attributed somewhat hesitantly to Giovanni Bellini, it is described as being in one of the last rooms in the museum, on the side overlooking the garden, together with the *Coronation of the Virgin* by Donato and Catarino.

It was only from the second half of the 1930s that the work began to be mentioned in city guidebooks as a piece by the Venetian master.[37] In 1946 it was exhibited in the first room devoted to the Renaissance together with the *Adoration of the Virgin* by Lorenzo di Credi, the *Madonna and Child*, then attributed to Giovanni Bellini, the *Portrait of Francesco Querini* and *Portrait of Paola Priuli* by Palma Vecchio and the *Judith* by Vincenza Catena (fig. 5).[38] In 1951 it remained in the same place, but with a photograph of the Berlin painting by Andrea Mantegna displayed next to it.[39] In the second half of the twentieth century, the work – still on an easel – was placed in a number of rooms that were subsequently involved in the architectural project implemented by Mario Botta (figs. 6–8). In the 1960s, the old easel was replaced by one designed by Carlo Scarpa and still used today for the public display. It was only in the late 1990s that a decision was made to showcase the panel by exhibiting it alone in a small room similar to a coffer, almost as if to emphasise its sacred subject matter.

Critical descriptions of the Querini panel have been somewhat complex over the years:[40] the first to agree with the 1809 inventory was Morelli, who described it as a copy after Mantegna in 1880, only ascribing it to the master himself in 1884 and 1893. Many of the subsequent critics agreed with Morelli, until Berenson, who attributed it to Giovanni Bellini in 1916. The difficulty that many critics have had in recognising the hand of the Venetian artist should probably be attributed to one or more nineteenth-century restorations that rendered the panel illegible. It was only in 1949, after the cleaning work carried out by Mauro Pelliccioli for the Giovanni Bellini exhibition in the Doge's Palace, that the *Presentation of Jesus at the Temple* revealed the colour and brushwork of the Venetian master, no longer allowing for any margin of doubt regarding its authorship.

The general apprehension in the art world and among critics regarding the work carried out by Pelliccioli was so great that Manlio Dazzi, director of the foundation at the time, provided a description of every single step in a detailed report that he published immediately after the restoration and that it is worth citing here:

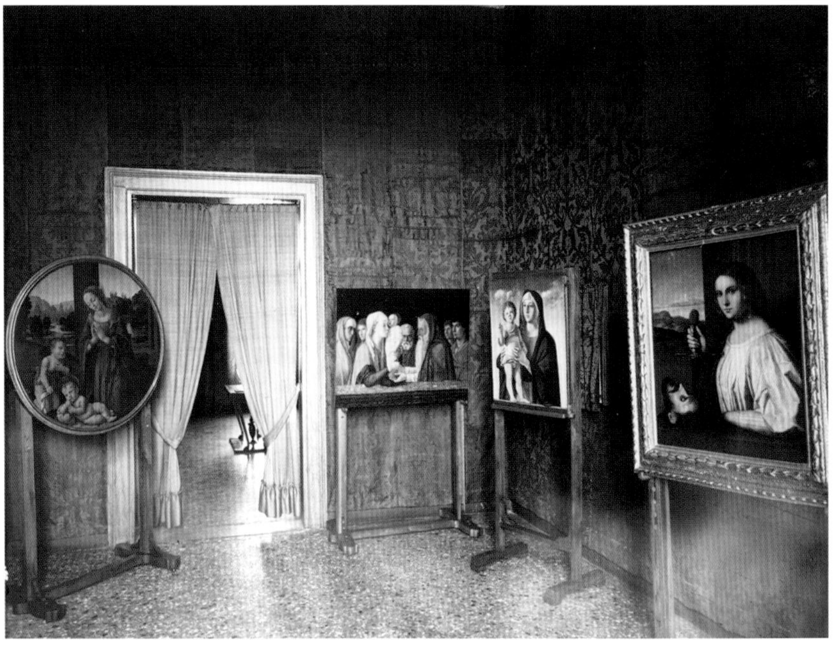

5. *Presentation of Jesus at the Temple* by Giovanni Bellini in the Museum of the Fondazione Querini Stampalia, Venice (Renaissance room). Set-up in 1946

The work was carried out by Prof. Pelliccioli in February of this year (1949), at the Galleria dell'Accademia, under the supervision of the Fine Arts Office and the foundation member appointed by the Collegio degli Accademici delle Belle Arti, and by the director of the Querini. The assays were performed with the greatest care: two square centimetres on the cloak of the Virgin and on her cuff. Amidst the academic bright blue, there appeared a poor, lean grey, beneath which the reddish ground could be glimpsed, while under the no less academic brilliant green there was a glaring yellow with heightening. This led to great perplexity. The entire tonal relationship seemed to be out of tilt. And if the repainting was so extensive and radical, should we not suspect that it had been done so as to pad out an actual painting that was in too great a state of disrepair? Other small tests, where the touch-ups were less profound and without alterations in colour, were encouraging; an assay on Simeon's right hand revealed a dead grey shadow. Another element of imbalance in a painting of bright colours. But it reminded us of the fundamental tones in Mantegna's *Presentation*. We wanted to uncover the Child's fingers, which were in a false pink. The solvents removed the recent paintwork very

6-8. *Presentation in the Temple* by Giovanni Bellini in the Museum of the Fondazione Querini Stampalia, Venice. Set-ups in the second half of the twentieth century

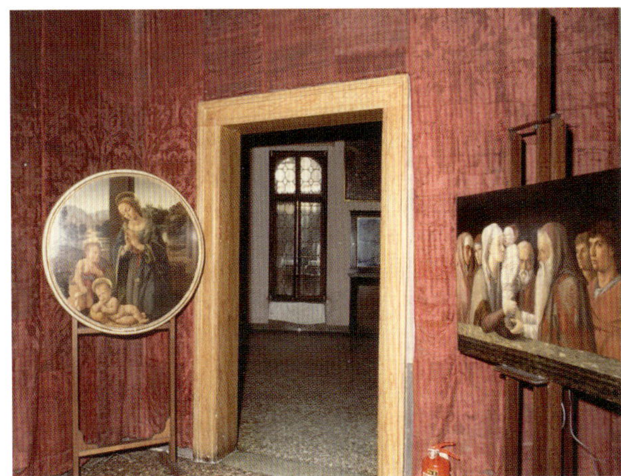

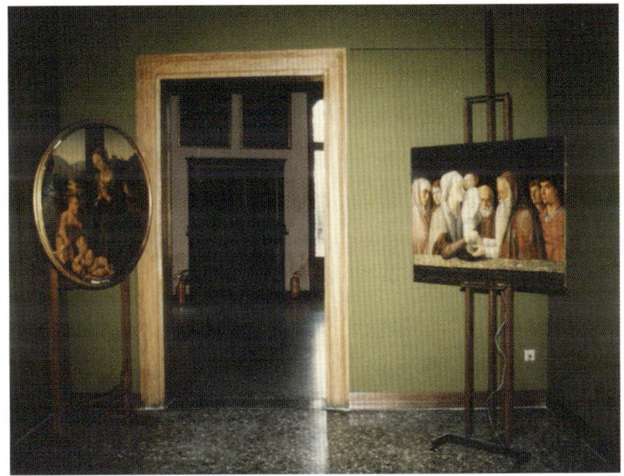

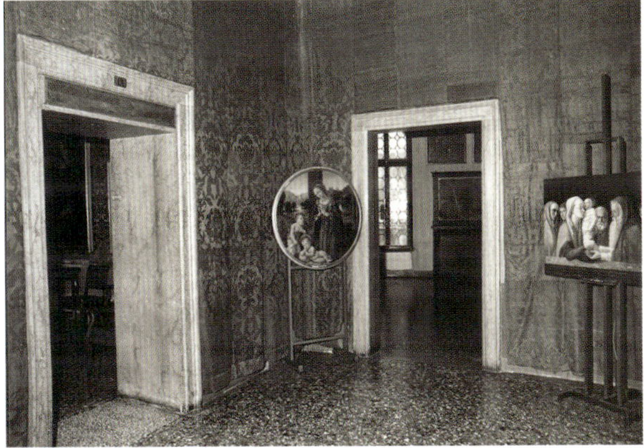

easily and, drying up immediately, they did not attack the older paint, which was clear-cut, smooth and clean. The Child's fingers appeared to be of that bluish grey that we see in the painting by Mantegna. It was now apparent that beneath the new paintwork there was another balance of tones, as indicated by the points we had uncovered. The underlying loyalty to the prototype guided our research. The hands proved to be the revelation: the earthy hands of Simeon, lacking in depth, had been enlarged, segmented by minute lines. Faced with such cold and precise delicacy, in a section that was still too small, we even suspected an eighteenth-century restoration, giving us the impetus to extend our research into the shaded area of the right hand. The solvents were no longer needed, it was time for the scraper, touching upon the panel primer. This was a happy mistake, because solvent proved to be the only means to be used. The thumbs seemed to come back to life, the golden stud on the Virgin's robes shone, the sleeves of the priest revealed the care with which they were drawn, the swaddling bands became lighter and once more revealed the fundamental elements of the bluey-grey shadows and the stripes, the shaded parts of the Virgin's hands appeared to be of wet clay, almost without any modelling, the beards stood out, the faces were lightened and the tones of the women's clothing became more muted. It was clear that a naive nineteenth-century painter had presumed to create a tonal balance between the female group and the more colourful male group, and had borrowed and imitated with a certain degree of technical ability the Bellinian colours of other Madonnas and had adopted them to complete Bellini's work, without suspecting that the softer colours of the female group might have a lyrical value. And he did more, he even painted quite good blonde curls on the temple of the Virgin, where both the originals simply showed the subtle shadow of the veil, so full of suggestion, on her bare temple. Bellini's work responded happily to our anxious research. There was no deterioration in the points that we explored, the application of colour, smooth as it was, gave no cause for concern. The cleaning process was now decided with touching peace of mind. There were no sensational revelations, no skies appeared, the marble did not change colour, but instead an intact Bellini shone before us (this is certainly true of the pale face of the Virgin, and those white bandages, the beards and the shirt) and in its original brushwork, highly detailed in the centre and becoming looser and more mannered at the edges, its melancholy intimate religiosity could be savoured.[41]

We may put forward a number of ideas regarding the identity of the naive nineteenth-century painter who presumed to establish a tonal balance between the female and male groups. Dazzi recalls that Elio Zorzi, in an article published on 28 July 1949, had attributed the restoration to Placido Fabris: "It is very well known, for example, how that beautiful painting of the Querini Stampalia, now displayed in the Doge's Palace, and entitled *Presentation of Jesus at the Temple*, attributed until quite recently to Andrea Mantegna, was then recognised as an early work by Giovanni Bellini, painted at a time when Bellini was still under the artistic influence of the great Mantuan artist. It is an exquisite work of beautiful pale tones, which are harmoniously concentrated. In the foreground is the figure of the Virgin, who holds and presents the Child. The Madonna's dress had sleeves lined in a silky fabric of soft green colour, draped in masterful folds. It was described as beautiful by critics and guides. But Mauro Pelliccioli did not believe in it. And with his implacable little knife he began to scrape away that green. The green came away and left in its place a beautiful ochre colour, with even more stylish and praiseworthy drapes, in that they are really those painted by Giovanni Bellini. The beautiful green had been applied just under a century ago by Placido Fabris, a reputable copyist and restorer of ancient paintings [...]."[42]

If it was really Placido Fabris, who died in 1859, who intervened so heavily on Bellini's work, how would we explain Morelli and Frizzoni's references to the tasks entrusted by the gallery management, and therefore after 1869, to a disastrous restorer? Frizzoni wrote: "This panel, together with other priceless works in this collection by the Venetian school, was entrusted by the Administration of the Institution with deplorable lightness to the hands of a disastrous restorer, who completely redid them so that it was almost impossible to recognise the hand of the original artist."[43]

As a result, if the restoration had been carried out after the establishment of the foundation, it could not have been by Placido Fabris, as he had died ten years earlier. It could, however, have been done by his brother Paolo Fabris,[44] a painter and professor of restoration at the Accademia di Venezia, who already frequented Palazzo Querini Stampalia, having been appointed to draw up the list of paintings in the legal inventory of the legacy left by Count Giovanni Querini in 1869. Nevertheless, this theory does not seem convincing given that Paolo Fabris, when he records the *Presentation of the Child to the Old Simeon* by Andrea Mantegna in the legal inventory, notes on the side that it has been "heavily restored," leading us to understand that he was not the author of the heavy restoration.

The panel probably underwent numerous restoration interventions at different times: some requested by the family and others commissioned by the foundation management. Even the restorer Mauro Pelliccioli, in a letter sent to Manlio Dazzi in 1946, just before taking on the job, emphasises how the extensive restoration work performed in the late nineteenth century was followed by other more recent work: "G. Bellini underwent restoration fairly recently, perhaps not more than fifty years ago. This led to the complete reworking of the Madonna's blue cloak and her green cuffs. Restoration work and too many layers tarnish the head of the second woman to the viewer's left. The head of St Joseph and his hands have also been the object of restoration and new outlines and there is other less extensive restoration work in other points of the panel. The surface of the marble parapet has also undergone considerable recent restoration work. The panel needs to have the old varnish evened out, together with the oxides and stains associated with it."[45]

The archives do not contain any documents that help us to identify "the inauspicious restorers," although indirect accounts allow us to theorise about numerous interventions between the second half of the nineteenth century and the first half of the twentieth century: a more secure and expert hand that took the liberty of reinterpreting the work, substantially modifying its characteristics, and other hands that intervened in a less invasive manner. The correspondence, the family inventories and the documents uncovered in the local area add no further information to that which has been set out above and do not help us to establish with any precision how and when the work by the great Venetian master entered the Querini home.

It seems very unlikely that the work was commissioned by the family. In this case, the work would have been mentioned in the inventories prior to 1809 and would, with all probability, have been attributed directly to Giovanni Bellini and not to his brother-in-law Andrea Mantegna or his school, and the estimates of its value would have been more accurate. Instead, it seems more plausible that the *Presentation of Jesus at the Temple* was purchased or inherited between the late eighteenth century and early nineteenth century by one of the more cultured family members, who unknowingly displayed in his home one of the finest works by the great Venetian master: Giovanni Bellini.

I would like to thank Angela Munari for her archive research.

[1] Sante Zago (Venice, c. 1500 – before 1568) was a painter who is not particularly renowned today. He was a pupil and follower of Titian, accredited with moderate success in the first half of the sixteenth century. See Gilbert 1952, nos. 21–24, pp. 121–129.
[2] Trevisan 2009, pp. 292–294.
[3] Francesco, son of Zanne Querini, was presented at the Balla d'Oro in 1523, married Paola Priuli in 1528 and died in 1554.
[4] Rylands 1988, pp. 37–38, 168–172.
[5] *Catalogo della Pinacoteca* 1979, p. 39, no. 9.
[6] Ibid., p. 38, no. 8.
[7] Ibid., p. 40, no. 11.
[8] Archivio Privato Querini Stampalia (hereinafter APQS), *Registro di spese di Francesco Querini Stampalia*, b. 4, no. 2.
[9] They include a depiction of Marco, the joint protagonist in the famous Bajamonte Tiepolo conspiracy of 1310; Romeo, whom the words in the painting attribute with the feat of having brought Robert, nephew of Charles II of Anjou, to the Hungarian throne in 1307; Nicolò, Francesco and Turno, three generations of prosecutors of San Marco in the first half of the fourteenth century; and Antonio, who entered the Church and took the name Girolamo, becoming patriarch of Venice from 1524 to 1554. See Busetto 2004, pp. 24–25.
[10] Bottacin 2000, pp. 239–255.
[11] *Catalogo della Pinacoteca* 1979, p. 71, no. 105. Polo Querini was born on 14 May 1654 and died on 12 July 1728.
[12] Ibid., pp. 70–71, no. 104. Gerolamo Querini was born on 12 March 1648 and died on 27 November 1709.
[13] Jesuit preachers.
[14] Biblioteca Querini Stampalia (hereinafter BQS), *Manoscritti*, Cl. VII, cod. XII(=366), coll. P, nos. 563 to 595, Letter from Giorgio Pagani to Polo Querini, Rome, 7 April 1708, no. 23 "To Your Most Illustrious and Excellent Gentleman and Most Honoured Master, I have not received letters from Your Excellency in this post. Although convalescent and lacking in strength, I did not wish to fail in my duty of wishing you a very happy Easter, with all the prosperity and long life that I would wish for you from Heaven. [...] I would like to make a suggestion for Your Excellency to think about, namely that you could build a chapel in a room of the Palace, where you could hear Mass at home at your convenience, like other great figures do. I would obtain the Apostolic Brief for you.
I would like to make another suggestion to Your Excellency for your amusement, like other great men, and that is to make a small gallery in a room of your palace, and decorate it with ancient bronze medals of popes, emperors, and other illustrious men. I would procure similar medals and small paintings for you in Rome at very little expense.
Now in Rome, due to great poverty, poor but noble people sell things for very little [...].
Rome, 7 April 1708 / Your Humble, Doting and Obedient Servant Giorgio Pagani".
[15] APQS, *Manoscritti*, Cl. VII, cod. XI(=365), coll. G, nos. 309 to 335, Letter from Flaminio Giberti to Polo Querini, [1688–90], no. 13 "To Your Most Illustrious and Excellent Gentleman and Most Honoured Master, I am sending these three precious paintings to Your Excellency, of which one is by the very famous man Liberi, the other long one by Cruschi, and the Madonna by the school of Liberi. Paintings worthy of your notice, and worthy of occupying two great places in some room in Venice: that is to say the large chamber [...] I do everything for Your Excellency, for fear that I would offend you on the Mezzanine [...] Your honourable, devoted and loyal servant, Flamminio Giberti [1688–90]".
[16] APQS, *Manoscritti*, Cl. VII, cod. XII(=366), coll. P, nos. 596–614, Letter from Bernardo Pecori to Polo Querini, Florence, 1697, 25 May "[...] If, therefore, Your Excellency has decided to proceed, you will be well served by sending me the portrait in the dress you wish to be worn by the figure, and the drawing in profile for the relief, since I will not be lacking in due attention on that occasion, so I can assure Your Excellency that I will always glory in your esteemed commands [...]. Florence, 25 May 1697". See also: APQS, *Manoscritti*, Cl. VII, cod. XII(=366), coll. P, nos. 596–389, Letter from Bernardo Pecori to Polo Querini, Florence, 1696, 2 February, no. 1. See also the letters: Florence, 1696, 9 March, no. 2; Florence, 1697, 25 May "Having had the good fortune upon my return to my homeland of being visited in this abbey by Father Don Angel Maria, son of Your Excellency, and having paid on that occasion [...] those expressions of deference, he even showed signs of pleasure but in few words, perhaps due to the presence of the master of the Novices who attended us. I give a part to Your Excellency so that you can observe how much I esteem the honour he was so kind to pay me, and when I will be able to show this again with the works produced in service to P and to Your Excellency [...] I will also say to Your Excellency that I visited Mr Foggin, sculptor, and, representing to him the wishes of Your Excellency, he replied to me that the portrait can very well be used to produce the statue, but that for the relief it is also necessary to have a portrait drawing in profile. That the usual price of statues, that is to say head with bust without arms in fine white marble, with fine coloured marble pedestal, is 70 Florentine piastre – but that as you are my friend he will accept 60 piastre – to be paid upon completion here, but he does not want to think either of taking it or of profit. When the sculpture is ready, I shall take Father Don Angelo Maria your son to see it once again, so that even he may be satisfied that it has been perfectly sculpted [...]. Florence, 2 Feb. 1696".
[17] Guerriero 2007, pp. 56–57.
[18] APQS, file 11.7, *Will of Polo Querini di Francesco*, Venice, 23 August 1727, fol. 22r [but 5r] "[...]I confirm the trust made in my will of silks, to which I add my gallery of paintings, not wanting that this collection or the paintings are divided, but that they are conserved, nor do I want them to be taken away from the home where I live, to be evaluated for some purpose, and subsequently at the home of Don Angelo Maria, now bishop of Brescia, and the cardinal my son, remaining subject to the trust".
[19] Guerriero 2007, pp. 50, 52.
[20] The family owned several more portraits of philosophers by Luca Giordano, probably sold off during the nineteenth century.
[21] Busetto 2004, pp. 29–32.
[22] Ibid., pp. 36–39.
[23] Venice 1995.
[24] Ibid.
[25] Venice 1998.
[26] Querini Stampalia 1914.
[27] Archivio Fondazione Querini Stampalia (hereinafter AFQS), file XLII, 21 *Inventario di quadri della galleria Querini e confronto con la consistenza nel 1810*, Venice, 1 November 1844. The date of 1810 can be brought forward to 1809, inasmuch as we can claim with certainty that the inventory was drawn up by Pietro Brandolese

when engaged in reorganising the Querini Stampalia library, prior to his death in 1809.

[28] *Pietro Brandolese* 1990.

[29] AFQS, file XXXIV, 9, *Inventario della sostanza mobile ed immobile lasciata da Gerolamo Querini di Zuanne, fatto da Giovanni Querini di Alvise, 1830*, 6. *Inventario della galleria*, entitled F, no. 6.

[30] AFQS, file XLII, 20, *Inventario di beni mobili del palazzo di S. Maria Formosa, già appartenuti ad Alvise e a Gerolamo Querini ed ora passati a Giovanni Querini di Alvise* (Venice, 1 November 1844); AFQS, file XLII, 22, *Inventario della sostanza mobile di proprietà di Giovanni Querini di Alvise nel palazzo di S. Maria Formosa* (1844).

[31] *Catalogo della Pinacoteca*, p. 40, no. 11. Now attributed to Bonifacio De' Pitati.

[32] AFQS, file W, *Inventario giudiziale della eredità abbandonata dal co. Giovanni Querini* (1869).

[33] *Catalogo degli oggetti* 1872.

[34] *Guida artistica* 1881, p. 205.

[35] *Pinacoteca Querini Stampalia* n.d. p. 46.

[36] *Venezia e dintorni* 1932, p. 71.

[37] *Venezia e dintorni* 1937, p. 80.

[38] *Galleria Querini Stampalia* 1946, p. 21.

[39] *Venezia e dintorni* 1951, p. 194. The work is also mentioned as being in the same room in the publication: *Venezia e dintorni* 1953 and Lorenzetti 1956, pp. 677, 679. The wish to record its resemblance to the work by his brother-in-law in a photograph is also documented in city guides up to at least the 1990s.

[40] Trevisan 2008, pp. 176–177.

[41] Dazzi 1949, pp. 153–158. The draft by Dazzi conserved in the foundation's archives adds the following to the published text: "The suspicion that an effective tonal imbalance would persist even after the colours of the male group had recovered their original hues, and that the necessary work of removing the overlaid colour would excessively reveal the yellow of the cuff and the ash grey and blue-grey grounds, led to very thin layers of barely coloured watercolour being added to the cuff, the fingers in shadow and the face of the pious woman behind the Virgin. Perhaps this is the way in which the only element of a tonal link between the copy by Bellini and the original by Mantegna was attenuated, while recognising that in our painting it had taken on an accentuation extraneous to the overall colouring, and not concealing the suspicion that the excessive removal of layers led to that tone in the background of the painting by Mantegna. Moreover, the scrupulous approach taken towards the revelations and towards the deployment of the subtle material used to restore balance, illustrates with what care matters proceeded, both in terms of the work of the excellent restorer and in terms of the responsibility involved in this restoration."

[42] Zorzi 1949.

[43] Michiel [1525-1528] 1884, pp. 44–45.

[44] Rollandini 2005, no. 327, pp. 51–68.

[45] AFQS, Letter from Mauro Pellicioli to Manlio Dazzi, Venice, April 1946.

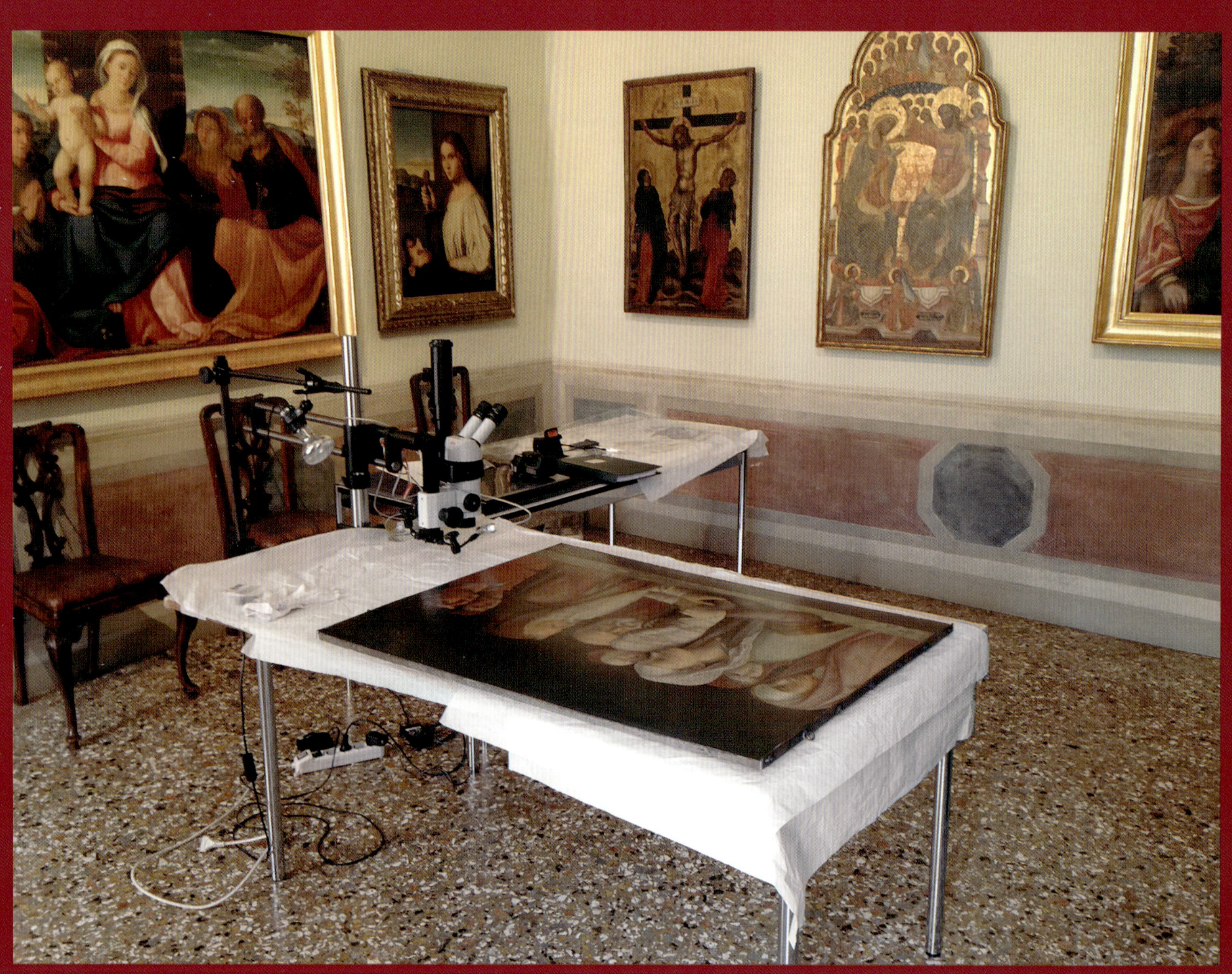

Andrea Mantegna's and Giovanni Bellini's *Presentation of Jesus at the Temple*. The Genesis and a Technological Comparison of Both Works

BABETTE HARTWIEG

The connection between the two paintings with the obviously related compositions has repeatedly been a topic for discussion throughout the history of art with very different conclusions.[1] While the Berlin painting has long been linked to Andrea Mantegna because of notes and seals on the back and archive documents, the painting from the Querini Stampalia collection has had a wide range of attributions right up to recent times. On the back of the wooden panel from the Fondazione Querini Stampalia, the name "Andrea Mantegna" is displayed in big letters (fig. 19), presumably from the eighteenth century. And in the inventory register from the nineteenth century, the painting also has the heading "maestro padovano" or "scuola del Mantegna."[2] But since Berenson first attributed it to Giovanni Bellini in 1916, it has remained unclear whether the painting should be seen as a copy of Mantegna's composition from the Bellini workshop or as a "paraphrase" by Giovanni Bellini's own hand.[3] This was the background against which the question of extensive studies using art technology was addressed to the author, first with Mantegna's painting in Berlin, then also, for comparison, with Bellini's panel in Venice.[4]

1. Stereomicroscopic studies in the Museo Querini Stampalia, Venice, June 2017

For these technical studies, we now have a variety of processes at our disposal: for the Berlin painting, in 2014, Christoph Schmidt's recently produced raking light, UV and X-ray photographs, as well as infrared reflectography[5] were analysed. Volker Schaible from the Stuttgart State Academy of Fine Arts took on the fabric fibre analysis. In 2017, in collaboration with the Rathgen Research Laboratory, Ina Reiche and Sabine Schwerdtfeger, micro X-ray fluorescence analysis (μRFA) could be carried out in conjunction with NIR hyperspectral imaging scans and Fiber Optic Reflectance Spectroscopy (FORS) point analysis by John Delaney and Francesca Gabrieli, National Gallery of Art, Washington, D.C., Scientific Research Department.[6]

But the systematic stereomicroscopic study by the author formed the basis of all the results presented here.[7] With the comparative studies in Venice, she could rely on the same microscope and analyse the IR-reflectography provided by Giovanni Villa (fig. 1).[8]

We will now present first the study results on Andrea Mantegna's *Presentation of Jesus at the Temple*, then those on Giovanni Bellini's panel and finally draw comparative conclusions.

The Painting by Andrea Mantegna from Berlin

The Presentation of Jesus at the Temple by Andrea Mantegna has been mostly described until now as "tüchlein."[9] It is a rare, early example of a painting on

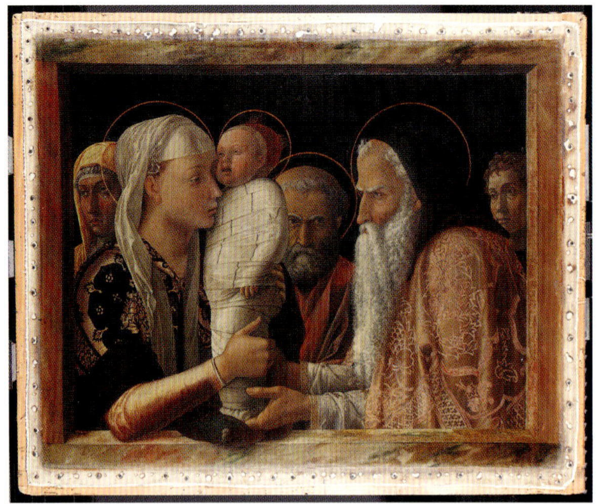

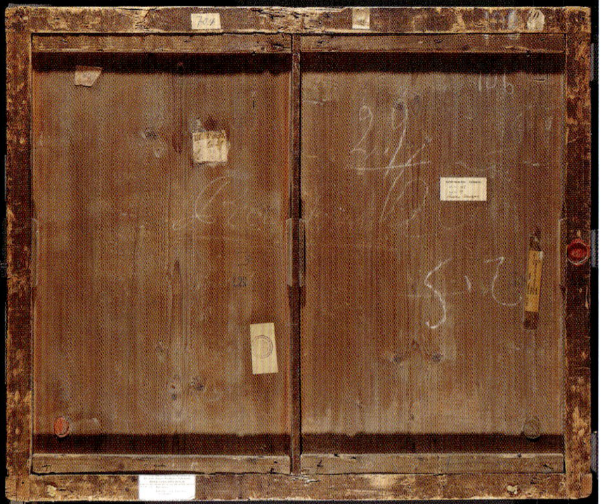

2. Andrea Mantegna, *Presentation of Jesus at the Temple*, with tacking edges on a frame system. Staatliche Museen zu Berlin, Gemäldegalerie, no. 29

3. Andrea Mantegna, *Presentation of Jesus at the Temple*, support frame from behind. Staatliche Museen zu Berlin, Gemäldegalerie

a fabric paint support with an originally preserved stretch system that is rarely absent from a technical history of panel painting.[10] The approximately 74 cm high and 91 cm wide piece of original canvas is nailed on to the front side of a large stretcher frame (fig. 2).[11] Due to the undulations on the surface, the picture tends to have more of the characteristic of a loosely painted fabric. The painted surface is around 69 x 87 cm in size. From the back, on the other hand, it gives you the impression of a wooden panel painting (fig. 3) which obviously gave further cause for confusion.[12] Here you can see the firm support which consists of a stretcher frame with a flush vertical strip of wood in the middle and two flush inserted spruce wood boards around 1 cm thick. [13] This construction acts as a protection for the back and supports the fabric at the same time. Thus more than 500 years ago, a preventive protection was already being produced as we restorers constantly recommend today to protect the fabric painting support against vibrations and variations in climate.[14]

On the right-hand board, raking light shows up rough, horizontal saw marks and vertical marks from the use of a scorper. A photo from 1961 records the state of the construction on the front side as well – at that time, the original painting support was removed because the nails had rusted and, as a result, the nail holes had eroded. In the raking light, you can also make out exactly the same saw and scorper marks on one of the boards. In addition, the knots of wood and a square insert appear in a corner on the left as well as – reflected and rotated – on the right-hand board. It allows you to deduce that both boards came from a single approximately 2.5 to 3 cm thick plank of around 69 x 41 cm which was sawn in the middle and worked on afterwards with a scorper.

The seals and labels on the back tell almost the complete story of the painting. A seal with the Gradenigo family's coat of arms (fig. 4) records that the painting had already passed in the 16th century from the ownership of Cardinal Pietro Bembo, as stated in the archives, to that of the Gradenigo family when they took over the Casa Bembo in Padua.[15] It was seen and described here again in 1803.[16] After its sale, the Accademia di Milano granted an export licence with a seal, whereupon the work left Italy between 1815 and 1819 (fig. 5).[17] In 1819, it is listed in businessman Edward Solly's storeroom in Berlin as "Andrea Mantegna" when the seizure of the unique, large Solly collection was pending. Here it includes an inventory note with measurements in feet ("pie") and inches (fig. 6).[18] After the Solly collection had been sold to the Prussian King Frederick William III in 1821, the painting was marked retrospectively with a small note with a seizure stamp on the upper side of the stretcher frame (fig. 7).[19] It can be inferred from the Gemäldergalerie's first directory, compiled up until the opening of the Königliches Museum in 1830, that the restorer Christian Xeller worked on the painting and a new frame was made.[20] During the cataloguing carried out systematically from 1833, the painting was given the inventory number "I 29" on both rear boards as well as on the stretcher frame (figs. 3, 8). In 1878, they broke the Königliches Museum seal, made theft-proof after drilling deep into the frame (fig. 8). After the fall of the monarchy in 1918, a new inventory note was added with the label "Staatliche Museen Berlin - Gemäldegalerie."

During the Second World War, the painting experienced the same fate as many others in the Berlin collection. It was deposited in the Merkers mine at Kaiserroda in Thüringen and after the end of the war it was taken to the Central Art Collecting Point in Wiesbaden. Here the painting was given the stamp of the customs office at Wiesbaden main station on a light paper sticker (fig. 3) before it was transported by ship along with around 200 other masterpieces from the Gemäldegalerie in December 1945 in a well organised US Army operation and taken to the National Gallery of Art in Washington, D.C. There the works were given new numbers (KFM106) which is marked in chalk on the back top right. According to the archives kept in the National Gallery of Art, it is documented in detail that the painting arrived without a frame, it received a new one and was X-rayed in 1947.[21]

From 17 March until 25 April, 1948, an exhibition of this collection took place in the National Gallery of Art that attracted many visitors, which made 13 other stops on its tour of the United States (fig. 9). For the Mantegna painting, however, it was reported by Karl M. Birkmayer that: "Because of the risks, it was excluded from the exhibition tour and was brought back to Germany on the first available transport after the exhibition in Washington." It was stated: "The painting is very loose on the stretcher

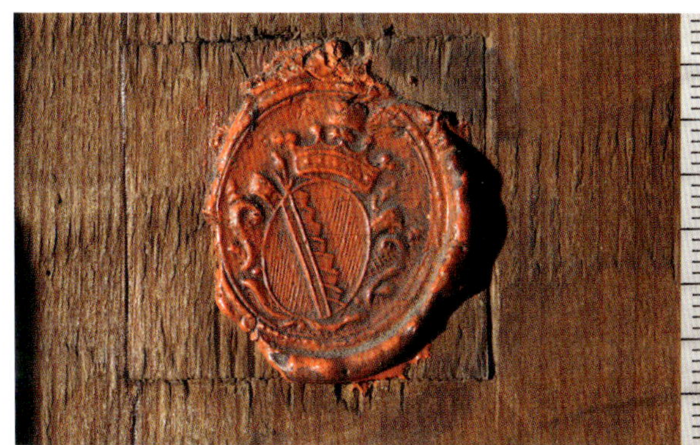

4. Gradenigo family seal, back of painting, lower left corner. Staatliche Museen zu Berlin, Gemäldegalerie

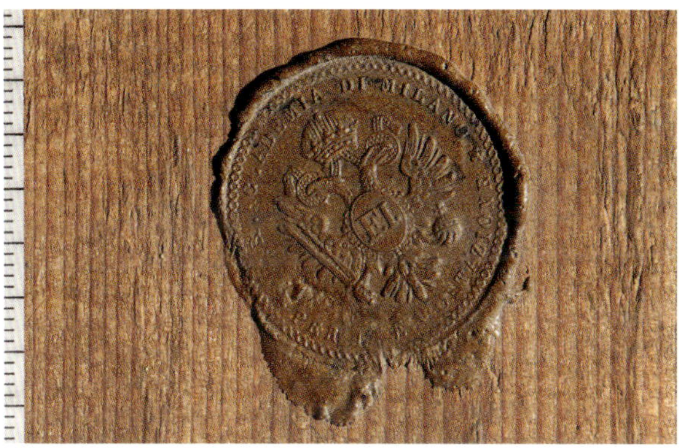

5. Accademia di Milano seal (export licence), back of painting, lower right corner. Staatliche Museen zu Berlin, Gemäldegalerie

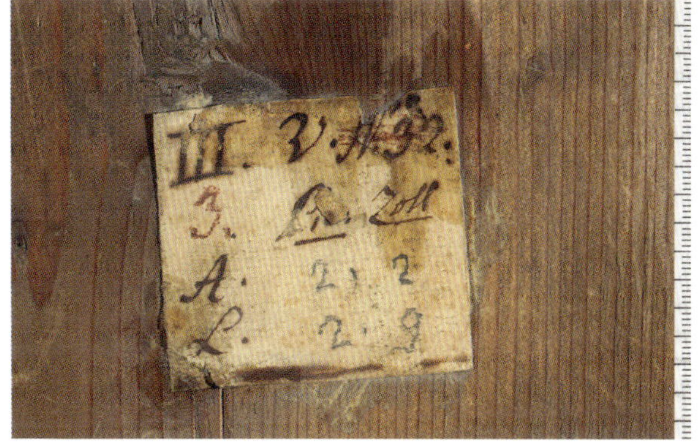

6. Inventory note with measurements from the Solly collection, back of painting, top centre. Staatliche Museen zu Berlin, Gemäldegalerie

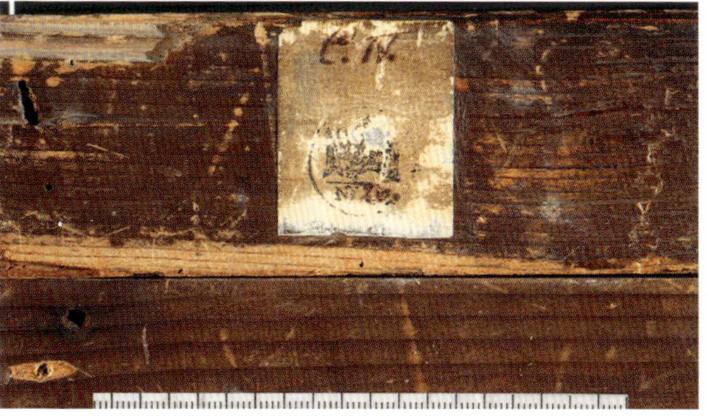

7. Seizure stamp which records the acquisition of the Solly collection, on the upper side of the stretcher frame. Staatliche Museen zu Berlin, Gemäldegalerie

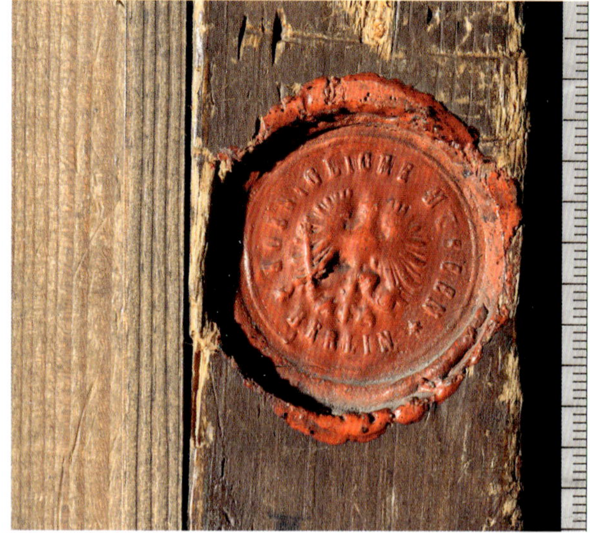

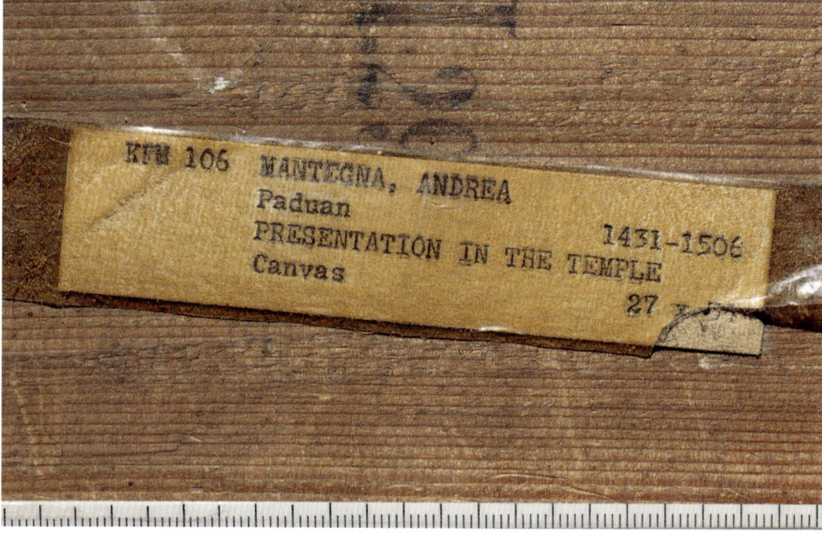

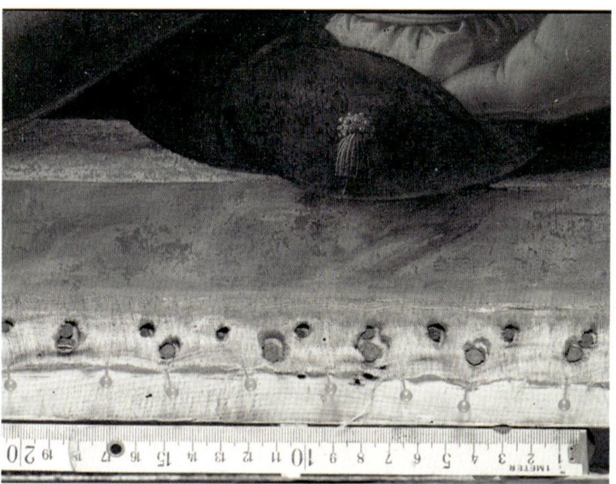

8. Inventory number and royal seal from the 1878 cataloguing on the right side of the stretcher frame. Staatliche Museen zu Berlin, Gemäldegalerie

9. Sticker from the exhibition of 200 masterpieces from the Gemäldegalerie in the National Gallery, Washington, D.C. in 1948 on the back of the painting, centre right. Staatliche Museen zu Berlin, Gemäldegalerie

10. Photo of its condition on July 7, 1957: securing the original tacking edges. Staatliche Museen zu Berlin, Gemäldegalerie, archive

frame" and recommended that: "The painting must be tightened."[22] After the exhibition of the first 50 returned paintings in 1948 at the Haus der Kunst in Munich, the painting was taken back to Wiesbaden until finally it was decided in 1957 that the pieces from the former Prussian collection that had fallen into the hands of the Western Allies should be housed indefinitely in Berlin-Dahlem.[23]

Immediately, in July 1957, attention was turned to improving the tightening of the loose canvas, as a photo shows (fig. 10). Until then the original nails, which had formed cusping in the fabric at regular intervals of about 4 cm, and a second row of nails were still present on the stretcher frame. To stabilise it, the tacking edges had a second canvas glued to the back (fig. 11 b).[24]

After this historical digression, we come back to our technical findings.

The original fabric is noticeably frayed when seen through a microscope which raises the possibility of a hemp fabric. However, the fibre analysis carried out was able to confirm a pure flax fabric of a very light, safely bleached linen.[25] The linen is thickly woven in a simple linen weave and has a selvedge on the left while the right edge is trimmed. The width of the material must therefore have amounted to more

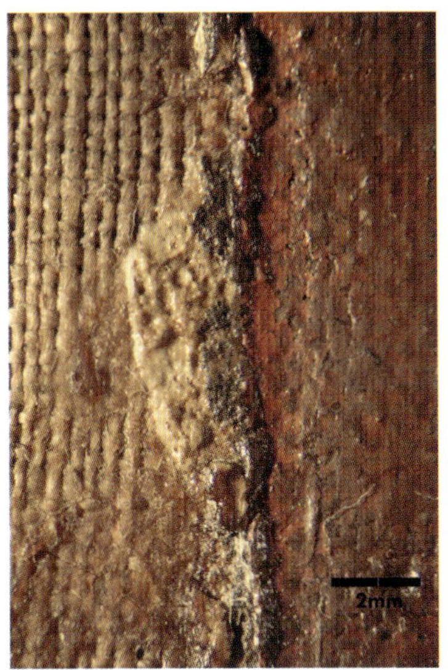

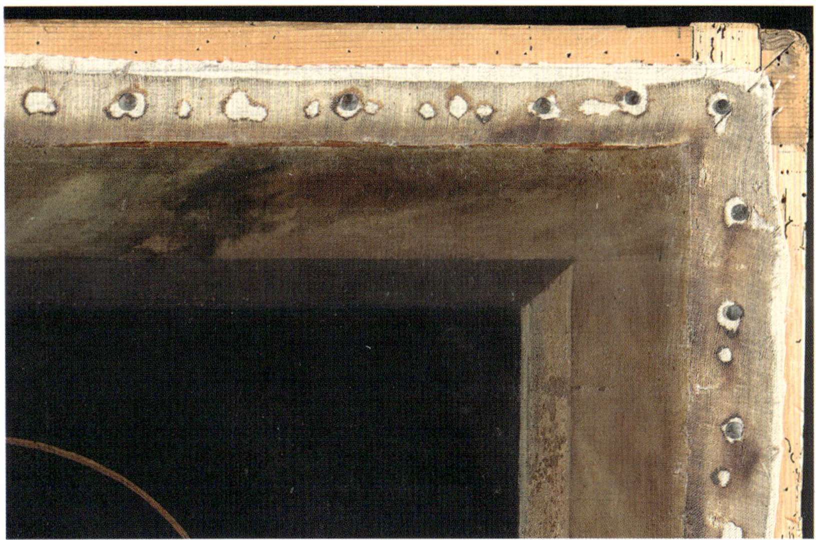

11. Stretching and framing: a) edge of ground from the left side of the painting b) chipped wood on the upper edge of painting from the original stuck on frame strips c) reconstruction drawing of the original framing, cutaway section. Staatliche Museen zu Berlin, Gemäldegalerie

than 91 cm. On the occasion of the Mantegna exhibition at the Louvre in 2008–2009, studies were carried out on the fabric painting supports of 17 of its works. They showed that for his later works from 1500 Mantegna obviously favoured a very fine and close weave with 24 to 36 threads per cm^2 whereas in the 1480s a more coarse weave with a close warp (around 19 threads) and a loose weft (around 12 threads) occurred more often. One exception is the large-sized canvas of *The Virgin and Child with the Magdalen and St John the Baptist* (The National Gallery, London) which is painted with egg tempera on a twill-weave fabric with 14 x 14 threads per square cm^2.[26] Our fabric, which has already been dated to 1453, thus attributed to the 22-year-old Mantegna, has a closely-woven structure by comparison with 21 vertical warp threads and 20–23 weft threads. The yarn is lightly spun in a Z-direction. The quality of the thread in the linen fabric emerges more clearly in the X-ray photograph because white lead apparently sticks to the threads, so we can assume it was not primed. Along the edges we find remnants of wood and brown adhesive as well as an edge of ground (figs. 11 a, b). Originally, therefore, strips of wood were glued on to the tacking edges and the stretcher frame, as was usually the case with

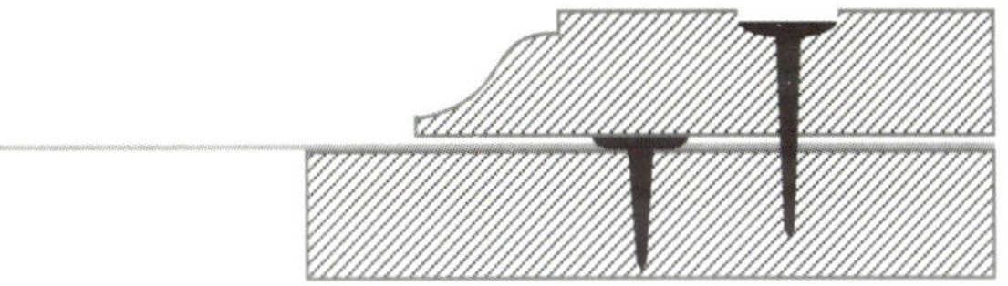

Italian wooden panel paintings of the time.[27]
Diagonal cracks on the corners of the stretcher frame can be explained by the mitre cuts of the frame strips (fig. 11 b). Even if the edges of the stretcher are not mounted, Andrea Rothe assumes that the frame strips did not protrude beyond these, therefore were not wider than around 4.5 cm (fig. 11 c).[28]
Fabrics and raised frames were both prepared with a ground. After removing the frame strips, the strong edge of ground remained for which gesso was detected (fig. 11 a).[29] The ground layer on the canvas, however, is so thin that the non-destructive study methods (µRFA, FORS) could barely detect the typical elements. A thin layer of gesso appears only to be rubbed deep into the fabric structure. This is also one reason for the assumption that we are dealing with a *tüchlein*, therefore matt distemper paint is applied directly onto the canvas with no

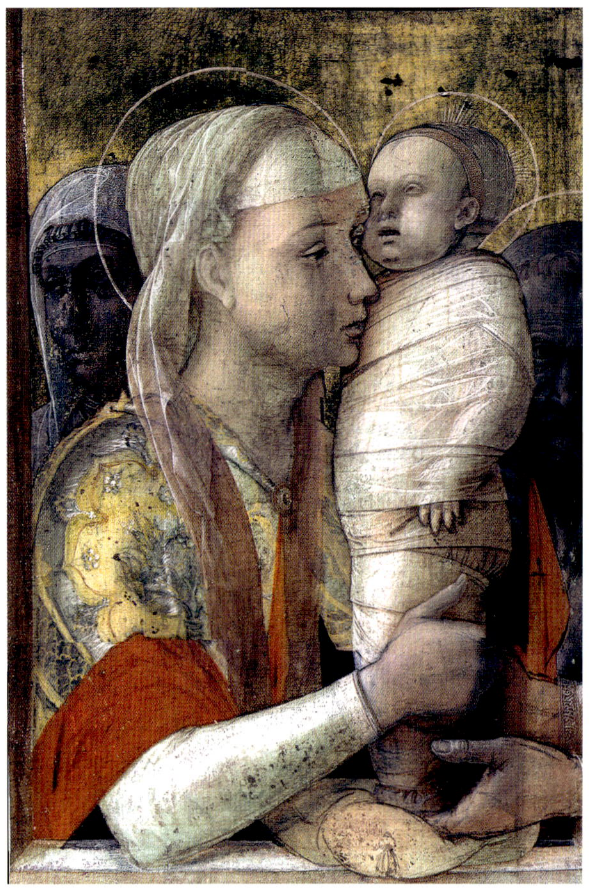

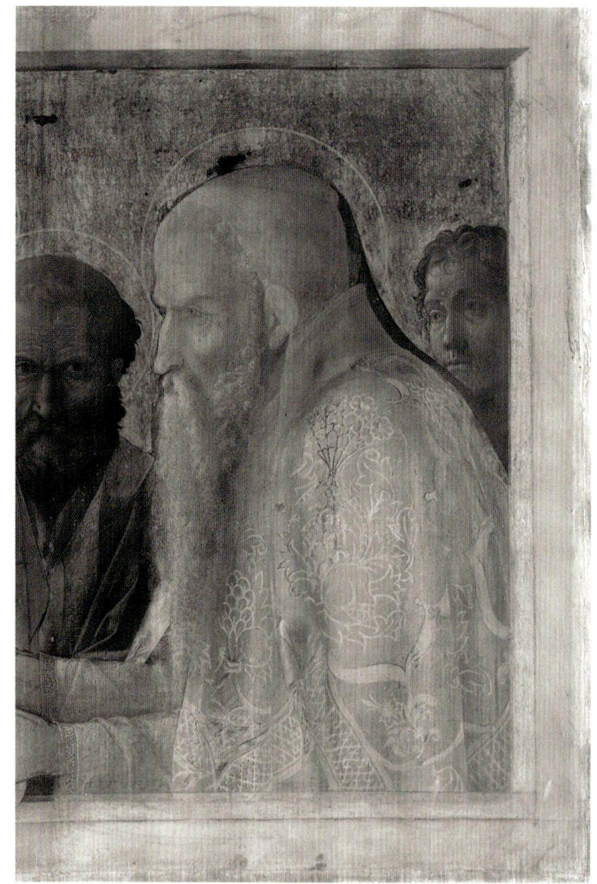

12. Infrared photographs: a) left half NIR false colour image (near infrared with the wavelengths – red 1650 nm, green 1300 nm, blue 1050 nm), generated from the hyperspectral image cube. The other underdrawings on Mary's face and in the brocade pattern of her gown become visible, azurite in the brocade pattern (yellow) and malachite on the sleeve cuff (red-brown). Data collection and analysis by John Delaney and Francesca Gabrieli, National Gallery, Washington, D.C., Scientific Research Department; b) IRR-photograph, Simeon's delicately handled curls become visible, as does the collar of his cloak, which were overpainted later with the headscarf; IRR. Staatliche Museen zu Berlin, Gemäldegalerie

ground preparation. The frame strips presumably had a somewhat heavier grounding and formed the stronger edge of ground.

One wonders what the setting of the profile frame might have looked like. There are no gold remnants on the edge of ground. Since the painted marble frame, from which the cushion and the Virgin Mary's elbow appear to jut out, is designed more to frame the picture and not as a window or – as is the case with Giovanni Bellini – as a parapet or altar table, a continuation of the marble on the frame strips was certainly conceivable.

The IRR image uncovers the outline of an underdrawing. Grey lines are visible which are drawn with a ruler and pencil in order to mark out the frame (fig. 12 b). On the lower edge, the inner line runs down without any mitring to the lower right-hand corner and indicates the height of the frame, which the paint initially overlaps, but which nevertheless was painted over again and corrected later. A further underdrawing with a brush is easily visible on Mary and Simeon's hands. Apparently, the Virgin Mary's forearm was also initially turned downwards (fig. 12 a). The very fine shading on Mary's face apparently stems from the hatched application of colour and does not point to a similarly heavy underdrawing as with the Giovanni Bellini piece (fig. 23).[30] As a rule, Mantegna prepared the drawing and underdrawing in his paintings meticulously, like, for example, in his painting *The Agony in the Garden* at the National Gallery in London (c. 1458–1460, see the contribution by Campbell in this book, fig. 1).[31] In our painting he gave some attention to the development of the drawing of the brocade pattern on the Virgin

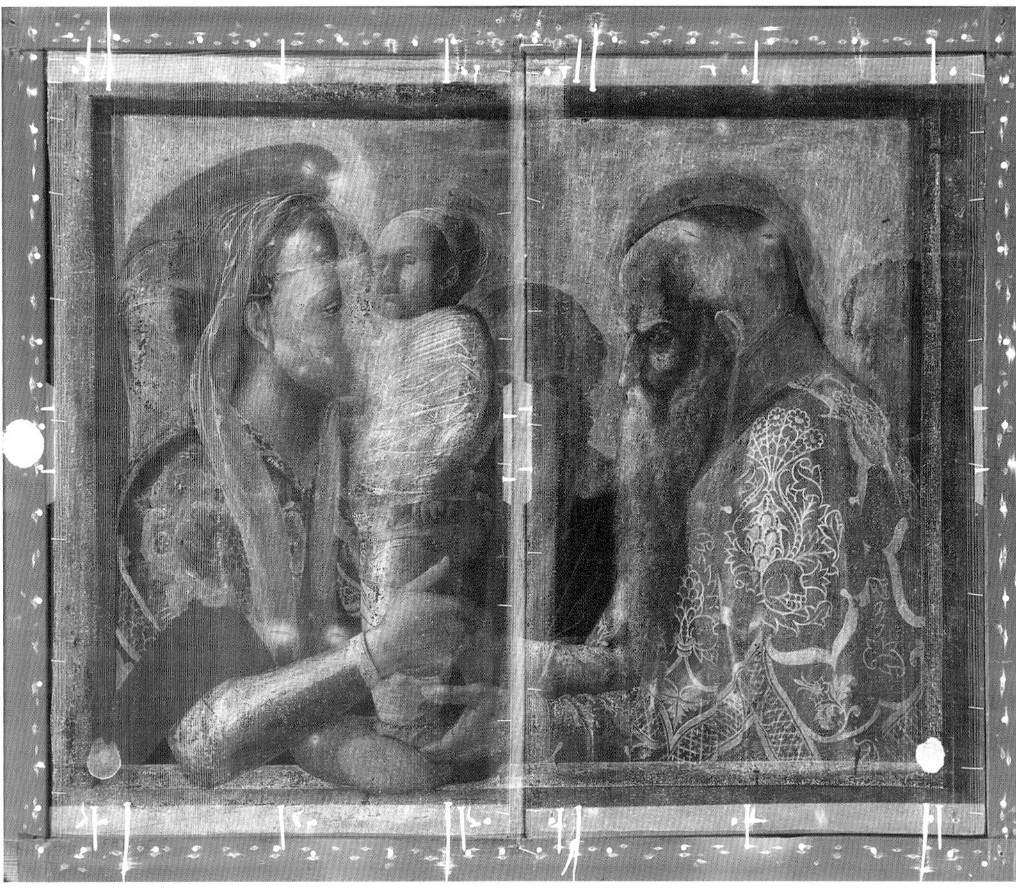

13. X-ray photograph. Staatliche Museen zu Berlin, Gemäldegalerie

Mary's garment which is made a lot clearer with the false-colour infrared image (fig. 12 a). At first, a different feathered pattern was planned. It is surprising that Mantegna carried out large-scale spontaneous changes to the paint support. On Mary's face, we can make out two different outlines of an underdrawing. The lines which become apparent on the forehead come from an initial drawing of the face which was clearly then drawn further to the left and so high that Mary and Child faced each other at eye level some distance apart. It was only later that Mantegna brought Mary and Child back together so they were touching each other.

The X-ray photograph is with respect to the genesis of the painting even more significant (fig. 13). The first steps in the painting involved applying probably a dark grey, white lead-based paint in the background which only left the heads of Mary, the Child and Simeon blank. The other three figures in which one sees the self-portrait of Mantegna to the right, his wife Nicolosia, Giovanni Bellini's sister, to the left and Joseph in the middle were not planned at the outset. There would have been no room for Nicolosia behind the Virgin Mary's head either, especially as the picture surface was smaller to begin with and the frame on both sides, left and right, was intended to be moved around 1.5 cm in the way. Above Mary's head, a blank space is apparent for a foreshortened aura. Simeon's head was also envisaged in the blank space to be higher and larger[32]. Then Mantegna painted the priest's head in fine detail below the Virgin Mary's eye level with his curly, white hair, a kippah-like head piece, his ear showing and a high, vermilion red raised collar on his chasuble with a leaf

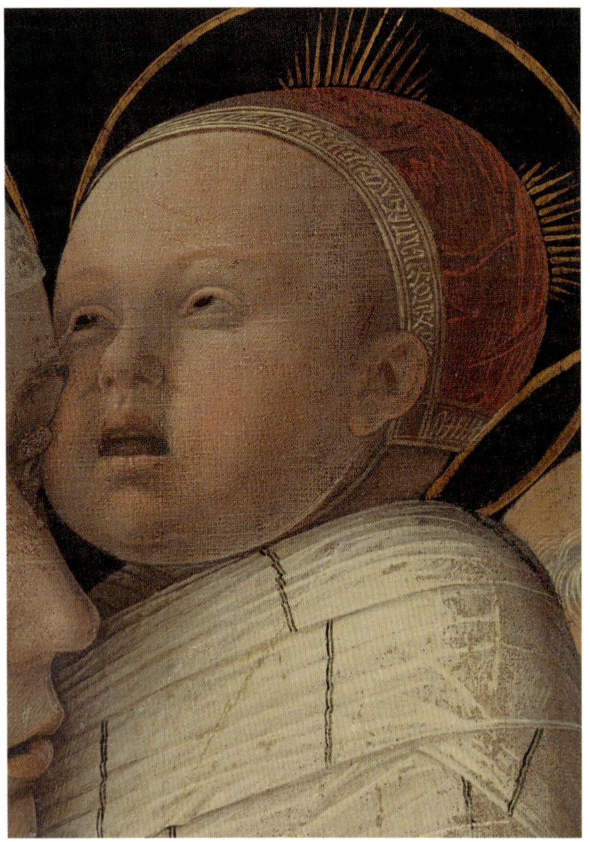

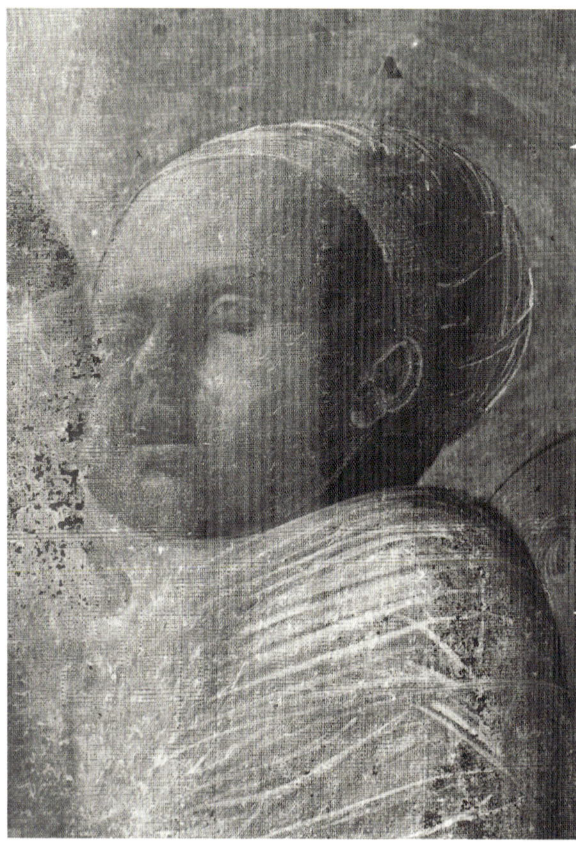

14. Detail of the Child:
a) incident light;
b) X-ray close-up that shows the delicate drawing of the bonnet. Staatliche Museen zu Berlin, Gemäldegalerie

or palmette pattern (fig. 12 b).[33] Only later did he decide to completely cover the back of his head and his collar with an azurite blue headscarf.

The colour of the painting as it appears today barely renders the colour effect that the artist intended, so severe are the later changes and signs of age. With the help of non-destructive study methods, some of the pigments used can be identified and under the microscope you can make out their different particle sizes. This makes an approximate reconstruction of its original colour possible. Large particles of azurite and correspondingly thick layers of paint appear in the background and in the brocade pattern on the Virgin Mary's garment, also in the thin, vertical lines of colour in the Child's swaddling and, as mentioned, in Simeon's headscarf. In the IR-false-colour image, the azurite sections appear yellowish (fig. 12 a). [34] Here you can also see the prominent cracks and imperfections in the background, which was apparently the reason for the overpainting of the entire background with a colour containing Prussian blue that now has a black effect.[35] When this reworking(s?) was carried out, we do not know, presumably in the 18th century.[36]

The golden auras with which the four biblical figures were honoured nevertheless resemble those which were added repeatedly during restorations of Italian works at the Gemäldegalerie before 1830. We find them for example on the *Presentation of Jesus at the Temple* from the Bellini workshop (Gemäldegalerie Berlin, cat. no. 36, fig. 31), which was also restored by Xeller between 1825 and 1830.[37]

While the background of Mantegna's painting now has a black effect due to the later application of varnish, the other blue sections mentioned appear green and therefore very similar to the inner lining of the Virgin Mary's cloak. As evidence of this, malachite, a bluish green, can be detected (reddish-brown in the IR-false-colour image (fig. 12 a).[38] The cushion on which the Child stands is produced, on the other hand, out of another green pigment containing copper.[39]

Even the red sections have undergone severe changes. Vermilion has become partly grey, partly almost blue-black. The once blue brocade pattern of the Virgin Mary's garment stood in front of a warm gold background for which vermilion, earth pigments and white lead could be detected, with lead-tin-yellow hatching on top for the woven-in gold lamé threads.[40] The delicate drawing of the Child's red bonnet can only be deduced from the X-ray image (figs. 14 a, b). Simeon's cope shows an especially elaborate construction of colour (fig 17). The brocade pattern is certainly drawn beforehand even if only a few lines of underdrawing can be made out on the back. The modelling of the bodies and folds in the garments was produced with a thin layer of subtle earth pigments and vermilion on to an initial grey underpainting. As with Mary, hatching with a fine brush and lead-tin-yellow is applied from the top right down to the bottom left, which repeats the direction of the gold lame threads.[41] The pattern was then painted on relatively thickly with white lead and is therefore shown clearly in the X-ray image (fig 13). It follows the form of the body and is certainly not applied with the help of a stencil or a cartoon.[42] The white lead simply acts as the reflector for a subsequent dark red lake that is painted on. This has now been mostly bleached out or flaked in isolated areas (fig. 15). On the lit-up parts of the garment, the pattern was at one time also made lighter with bright red, delicate brush strokes; the light-dark values now are reversed because the vermilion has blackened to a large degree (fig. 16). You can get a general idea of the original appearance of the painting by comparing it to Saint Gregory's cloak in the San Zeno Altarpiece in Verona, which Andrea Mantegna produced from 1457 to 1459 (fig. 18).[43]

Nicolosia's headscarf which is painted with lead-tin-yellow best conveys the original colour effect. The striking "granular" quality of the pigment under the microscope points to the typical formation of "protrusions" which – as we now know – are formed during the ageing process from the chemical combination of lead and an oily component of the binding medium.

A crucial question which was raised again and again for this painting concerns the binding medium used. In the Gemäldegalerie's first directory, the technique is characterised as "on canvas and in oil." After the restoration, presumably with the removal of varnish, it states in the first printed catalogue by Gustav Waagen in 1830: "Dark ground. In distemper. Canvas on wood."[44] Because of the very thin and hatched application of paint in some parts, the use of a water-based binding medium is obvious.

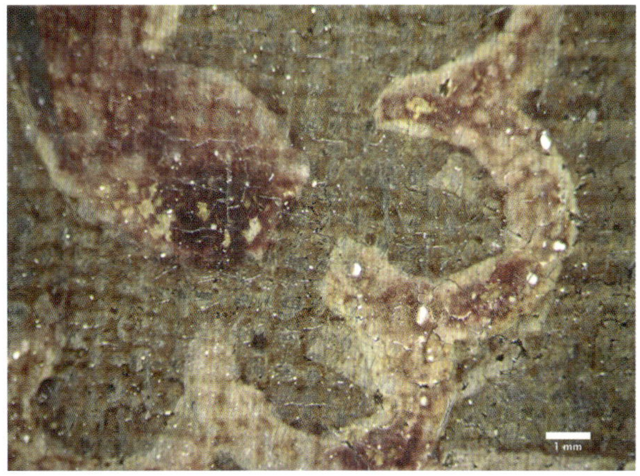

15. Detail of the priests's brocade cloak from fig. 17: bleaching and flaking of the red lake paint on the white pattern drawing, microphoto (magnified 6.5 times). Staatliche Museen zu Berlin, Gemäldegalerie

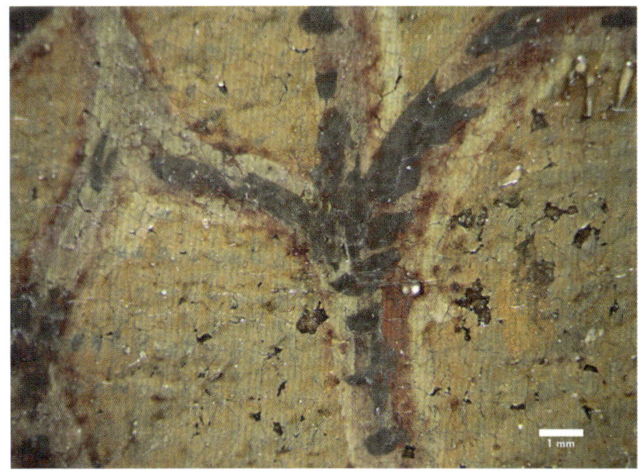

16. Detail of the priest's brocade cloak from fig. 17: blackening of the formerly vermilion red hatchings on the pattern drawing, microphoto (magnified 6.5 times). Staatliche Museen zu Berlin, Gemäldegalerie

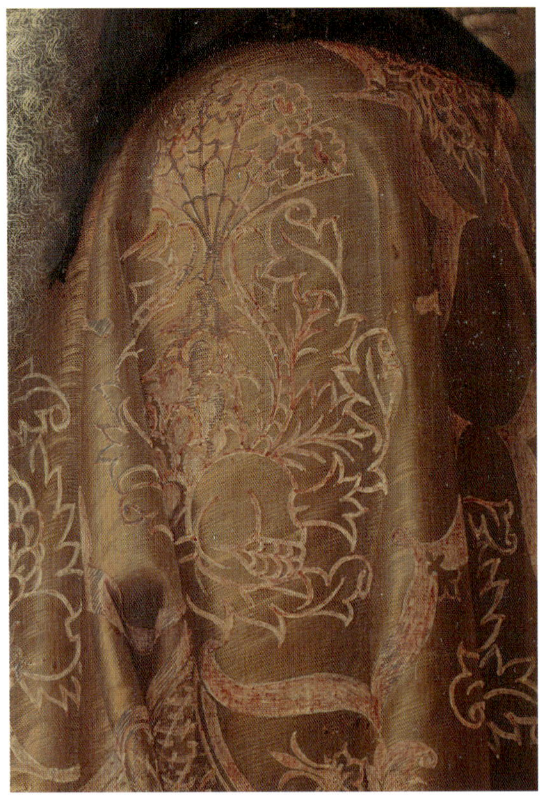

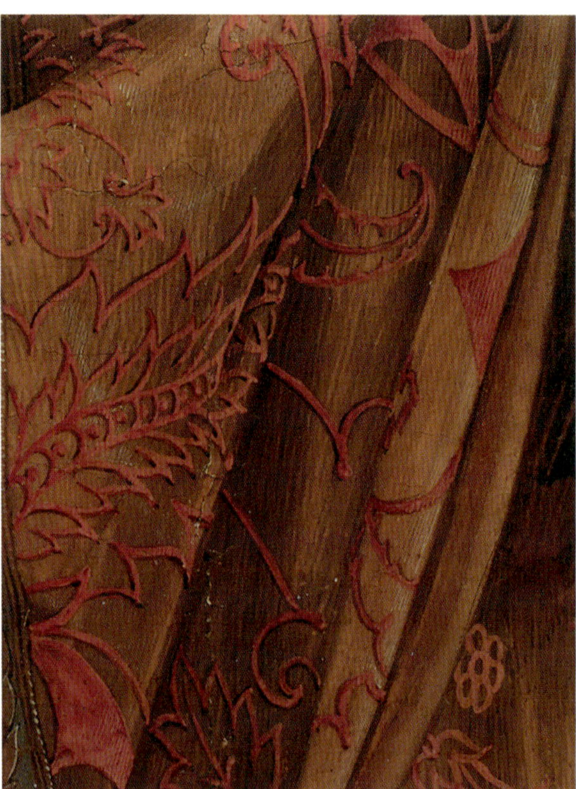

17. Simeon's brocade cloak. Staatliche Museen zu Berlin, Gemäldegalerie

18. Andrea Mantegna, *Pala di San Zeno*, right panel, detail of St Gregory's garment, pattern colour almost unchanged. Verona, Basilica di San Zeno

Rothe used the few established facts on the binding medium carried out by the Getty Conservation Institute in 1991, although it was far from clear, to confirm his assumption, that it concerned distemper paint.[45] What it indicated, for example, on the covering qualities of some areas of colour, especially with regard to compositional changes, can now be confirmed with the new methods of analysis: at least in some parts, like Simeon and Mantegna's flesh tones and Simeon and Joseph's red garments, the use of egg tempera is clearly proven.[46] As Dietemann explains scientifically, egg tempera contains all the optical characteristics of a water-based binding medium.[47] Certainly it may be that not all colours were blended using the same process or mixed with binding medium. In view of the existence of a thin ground layer and the egg tempera medium, one may no longer talk about a "*tüchlein*" with regard to Mantegna's *Presentation* – it is much more like an early canvas painting. Scientific analyses also led to this correction on other paintings by Mantegna.[48] It can no longer be deduced whether the artist intended to have a matt surface and left the painting unvarnished. The varnish that exists today has penetrated into the canvas and darkens the fabric and colours by changing the refractive indices.

Giovanni Bellini's Panel Painting in Venice

In contrast to Mantegna, Bellini used a poplar wood panel with a correspondingly smoother surface as the paint support for his *Presentation of Jesus at the Temple*.[49] At 81.5 x 105.5 cm, the panel is distinctly larger and provides room for two additional figures on the right and left. The panel consists of two boards joined horizontally: the upper one around 33 cm, the lower one 48 cm high, whereby the joins are barely visible from the front.[50] On the back, the join is secured with four approximately 9 cm long dovetails (fig. 19). There are not the usual fitted or inserted transverse strips here. On the back, bright

19. Giovanni Bellini, *Presentation of Jesus at the Temple*. Venice, Fondazione Querini Stampalia, back of panel

20. Andrea Mantegna, detail of *Mary with Child*. Staatliche Museen zu Berlin, Gemäldegalerie

21. Giovanni Bellini, detail of *Mary with Child*. Venice, Fondazione Querini Stampalia

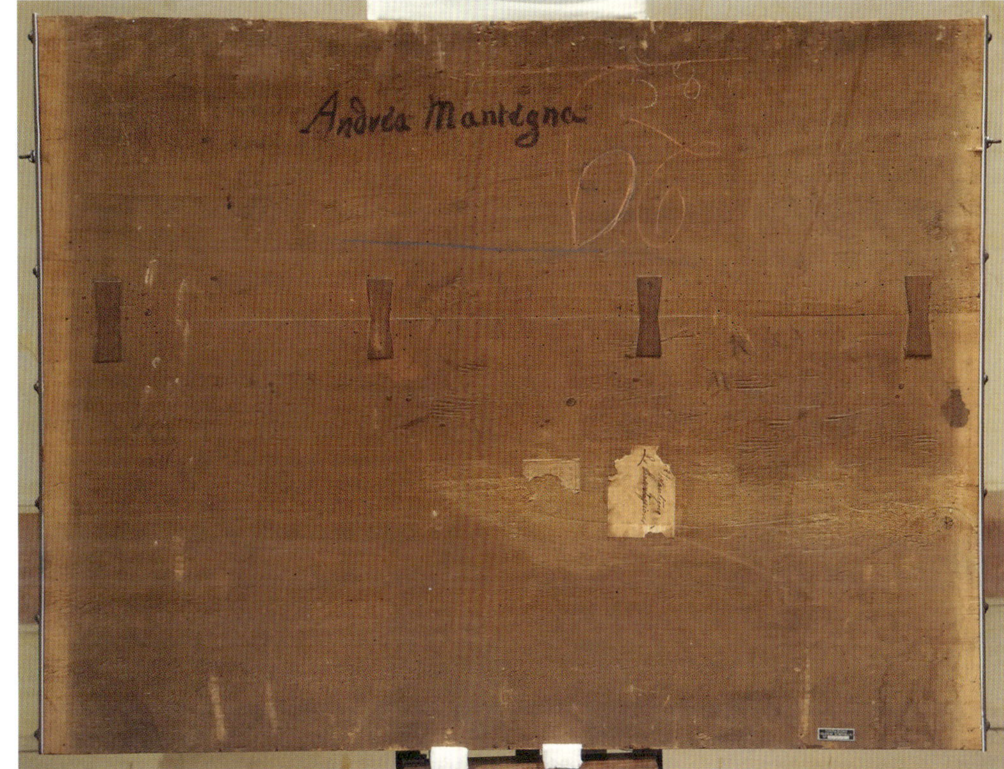

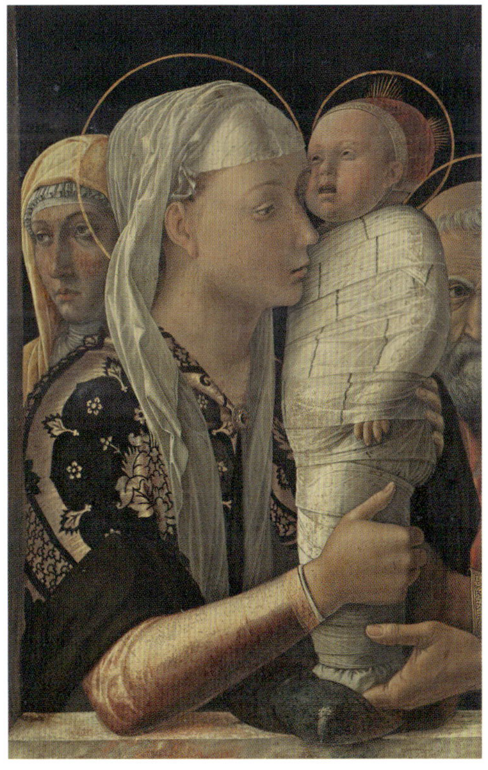

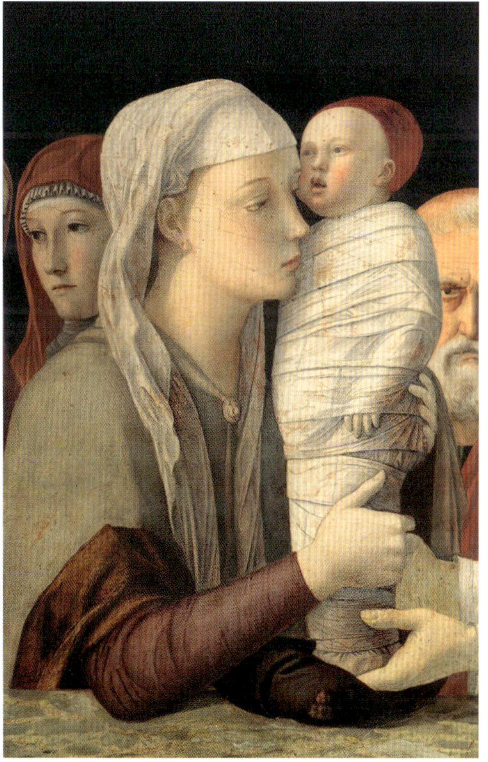

areas, so-called light edges, are apparent on both narrow sides, which however point more to a cover in a frame than to support strips attached to the outer edge.[51] The panel is relatively thin at 16 mm. But clearly it shows original, rough marks from being worked on and many very old inscriptions, including figures sketched in black pen, which are very much reminiscent of the sketches found on the back of triptychs from the Santa Maria della Carità church (now Gallerie dell'Accademia, Venice).[52] All edges are lightly cut.[53] Neither a visible wooden edge nor a ground margin from an integrated frame are present here, as would usually be the case. On all edges, lines are scratched into the already dry paint. They do not run exactly parallel to the edges and indicate that the panel was skewed slightly to the left when the edges were planed.

The ground is off-white and around 1 mm thick. The material is probably gesso. The surface was presumably smoothed with a flat iron. In Mary's garment, subtle, parallel grooves are apparent, which are typical for removing with a flat blade, as well as short, soft scores using a knife with an approximately 8 mm wide blade (fig. 22). The latter could result from the use of a "raffietto," as Cennino Cennini describes it in his painting handbook *Il Libro dell'Arte* from 1390/1400.[54] A primer was not visible on the cut edges with the methods available; an isolation of the ground is probable, however, as the binder does not appear to have penetrated deep into the ground.

Studies of the Mantegna painting in Berlin prove, because of the many compositional changes, that Giovanni Bellini and his workshop cannot have had a cartoon developed by his brother-in-law Mantegna to use as a template, but rather that the painting in its finished state was the model. Only by placing a transparency of an outline drawing from Mategna's painting on the surface of the panel in the Querini Stampalia the studies confirmed that a tracing from Mantegna's painting on a 1:1 scale was used for a detailed reproduction of the composition on the primed panel (fig. 24). A series of dots from a tracing using the "spolvero" process are not visible. Instead, the composition was obviously scored in the ground with incredibly powerful impressions using a tool with a round point, possibly with the help as well of a blackened reverse side or carbon paper. Evidence of this at least are the heavily engraved lines in Mary's headscarf and along the outline of her face, the curly hair of the priest, Joseph and the second man on the right, whose larger eyes and Simeon's beard are also drawn deep into the surface. In the X-ray photo, the deep lines in the area of the Child's swaddling appear white because they are filled in with white paint.[55] The outlines, for example, on Mary's arm are so broad that they could be described as knife scrapings (fig. 22). Since there are scratch lines from several stages of the painting's development, as will be shown below, one must examine the allocation of these scratch lines as accurately as possible.

The comparison of the outline drawing from the Berlin painting with Bellini's painting also showed clearly how the copy proceeded and where divergences arise. They began by placing the group of Mary, the Christ Child and Simeon. Then the drawing was moved down a little and the heads of

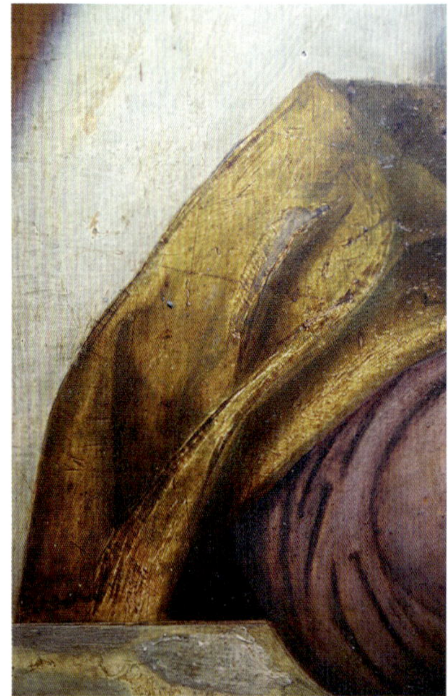

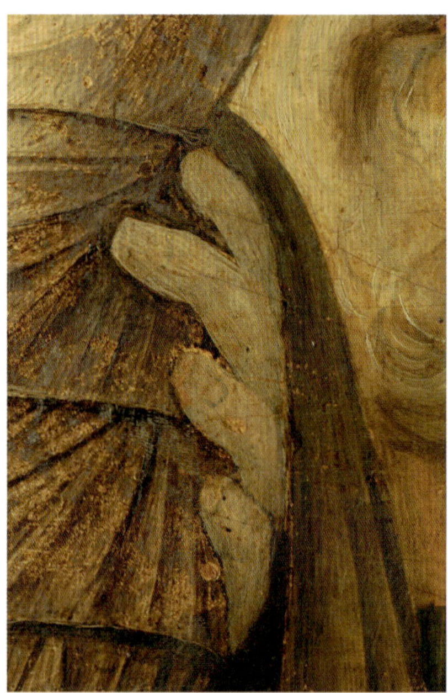

22. Detail from fig. 21, the Virgin Mary's cloak cuff: fine, parallel notches from smoothing out the ground, centre right, deep scratch lines and notches from copying Mantegna's composition drawing on to the ground

23. Detail from fig. 21, Mary's hand and Child's swaddling with considerable flaking of paint which makes the heavy brown-black underdrawing visible

24. Giovanni Bellini, *Presentation of Jesus at the Temple*, section with Mantegna's outline drawing

25. As fig. 24, Mantegna's outline drawing moved
a) Mary's arm;
b) Mary and Simeon's hands

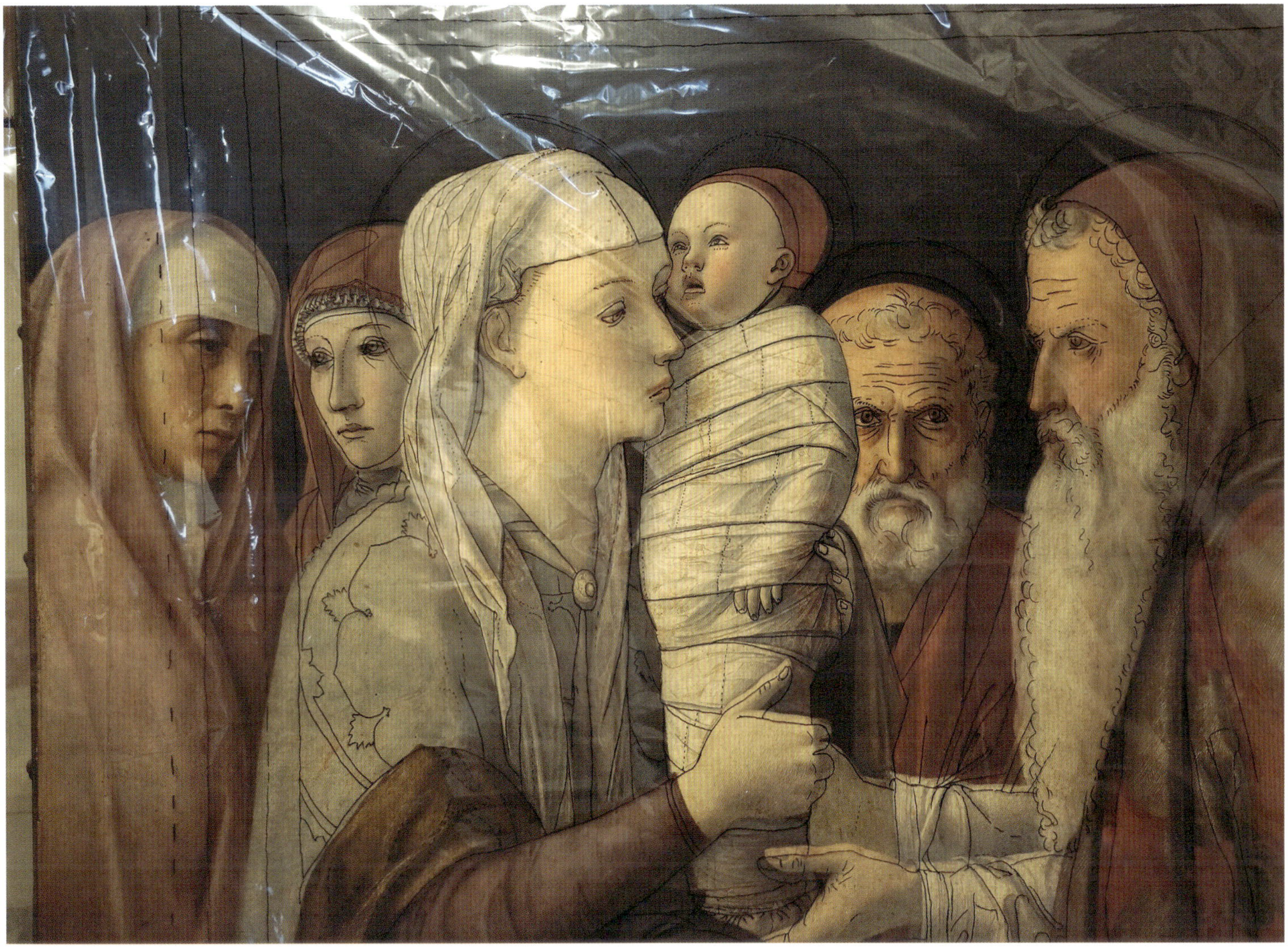

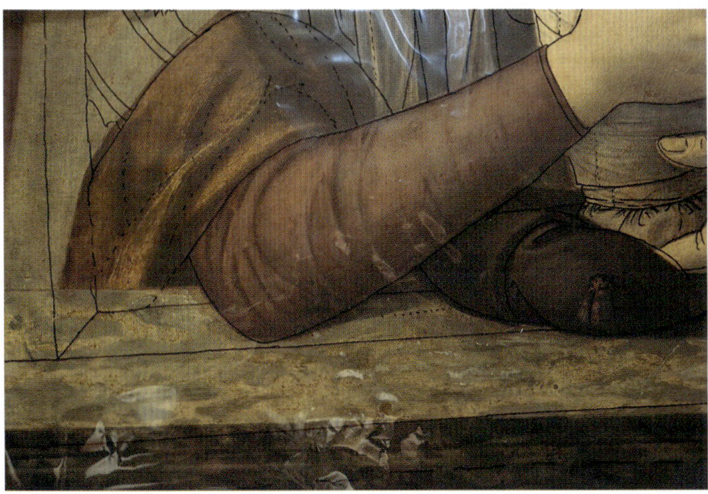

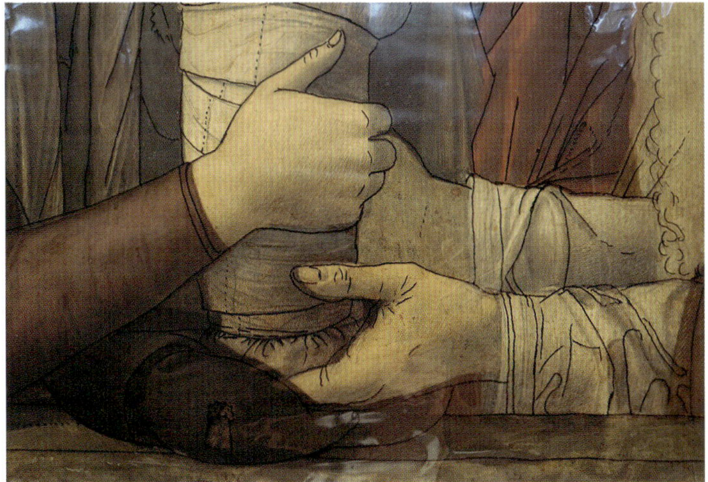

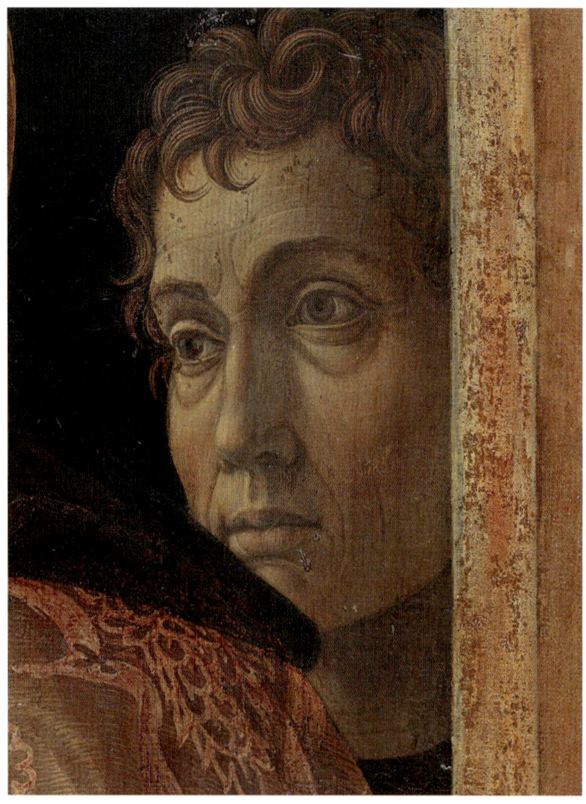

Joseph and the woman on the left (Nicolosia) were also gone over in just as precise detail (fig. 24). Mary and Simeon's hands are moved up a little, so that the Virgin Mary's forearm had to be bent more by turning the tracing to the left (fig. 25). As for the face that is considered to be Mantegna's self-portrait, initially only the right profile and the mouth were carried over (figs. 26, 27 a). Eyes and nose were only traced after the drawing was turned clearly to the right and the eye section horizontally. In the underdrawing, the line of vision follows Mantegna's template (fig. 27 c); only in its painting does Bellini fundamentally change the man's head. This process of adapting a prepared drawing in a variety of ways by moving and turning individual elements was an effective and surprisingly widespread method which could be demonstrated repeatedly in the case of contemporaries and also in northern Europe.[56]

The composition set up is then worked on with a brush underdrawing modelled in great detail. The heavy hatching with brown-black ink is displayed in a few outbursts, especially in the Mary and Child grouping (fig. 23). As they are only thinly overpainted in the light-coloured sections and the lead-white oil paint has increased in transparency, they can be judged even better with the naked eye than in the IRR-photographs. This type of chiaroscuro underdrawing is typical of Giovanni Bellini: it is striking in the IR-reflectography of his *Pietà* in the Pinacoteca di Brera in Milan and in his other paint-

26. Mantegna, detail of self-portrait from the right edge, incident light. Staatliche Museen zu Berlin, Gemäldegalerie

27. Bellini, detail of the men on the right:
a) with outline drawing from Mantegna's composition;
b) with the outline drawing turned to the right;
c) IRR-photograph

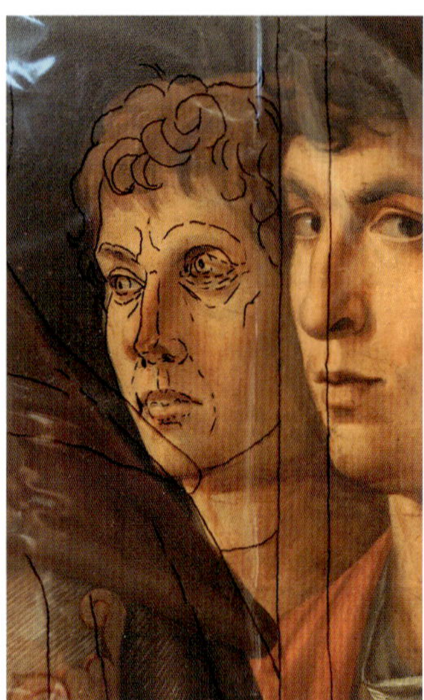

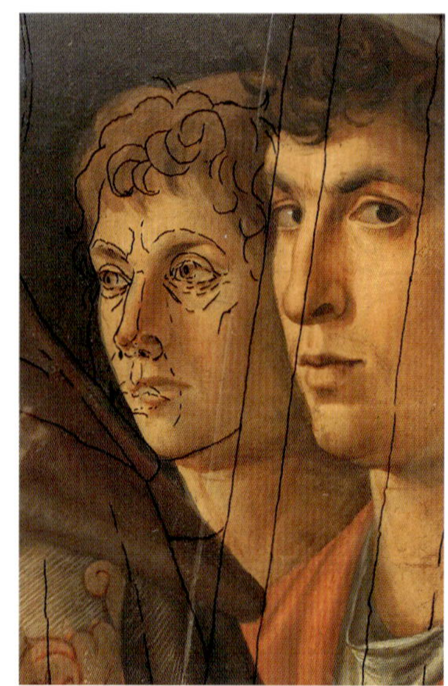

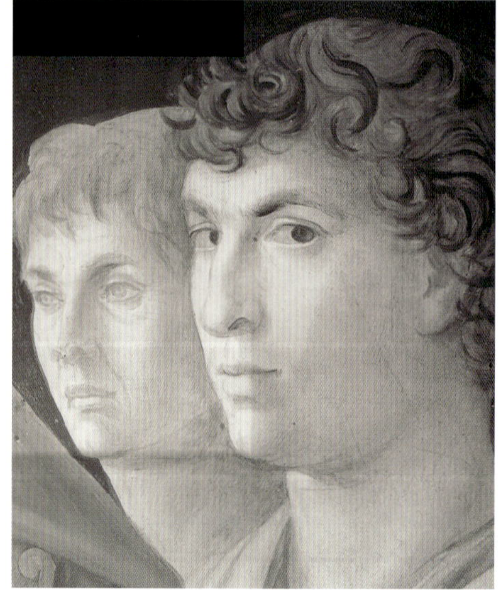

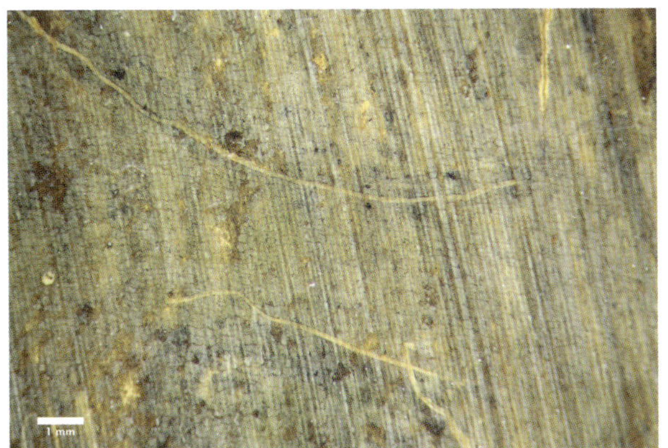

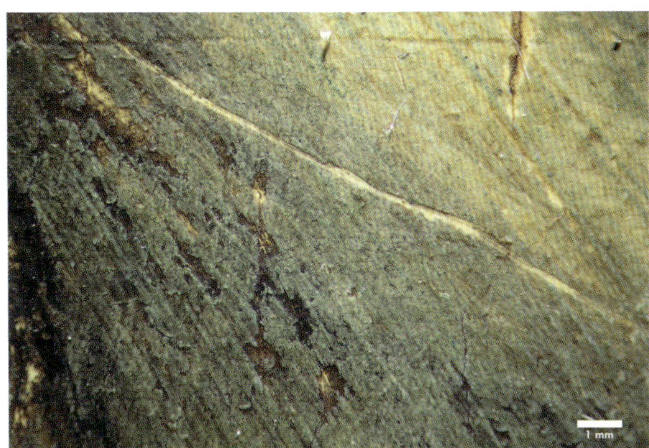

28. Bellini, scratch marks, a) detail of Mary's headscarf: scratch lines on the underdrawing, originally overpainted; b) detail of a section of Mary's cloak: transparent black underdrawing and later scratch lines in the dry paint, microphotos (magnified 6.5 times). Staatliche Museen zu Berlin, Gemäldegalerie

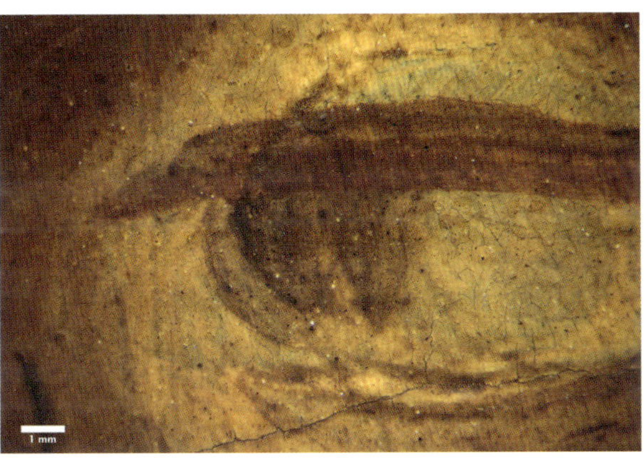

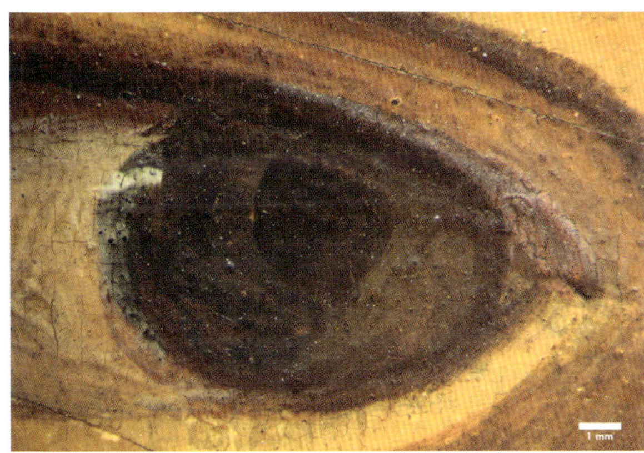

29. Eyes of the men on the right of the picture: a) fleetingly painted left eye of the man on the left; b) left eye of the man on the right painted in detail, microphotos (magnified 6.5 times). Staatliche Museen zu Berlin, Gemäldegalerie

ings.[57] Interestingly, scratches are apparent in this heavy underdrawing beneath the painting which one must distinguish from further scratch lines in the finished painting from various later copying processes (figs. 28 a, b). Obviously, for its part, the worked-on underdrawing was already copied in the Bellini workshop.

In the base section, original scratch lines are drawn along a straight edge. They define the upper edge, the front edge and the lower edge of the thick tabletop.[58] Further scratch lines are added later when the outline of the tabletop was subsequently altered.

The painting shows all the characteristics of oil painting techniques, as can be seen, for example, from the type of brushwork, its fluidity and transparency. This becomes especially clear in comparison to Mantegna's careful and consistently hatched brushwork in the group of figures (figs. 20, 21). Bellini's brushwork is not consistent. In the Child's swaddling and in Mary's headscarf, the thin white colour is applied quickly with a broad brush over the detailed underdrawing (figs. 23, 28a). Blueish hatching results from the "optical grey" alone, therefore due to the translucency of the brown-black underdrawing without the addition of azurite. Only a few sections are remodelled with hatching. The translucency of the elaborate underdrawing was certainly intended by the artist and can only be partially attributed to chemical changes in the paint and damaging restorations. The brushwork on the man's head behind Simeon is similarly thin and fleeting (figs. 27 b, c, 29a). But here the underdrawing has less of an influence on the surface. This feature of the brushwork leads repeatedly to the assumption that the painting is unfinished.[59] On Mary's face, the underdrawing was partially covered, firstly with a thin, light layer and the skin colour only applied on top of that. The skin colour of the woman on

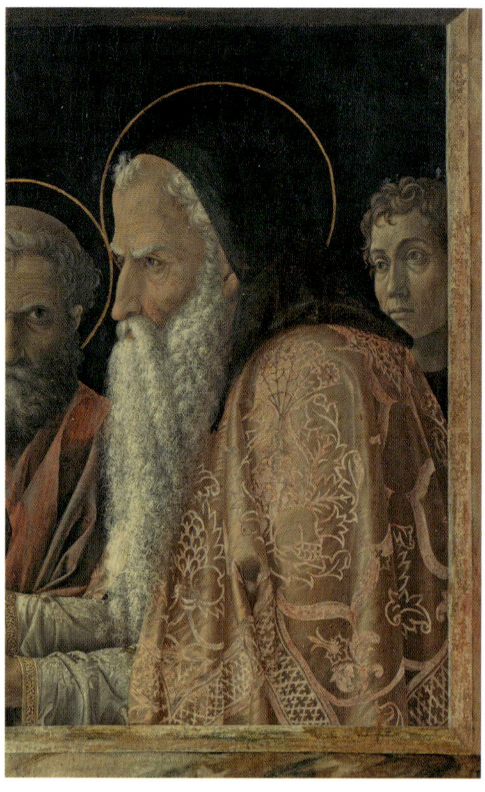

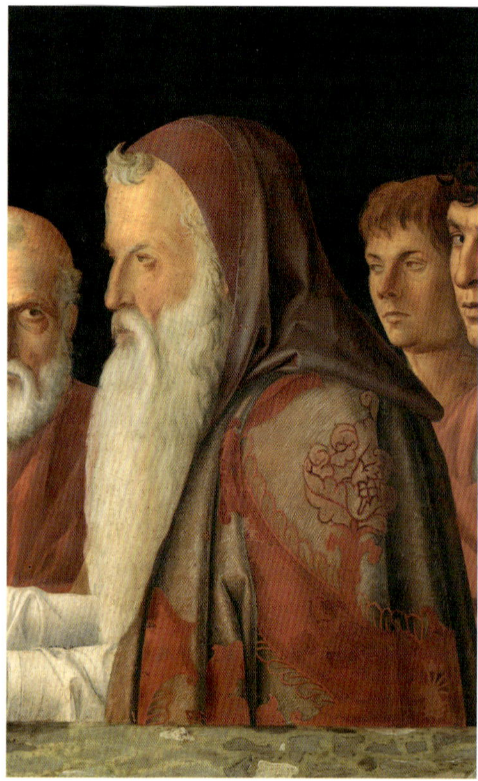

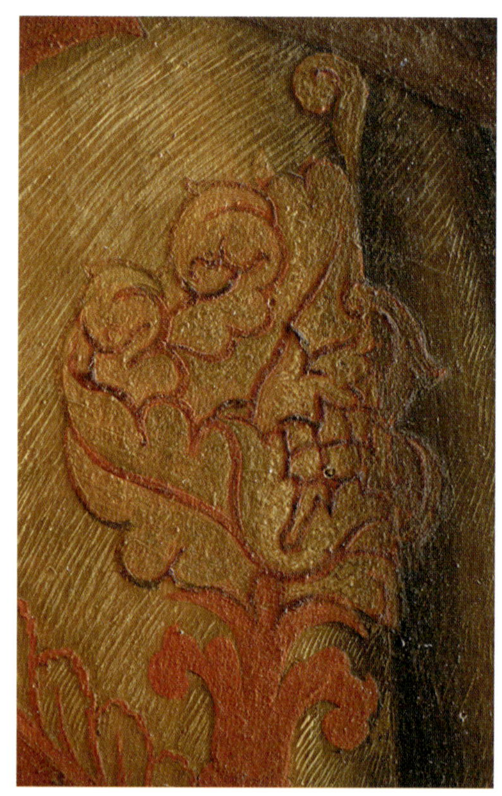

the left edge is put on with broad, flat brushstrokes. Her red garment was painted on after Mary's blue-grey garment, subsequently Nicolosia's red-brown headscarf was added. On the other hand, on the far right, the red gown of the man who looks directly at the viewer is applied first. A fold in his collar was placed initially right in front of Simeon's back, but was then painted over with the brocade garment. The man's face is worked on particularly delicately. He has almost portrait-like brushstrokes and, with the reflections in the eye and the stubble that is applied with an especially fine brush, it is realistic in a way that is reminiscent of Antonello da Messina (fig. 29 b).

The representation of the priest's garment, an embroidered velvet in front of a gold background, is done lavishly and tries hard to imitate the texture of the material with varying paint techniques (fig. 31): an initial light underpainting has left behind a thick, streaky effect from the brushwork, then followed a brown-green layer of paint with fine particles of earth pigments; the red patterns have – as with Mantegna (fig. 30) – white painted underneath, the vermilion red partially glazed with dark red lake. Hatchings in yellow (presumably lead-tin-yellow, white lead with a few red pigments[60]) represent the gold lamé, they drip off in parts from the ground and may have been deliberately applied very dry or with a water-based binding medium on an oil ground. In the large stylised flower pattern, the paint is jabbed on, probably in order to reproduce a special textile technique (*bouclé*, *allucciolato*).[61] Some parts of Mantegna's template were not understood by Bellini: Mary's open gown was painted in dark above her forearm, but then blended in with the grey colour of the cloak (figs. 20, 21). Above the inside of Simeon's right elbow, the triangle underpainted in the colour of the sleeve was reinterpreted only at the end with a brown overpainting of the cloak lining. Joseph's red garment is treated in keeping with Mantegna's

30. Mantegna, detail of the priest. Staatliche Museen zu Berlin, Gemäldegalerie

31. Bellini, detail of the priest:
a) incident light;
b) detail of brocade gown in raking light with varied application of paint

template, and by broadening Simeon's white beard as well Mantegna's sharp angles disappear (fig. 30). The stone balustrade is painted very coarsely and effectively: the light patches on the green marble are initially painted on flat in the whole base area, whereupon the front edge of the tabletop and the front underneath both original scratch lines were shaded with a brown-black semi-transparent colour. The lead-white pigment used here is noticeably coarse.

The inconsistency in the degree of finish is not unusual in Giovanni Bellini's work. For example, in the *San Giobbe Altarpiece*, you can see a clear difference between the delicate treatment of the Madonna on the throne and the liberal application of paint for the angel musicians.[62]

Giovanni Bellini's panel was restored by painter, copier and restorer Placido Fabris at the end of the 19th century.[63] Damage from an aggressive removal of the varnish and the thin, black overpainting of the original black background presumably stems from this time. In 1949, Mauro Pelliccioli carried out a further restoration. The removal of varnish and extensive overpainting is recorded with black and white photographs.[64] He was very sparing with his retouches. There are hardly any changes to the heads of the donor figures at the edges of the painting, which had been assumed on many occasions.[65]

Mantegna's and Bellini's *Presentations*. A Summary and Comparison

With the same composition, the two paintings differ considerably in the colour palette as well as in the application of paint. The different binding mediums – egg tempera with an aqueous, subtle hatching technique and opaque colours for Mantegna and the longer-dispersing oil-based medium for Bellini – contribute decisively to the different characteristics.

In the Mary with Child group, Bellini comes closest to the template because the transparent texture of his heavy underdrawing is closely related to Mantegna's hatched application of paint (figs. 20, 21). But the comparison of the painting of Simeon's head shows clearly Bellini's very painterly handling of colours compared to the dry, linear approach of Mantegna's painting (fig. 30). In view of the stylistic qualities of the underdrawing and the painting, Bellini's panel – according to the general consensus of art historians – has to have originated only around 20 years after the accepted date of origin of around 1453 for Mantegna's *Presentation of Jesus at the Temple*.

Mantegna's painting was really colourful in its original appearance. He gave Mary a cloak made of embroidered velvet with a large blue pattern contrasting with the gold ground and a green lining with a ruby brooch. Facing her, the priest has similarly sumptuous clothes with a material of red tones with large repeat linear patterns.[66] The composition has such a lavish effect, yet Mantegna didn't use expensive paint materials[67]: he used neither ultramarine blue nor shell gold in his delicate drawing, a technique which he readily employed in his *Agony in the Garden* (The National Gallery, London), as well as in his later works.[68]

Mantegna's work seems to have been created for more private purposes as it is developed so freely on the surface of the painting. But what caused Bellini to tackle the same composition again after such a long period of time? His use of colour is not just completely different because of the different binding medium and state of preservation: red, brown and purple colours dominate the tonality. Bellini also decided against ultramarine blue, whose use he otherwise valued so much. Mary's garment remains very modest in its colour and material compared to the priest's lavish gown. Did Bellini really have Mantegna's painting in front of him or just a line drawing on which there was no outline of the brocade pattern?

The use of half-length figures in *the Presentation of Jesus at the Temple* offered so much opportunity for the integration of a family portrait that it obviously came into fashion for this very purpose. Bellini developed a variation on this composition with the same pictorial theme in which the Child is

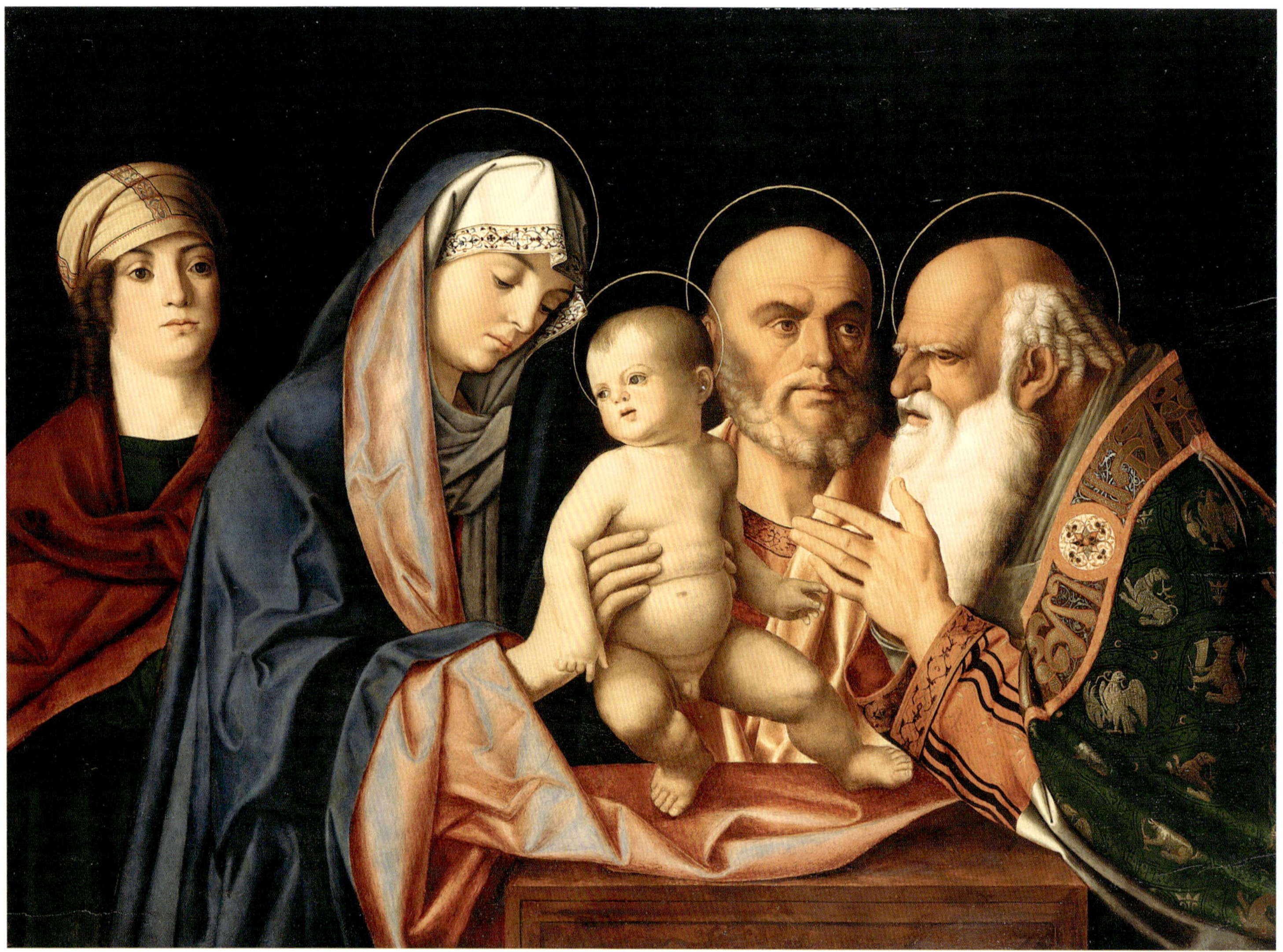

32. Giovanni Bellini (Atelier), *Presentation in the Temple*. Staatliche Museen zu Berlin, Gemäldegalerie, no. 36

presented more openly to the viewer, accompanied by the four biblical figures to the left of a person that varies in accordance with the client's wishes (fig. 32). Around 30 replicas and copies of this composition have survived.[69] The underlying compositional drawing was also used by Bellini's pupils and followers.[70] The varied use and re-use of one composition idea has also been verified on other often requested pictorial themes for Bellini's great workshop.[71] It was common workshop practice in the 15th century and did no harm to the appreciation of painting.

[1] See Neville Rowley and Babet Trevisan in this volume.
[2] See Trevisan 2008, entry no. 13, p. 176.
[3] Ibid.
[4] Stefan Weppelmann, as curator at the time of Italian painting until 1500 at the Gemäldegalerie in Berlin, initiated the studies in 2013 and together with the author as chief restorer at the Gemäldergalerie set up a workshop on 13 June 2014 at which the author presented the first results of her studies and discussed these with Brigit Blass-Simmen, Jill Dunkerton, Volker Schaible, Regula Schorta, Giovanni C.F. Villa. She presented further results under the title of "Andrea Mantegna's and Giovanni Bellini's *The Presentation of Jesus at the Temple*. The Genesis, Correspondence and Difference of Two Paintings in Berlin and Venice" at a session of the Renaissance Society of America (RSA) in Berlin on 28 March 2015.
[5] Analogue X-ray photograph on 1m-wide film material, IR-reflectography with XEVA-FPA-1.7-640 camera, InGaAs chip with sensitivity of 900 to 1700 nm.
[6] µRF analysis with a portable ArtTax Pro spectrometer with a molybdenum tube carried out by S. Schwerdtfeger on 21 June 2017. See S. Schwerdtfeger, I. Reiche, Rathgen Research Laboratory SMB, study report 71_062117 from 30 August 2017, unpublished. NIR hyperspectral and FORS spectroscopy carried out by J. Delaney on 5.07.2017, analysis by J. Delaney, F. Gabrielli on 19 December 2017, seven pages, unpublished.
[7] WILD M3Z stereo microscope with 6.5x to 40x magnification, eyepieces with 10x magnification, micro photographs with the digital single-lens reflex camera Canon EOS 5D Mark II
[8] For making it possible to carry out these studies from 7 to 13 June 2017 in the Querini Stampalia Museum, I want to thank Marigusta Lazzari and Babet Trevisan; together with them and Caroline Campbell, Jill Dunkerton, Birgit Blass-Simmen, Neville Rowley and Giovanni Villa, the results were discussed in front of the painting on 12 June 2017. The author is very grateful to Villa for the IRR photographs. In Villa 2007, p. 10, he mentions that he worked with the same InGaAs-Chip as Schmidt in Berlin (see note 5), but in two spectral ranges from 850-1000 nm and 1000-1700 nm.
[9] See Rothe 1992, pp. 82ff.
[10] See Wolters 1960, p. 161; Straub 1984, p. 154.
[11] Size of the stretcher frame: height 77.5 cm, width 94.4 cm, depth 2.8 cm.
[12] For the first mention of this painting, in around 1520–1530 Marcantonio Michiel described a *Presentation at the Temple* in the home of Pietro Bembo in Padua as "una tavola piccola"; see N. Rowley in this catalogue. In the Gemäldegalerie's first directory with details of restorations carried out between 1824 and 1830, it is written "on wood" which is scored out and corrected to "on canvas." Berlin State Museums, Central Archive I GG 25/1, leaf 19; I thank Ute Stehr for pointing this out.
[13] Wood identification by Peter Klein, unpublished report from 5 January 1980.
[14] Straub points out that amongst others Albrect Dürer's *Dresden Altarpiece* (central panel from 1496, side panels 1503–1504) was also painted on fine "*tüchlein*" and stretched on to wooden boards until 1840, Straub 1984, p.154
[15] Lightbown 1986, p. 405. Already mentioned in the Bembo collection around 1520–1530, see note 11. Because the Gradenigo seal is placed precisely on the square wooden insert, there was speculation about a later addition, but for the abovementioned technical reasons (the same shape of insert is mirrored on the second back board) I think it can be ruled out.
[16] Letter from Giovanni de Lazara to Giovanni Maria Sasso in 1803, in Campori 1866, p. 351.
[17] Seal with Austrian crowned double-headed eagles, in the middle "FI" for the kingdom of Lombardy under Franz I. (reigned from 1815–1835) and "C.R. ACCADEMIA DE MILANO* PER L'ESPORTAZIONE*" written around it.
[18] In the list drawn up by Friedrich Schultz regarding the Solly collection of around 150 paintings; the note with measurements comes from the period of 1821–1824 when Alois Hirt broke up the collection, Skwirblies 2009, pp. 71 and 80 (no. 61).
[19] Ivi, p. 71, mentions that the paintings pledged in 1819 were given an eagle stamp and catalogue number in around 1830. Here "C. IV.," presumably for 4th class, and the cat no. 26 are indicated. Another label of a similar age with the hand-written entry "No. 2" could not be attributed or dated up to this point.
[20] First directory of the Gemäldegalerie naming the restorations carried out between 1824 and 1830, Central Archive SMB, as note 12; Christian Xeller, summoned from Heidelberg, worked from August 1825 until December 1830 for the Royal Collections, then was employed until 1872; see Stehr 2012, p. 56.
[21] National Gallery of Art, Washington, D.C., Gallery Archives Series 17A5 Box 14 64041, according to the author's research of the archives on 12 October 2017.
[22] All three entries on loose-leaf paper with reference to reports by Taggert, Birkmeyer, Böhm-Sommerfeld, Ordner, "Restoration reports 1946–1950," Gemäldegalerie, Department of Restoration and Art Technology, archive; see also Birkmeyer 1949, p. 13 in no. 33.
[23] Exactly when Mantegna's painting was brought back from Wiesbaden to Berlin is not documented. It was at any rate part of the *Masters of Italian Art* exhibition that was held at the Neues Museum in Wiesbaden in 1953.
[24] Based on the photos this measure can be dated to 1961. Prof. Volker Schaible, Stuttgart State Academy of Fine Arts, verifies that protein was used as an adhesive (email of 22 November 2016), no starch or BEVA adhesive as assumed by the analysis of the Getty Conservation Institute in 1991.
[25] Fibre analysis carried out by V. Schaible, as note 24
[26] C. Naffah, in Menu, Ravaud 2009, p. 4.
[27] Botticelli's *Profile Portrait of a Young Woman* (Simonetta Vespucci?) from 1480–1485 (Gemäldegalerie Berlin, cat. no. 106A) shows comparable findings: wooden nails and cracks from mitred frame strips can still be seen on the approximately 4 cm wide wooden edge, but the frame strips have been lost.
[28] The distances between the outer edges of the stretcher frame to the ground edge are 4 to 4.2 cm on the right and left and more like 4.5 cm at the top and bottom. This is possibly explained by the fact that the canvas is shrunk more in the vertical warp direction. Rothe assumes that the nails, which do not relate to the cusping, stem from the fixing of the frame profiles. So many nails are not needed when gluing at the same time and in comparison with wooden panel paintings (see note 27) unlikely. See Rothe 1992, p. 83, with reconstruction drawing.
[29] Proof of Ca and S for gesso thanks to µRFA-measurements, Schwerdtfeger, Reiche 2017, pp. 5, 8 (test point 1).
[30] Further IRR-photographs from Trevisan, n.d., pp. 17ff and Villa 2009, pp. 52–53.
[31] Dunkerton, Hartwieg 2018.
[32] In my opinion, the blank space was not intended for a flat, parallel image of an aura above Simeon since the foreshortened ellipsoid aura above the Virgin Mary would have been barely conceivable beside a flat, round aura.

[33] Proof of Hg (quicksilver) from cinnabar alongside Cu as a result of µRFA measurements, Schwerdtfeger, Reiche 2017, pp. 6, 21ff (test points 28, 29).
[34] The establishment of azurite was only possible by analysing the hyperspectral imaging, Delaney-Gabrieli, see note 6.
[35] According to the analysis of a test (#E4) on the upper left corner by the Getty Conservation Institute, Analysis Report #794-P-91 from 14 August 1991 (M. Derrick, M. Schilling, E. Doehne): "The sample contains a protein and oil binder. The blue particles in the top layer of the painting are Prussian blue. Phosphorous was not found in the sample, thus it is unlikely egg yolk was used as a binder." Prussian blue and black are also possible according to the analysis of the Hyperspectral Data Cube spectra, email with spectra from F. Gabrieli, NGA Washington, D.C., 18 January 2018.
[36] Prussian blue has existed since around 1710. Since Xeller and the restorers working before the opening of the Königliches Museum in Berlin in 1830 used ultramarine and later cobalt blue, but not Prussian blue, overpainting by them is less likely, see notes 11 and 18, as well as, on the pigments used, Stehr 2012, pp. 115ff.
[37] Au (shell gold) according to the µRF analysis on Mantegna's *Presentation*; Schwerdtfeger, Reiche 2017, pp. 5 and 10. First, a fine, approx. 1 mm wide circle is drawn with a brush, which was then broadened to 2–2.5 mm. With cat. no. 36, they kept it to a simple, approx. 1.5 wide line. Mention of restoration in the first Gemäldegalerie directory right after Mantegna, as note 12, research in the SMB Central Archive as well by U. Stehr.
[38] Delaney, Gabrieli as note 6, p. 4.
[39] Possible mixture of azurite and malachite according to J. Delaney in a private conversation.
[40] Schwerdtfeger, Reiche 2017, pp. 5, 14 (µ-RFA test points 13 and 14).
[41] Ivi, pp. 6, 20, 22 (µ-RFA test points 24–26 and 30).
[42] In northern European painting, the rendering of flat brocade patterns persisted for a long time in the 15th century. In old German painting, folds and areas of shadow were mostly indicated by overpainting with coloured lustres (Hartwieg 2015, pp. 357–361). In Dutch painting, the patterns were transferred more often to the edge of the folds, only from around 1480 were the patterns distorted in keeping with the body shape (Van Duijn 2013, pp. 28, 50–54).
[43] Ciatti, Marini 2009, fig. 23.
[44] Directory as note 12, Waagen 1830, p. 23.
[45] Four samples had been taken from the left and right edges of the painting. Their results are not totally clear. The FTIR analyses at the time revealed "protein with traces of wax," "no cholesterol found." Accordingly, egg tempera was excluded. Unpublished report and Rothe 1992, p. 82.
[46] Evidence on the basis of the spectral bands characteristic of eggs (2309, 2352 nm), by Delaney, Gabrieli, as note 6, pp. 3–6. Possibly the azurite parts are also done in egg tempera. In any case, it is not the chemical change in the egg binding medium that is responsible for darkening the background, as Blass-Simmen writes (Blass-Simmen, Weppelmann, p. 17, note 39), but rather the overpainting and saturation in varnish.
[47] Dietemann *et al.* 2012, pp. 84ff, 288ff, and Dietemann, Fischer, Karl 2017, pp. 94–96.
[48] Establishing the existence of egg tempera, e.g. in *Ecce Homo* (around 1500–1502) at the Musée Jacquemart-André, Paris, that has long been considered the best preserved example of Mantegna's distemper paintings, as well as in *Madonna della Vittoria* and *St Sebastian* at the Musée du Louvre, Paris; see Ravaud *et al.* 2009, pp. 27–34.
[49] Presumably Populus sp., no wood identification.
[50] Slightly diagonal join: lower board 48.6 cm to the left, 48.1 cm to the right, upper board 32.6 cm to the left, 33.5 cm to the right.
[51] The iron plates screwed into both cross-cut wooden edges, with a hard, white plastic strap placed underneath since being loaned to Rome in 2008, are supposed to keep the board level, probably since it was exhibited without a frame on the easel designed by Carlo Scarpa (1960s).
[52] Images of these sketches in Venice 2000, p. 123.
[53] Can be made out on the open worm-damaged parts above and below and on the cut paint and ground layer.
[54] Cennini (Ilg) 1888, chap. CXXI, p. 105.
[55] The white lines are not evidence of the use of a lead pencil "punta di piombo." This false interpretation of the X-ray details was provided by Bagarotto *et al.* 2000 p. 188, fig. 26.
[56] For Giovanni Bellini, *Madonna degli alberetti*, *Madonna and Child with Saints Paul and George*, see Bagarotto 2000, p. 189, for the example of Raphael and his teacher Perugino, Hiller von Gärtringen 1999; the author's studies on Botticelli and Verrochio brought similar results; on the use of face templates in north German painting around 1425, Hartwieg 2015, pp. 342–346.
[57] Villa 2008, p. 38, fig. 1; *Pala di Pesaro* and *Cristo morto*, Galleria degli Uffizi, Florence, Poldi, Villa 2009, pp. 60, 64.
[58] The upper edge is corrected from the left side of the picture to the cushion with a second tilted line of a maximum of about 2 mm.
[59] Luca Caburlotto with regard to Goffen, Tempestini, Christiansen in: Venice 2000, p. 151.
[60] In the microscopic image, very typical "protrusions," chemical changes in the pigment are visible.
[61] See Davanzo Poli, Moronato 1994, pp. 42, 50: "Velluto controtagliato o alto-basso, di seta, allucciolato con oro filato, Venezia, seconda metà del secolo XV." For details about the materials represented, I thank Christine Waidenschlager, Museum of Decorative Arts, Berlin, email 26 January 2018.
[62] See Dunkerton 2004, p. 212.
[63] Trevisan n.d., p. 11; and Villa 2009, pp. 47, 48.
[64] Trevisan n.d., pp. 11–14.
[65] Most recently, Villa 2017, p. 83.
[66] Probably also embroidered velvet in front of a gold ground or damask.
[67] The assumption "un dipinto costoso e ordinato da un committente benestante" has to be put into perspective. Schmidt, Arcangeli 2015, p. 321.
[68] Dunkerton, Hartwieg 2018.
[69] Heinemann 1962 lists 29 replicas; see also Schmidt, Arcangeli 2015, p. 180ff.
[70] A version, which supposedly originated after 1488 in the Museo Civico, Padua, is signed by Vincenzo dai Destri (Schmidt, Arcangeli 2015). In Gallerie dell'Accademia, Venice, there is a Francesco Bissolo's version with three people on the left-hand side (79.8 x 119.4 cm, cat. 93).
[71] Golden 2004.

Album

MANTEGNA

BELLINI

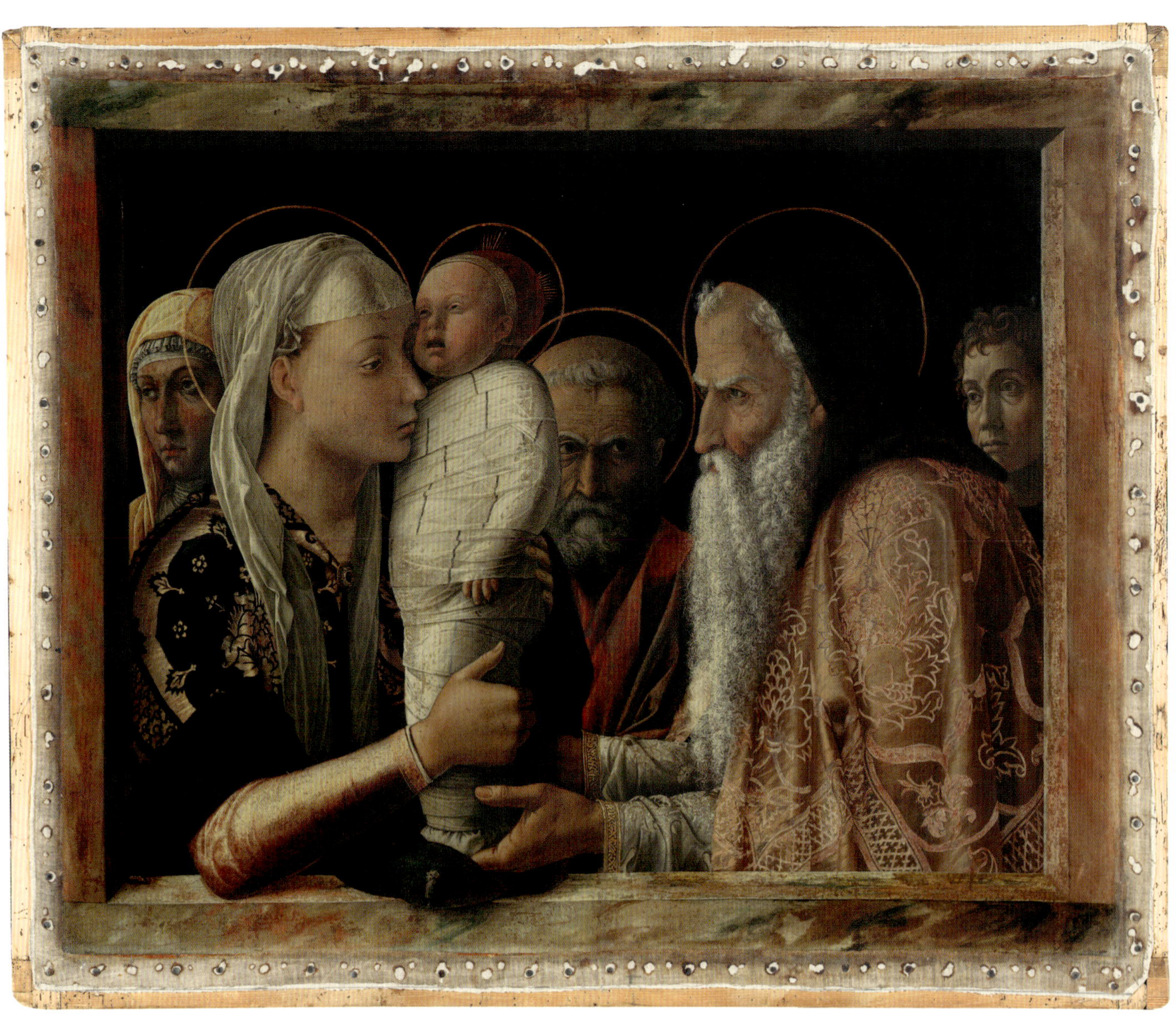

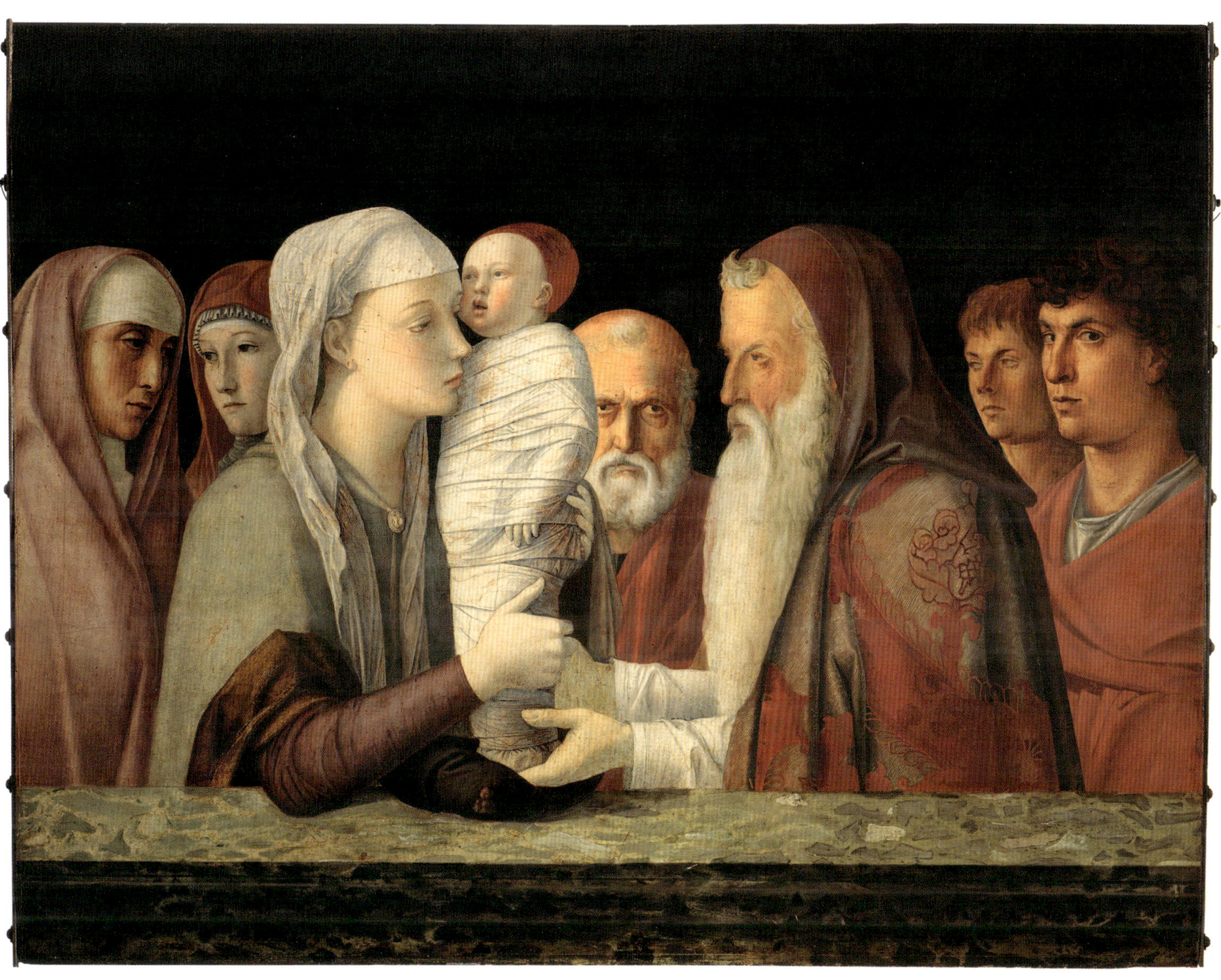

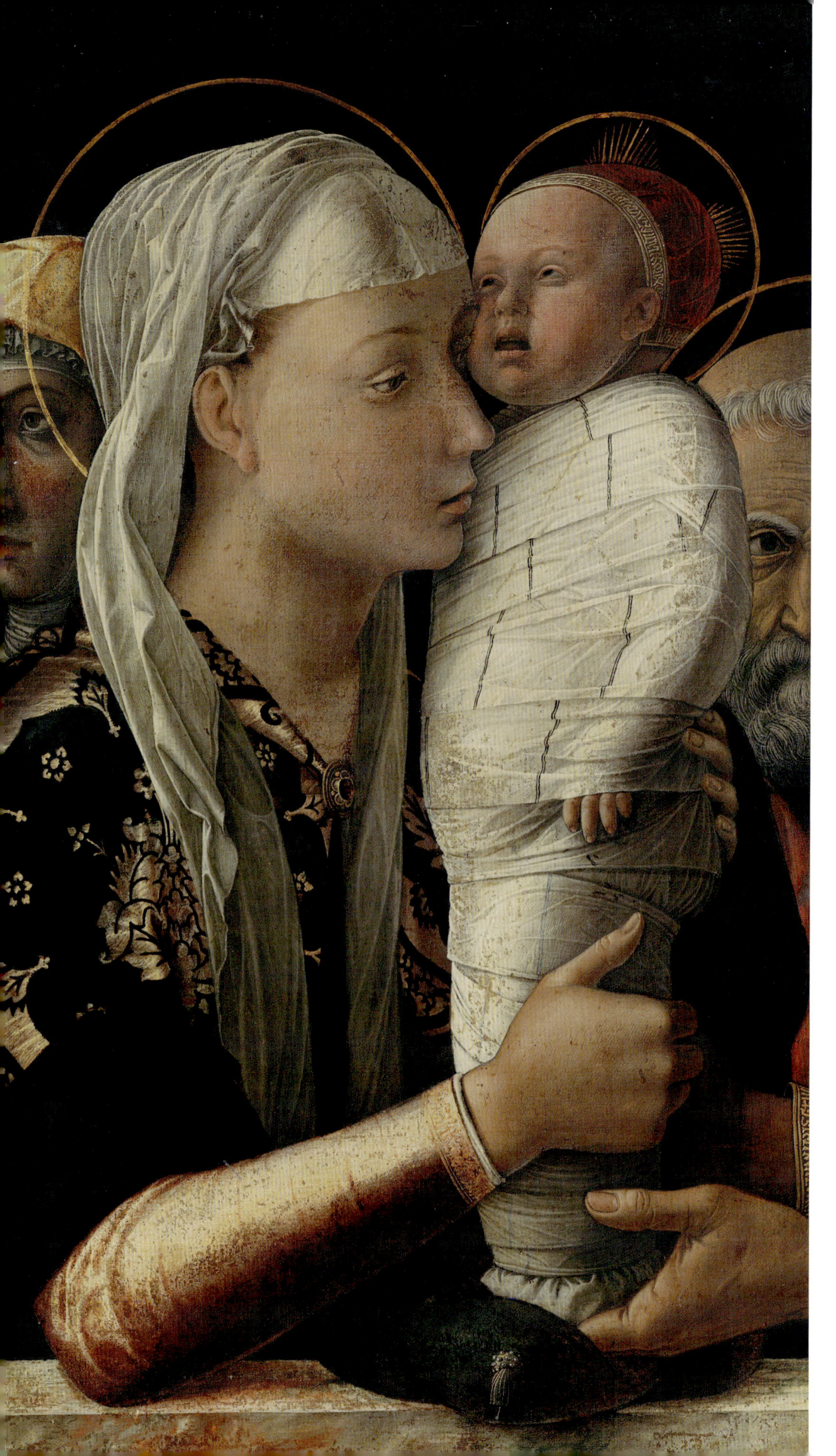

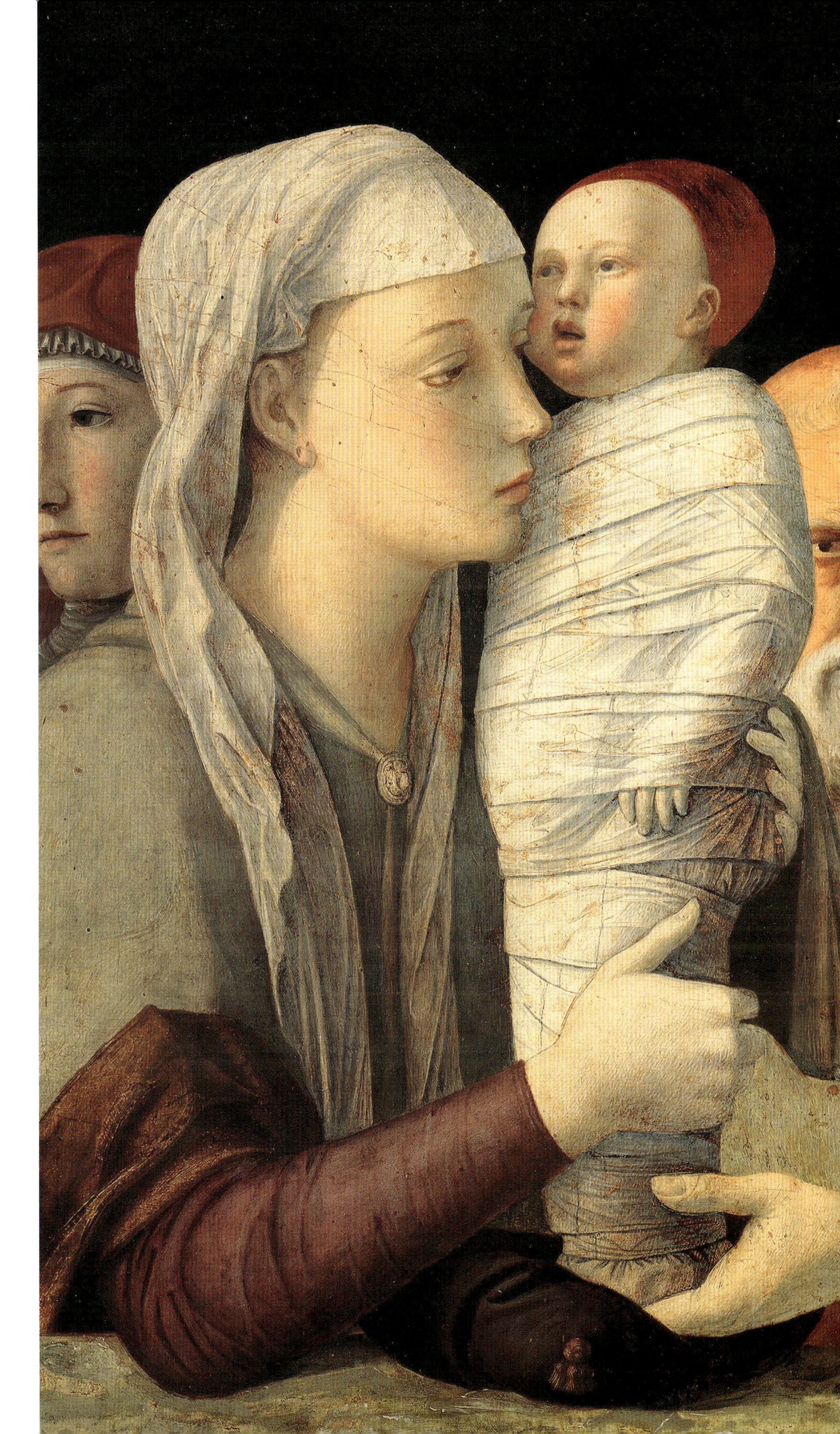

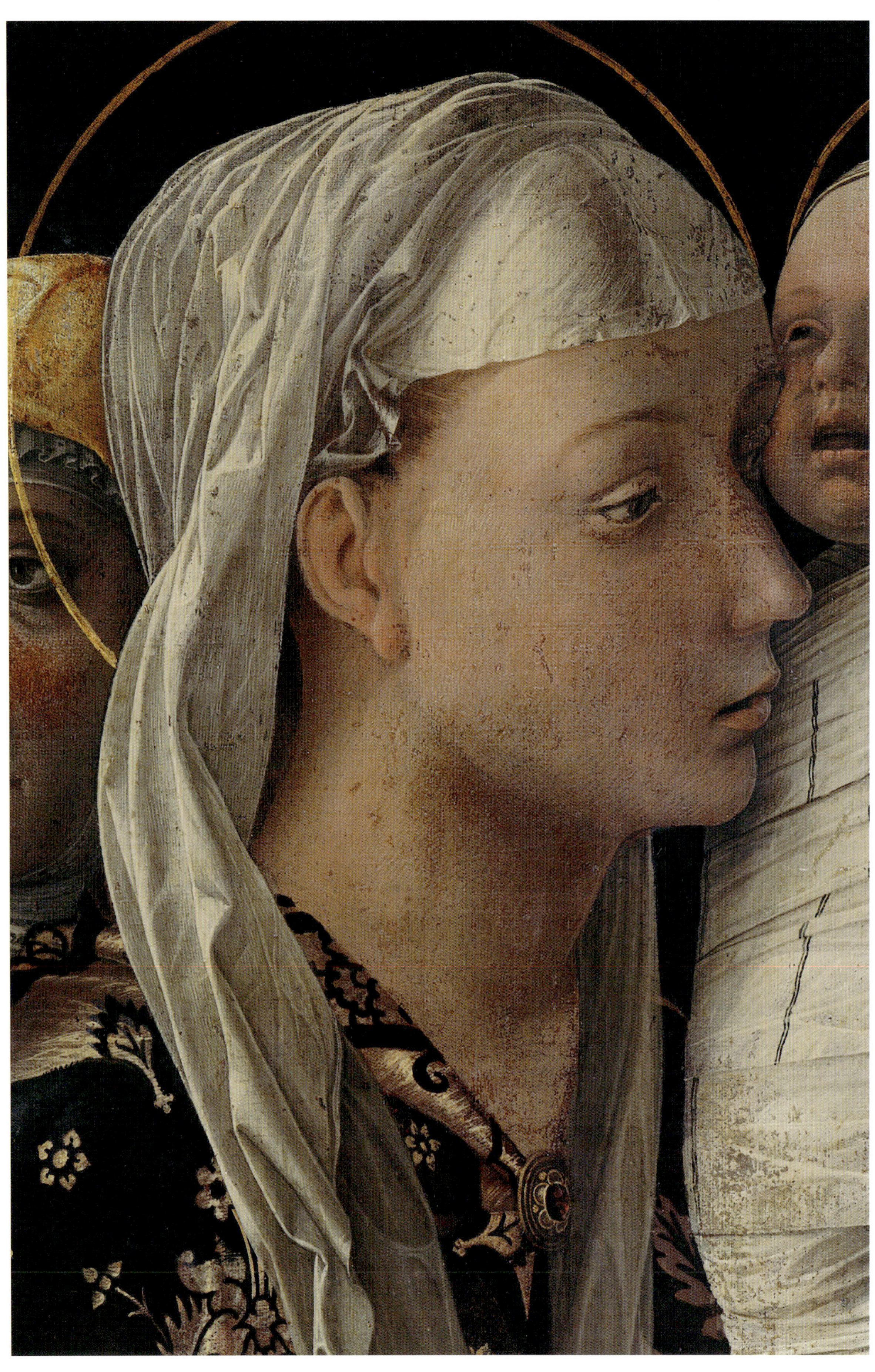

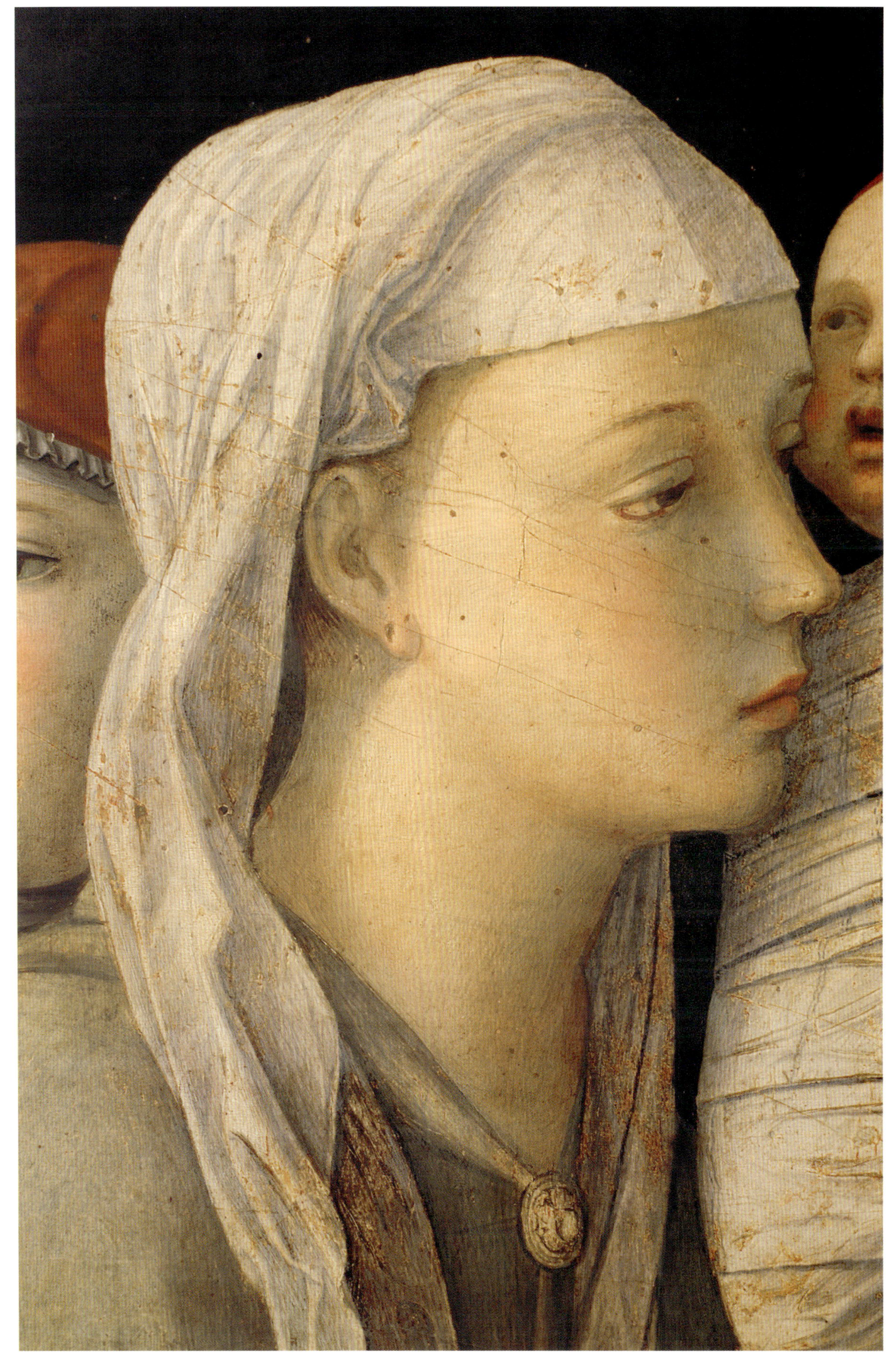

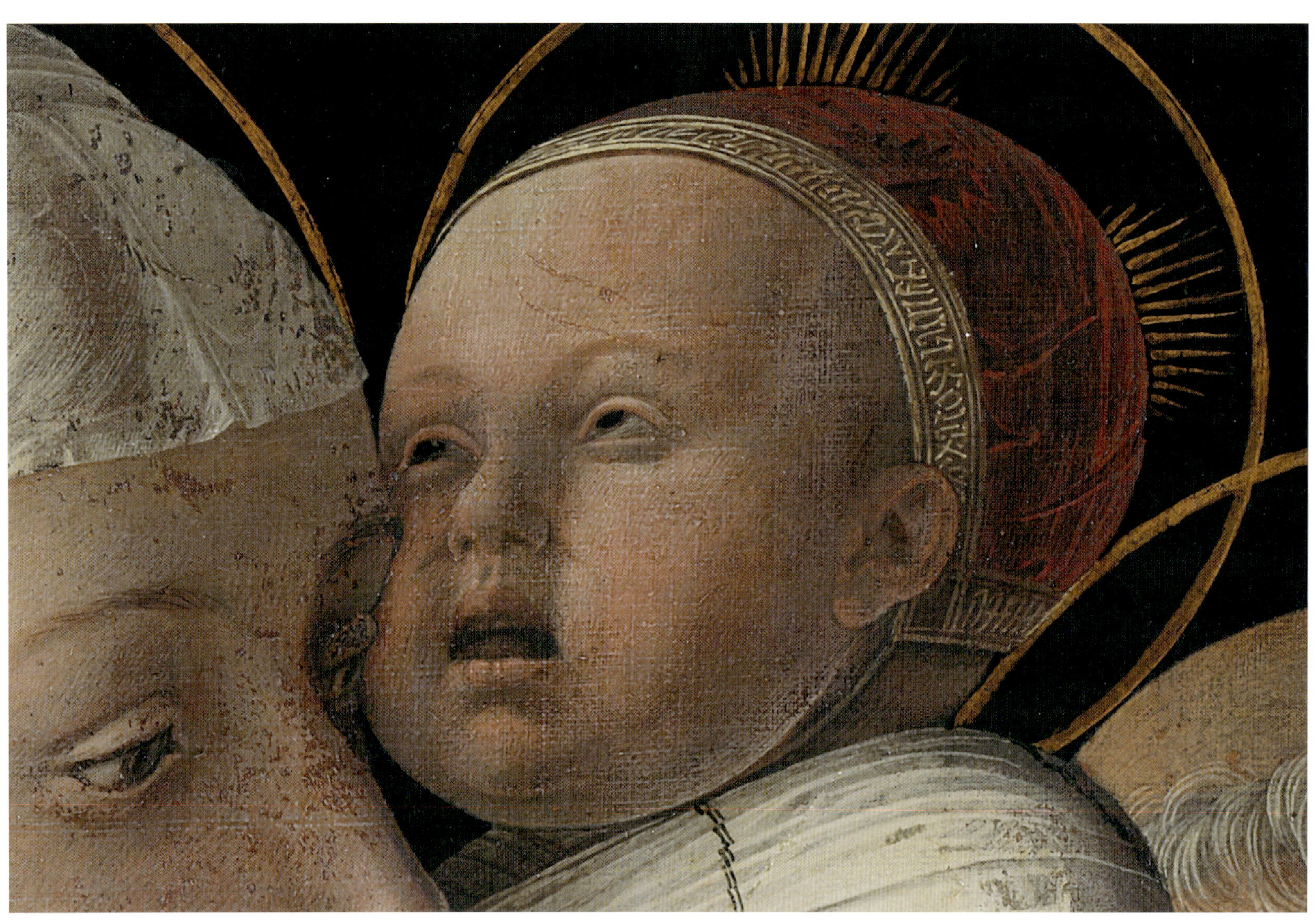

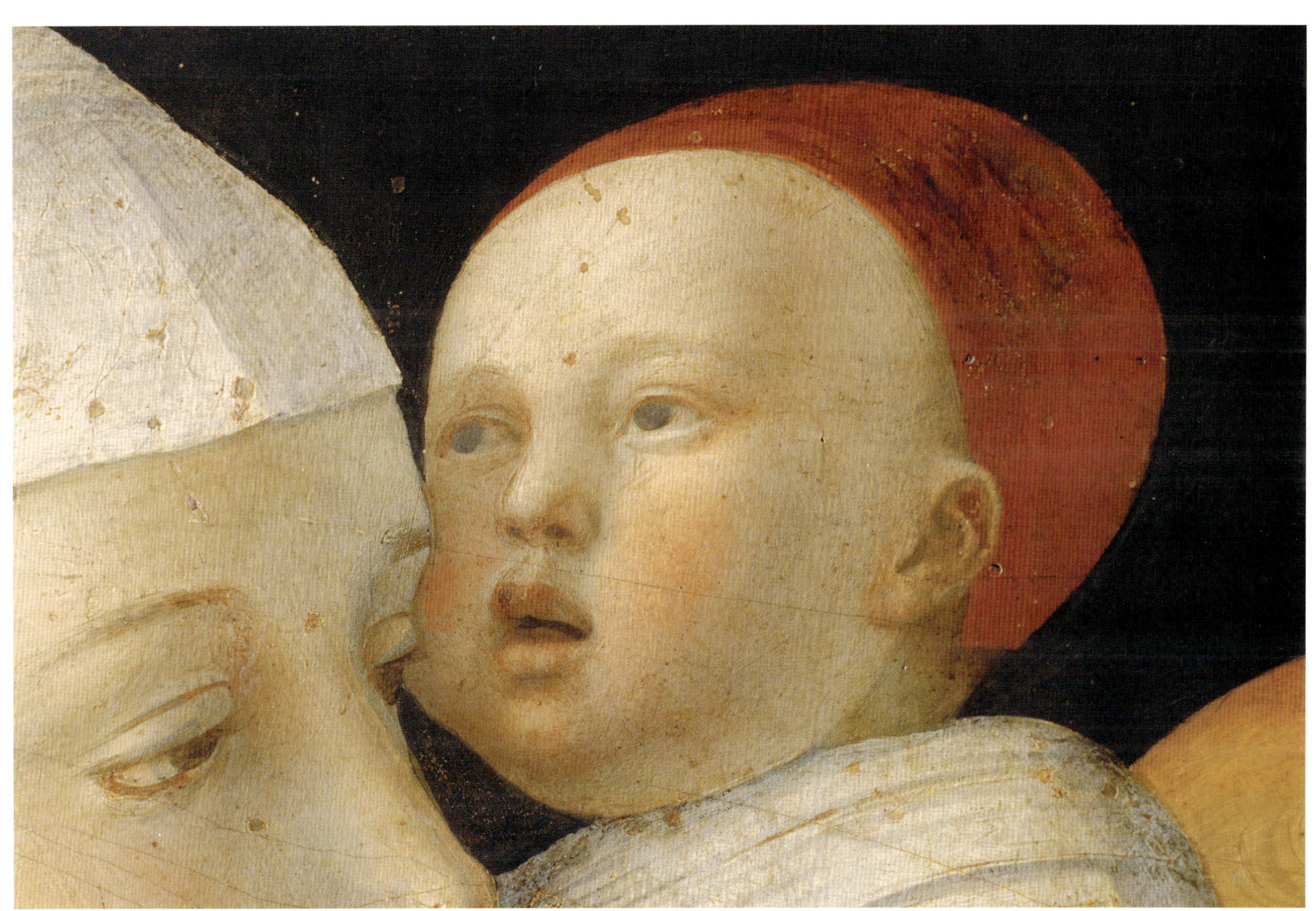

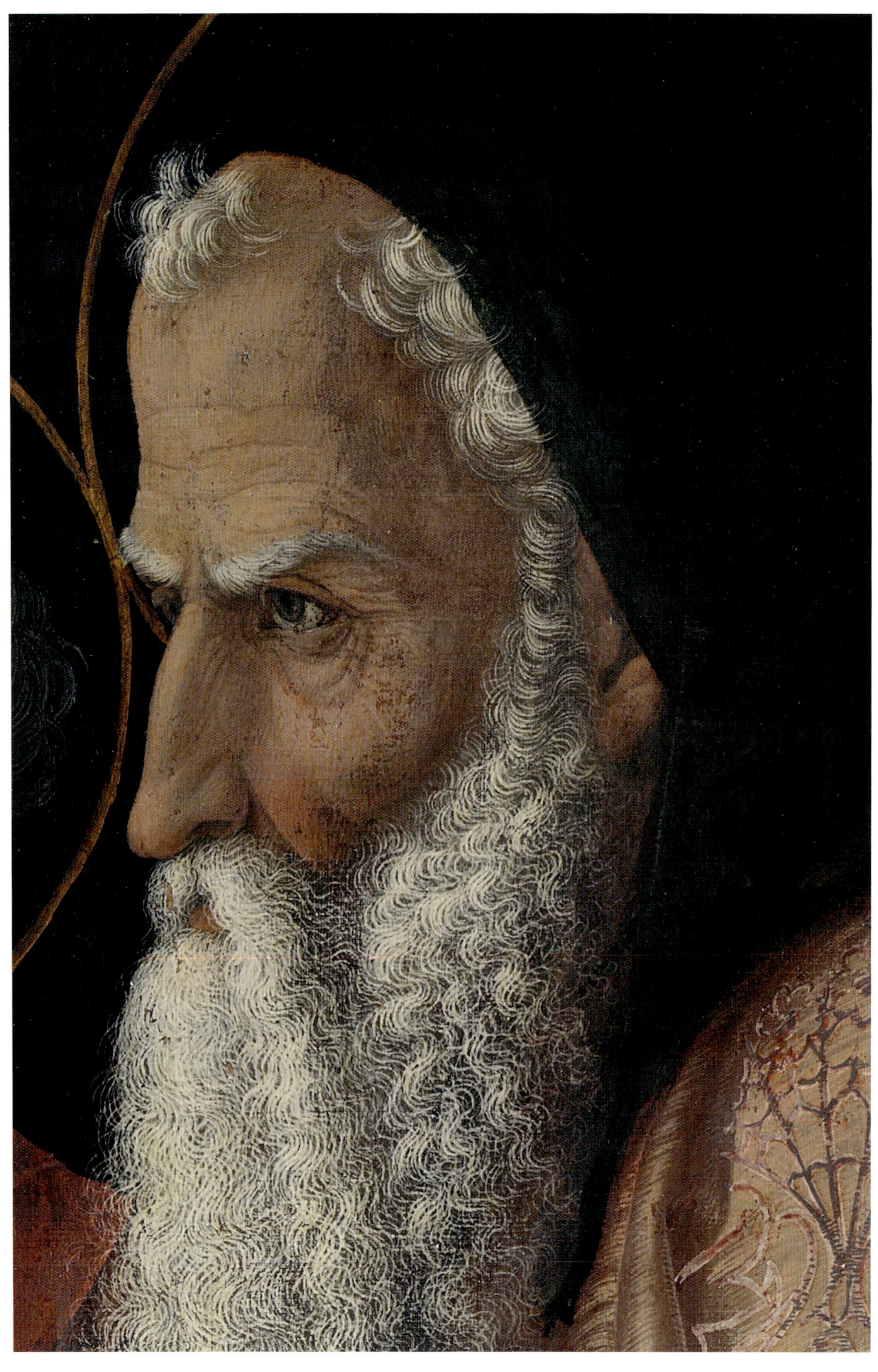

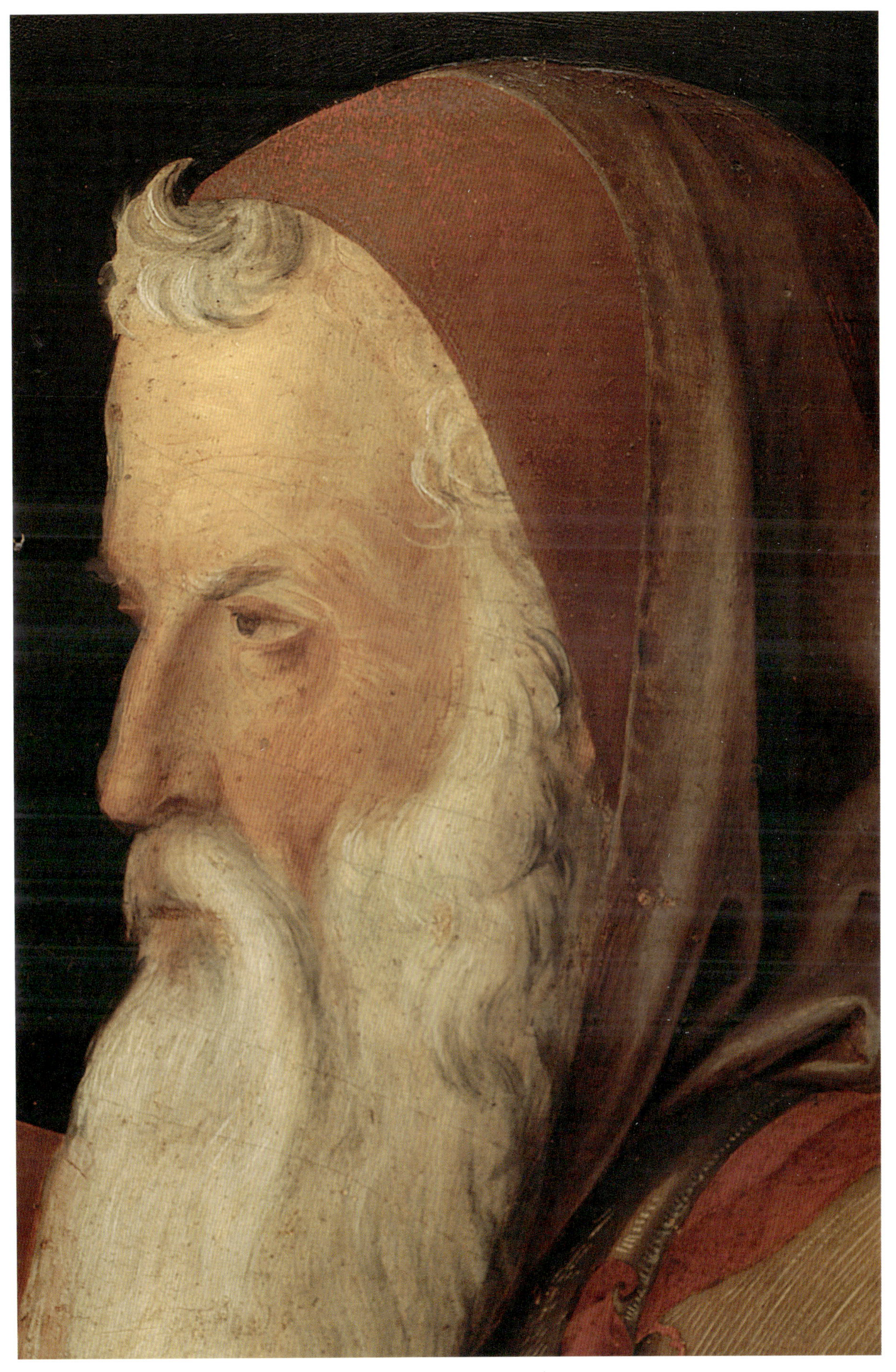

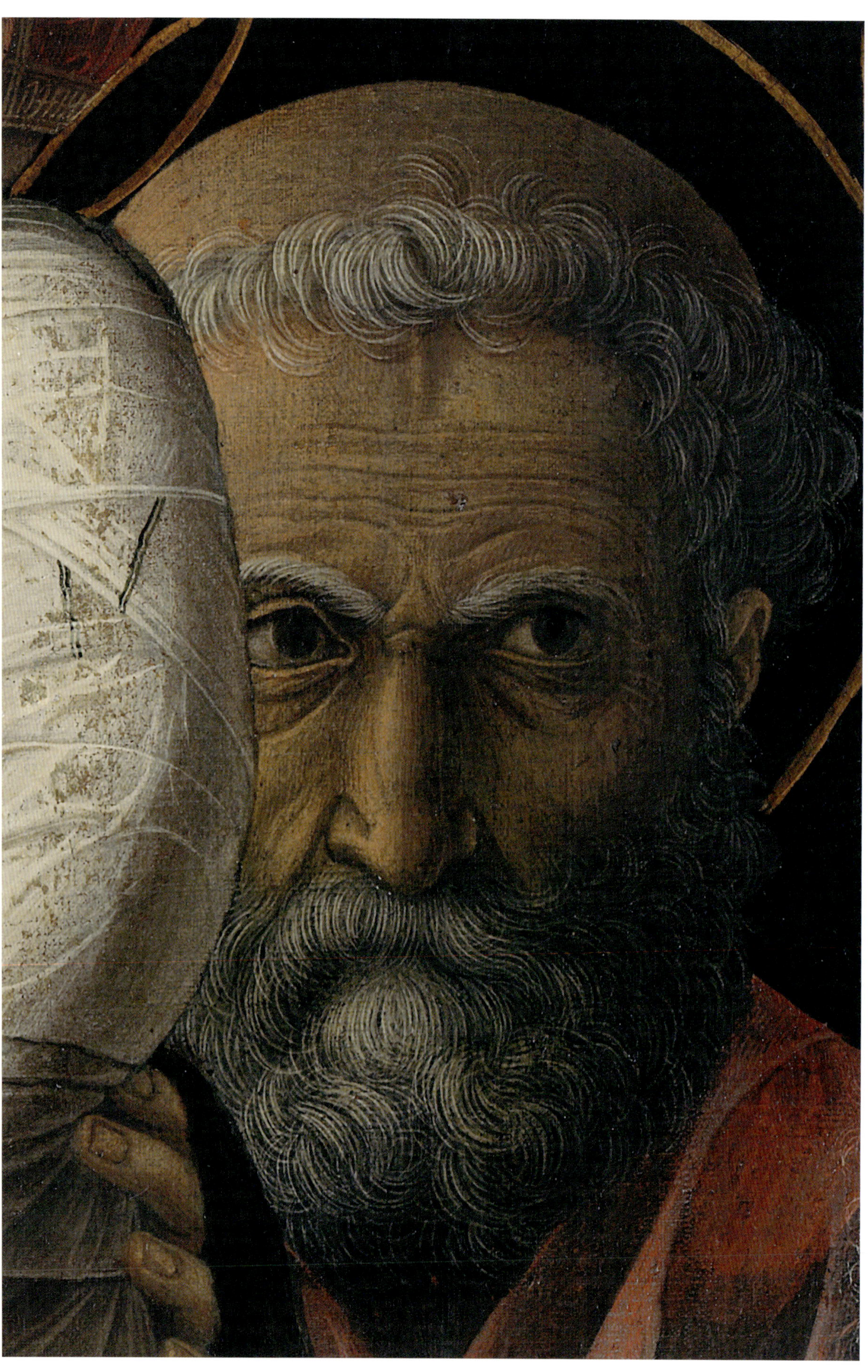

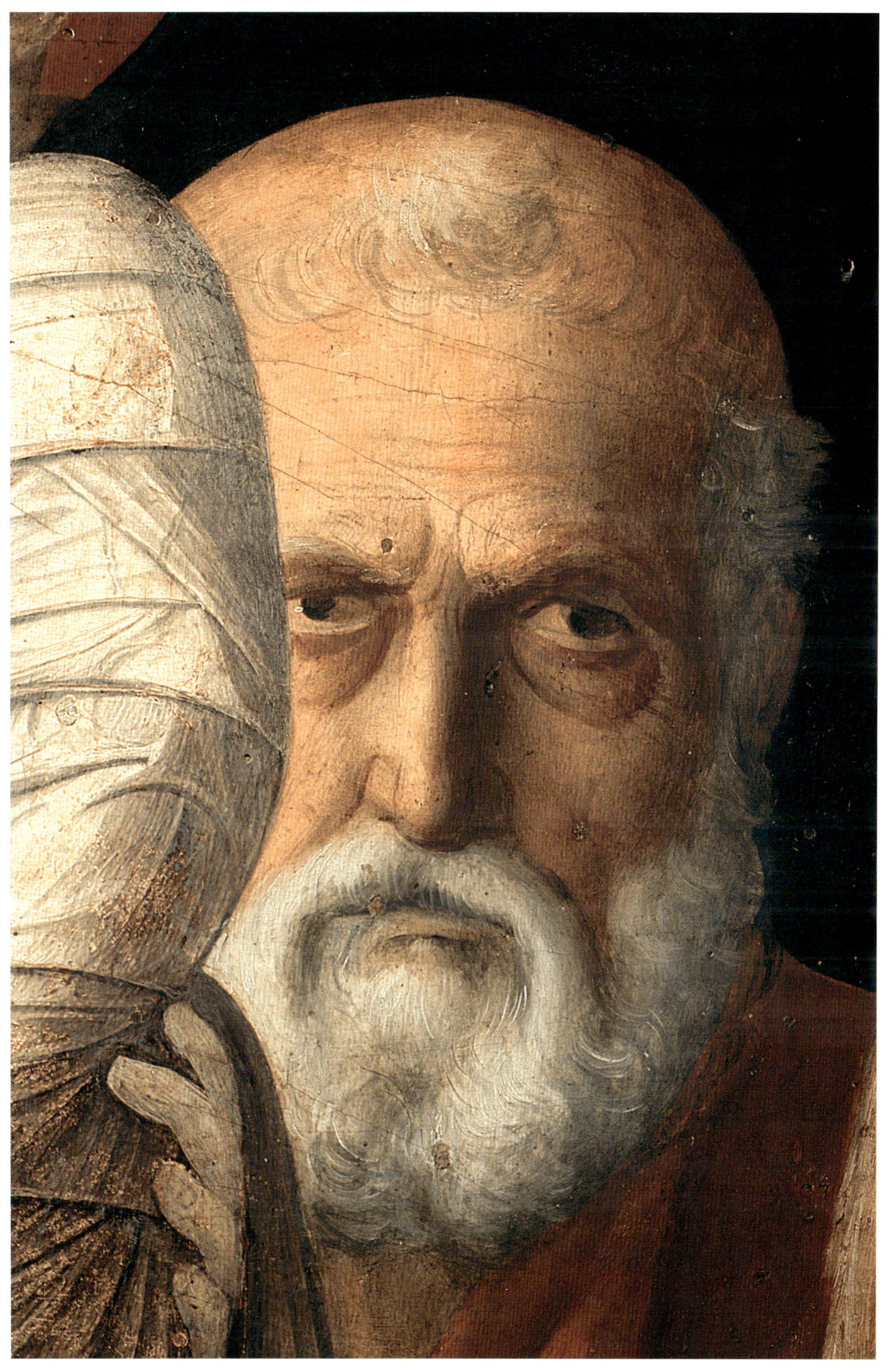

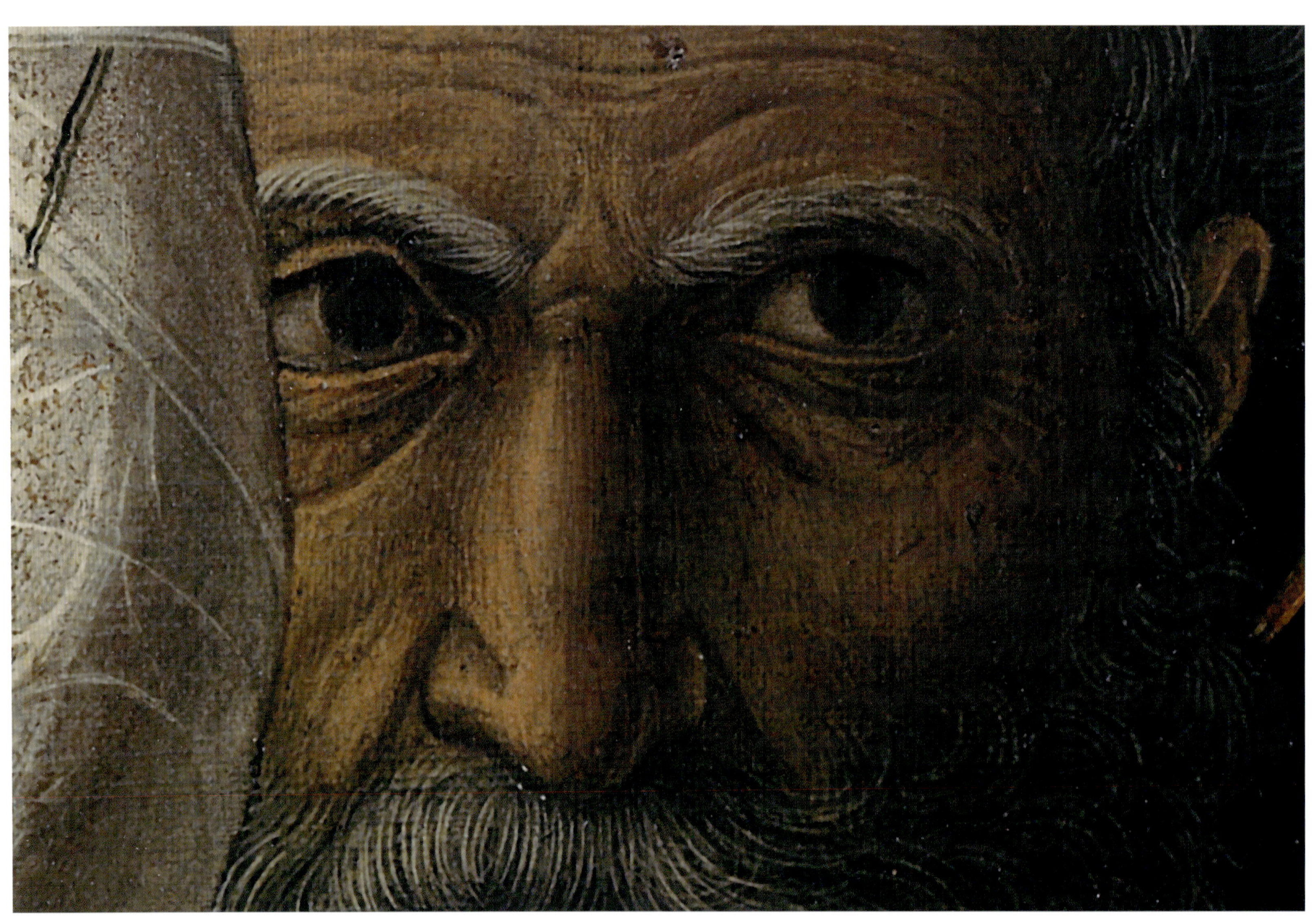

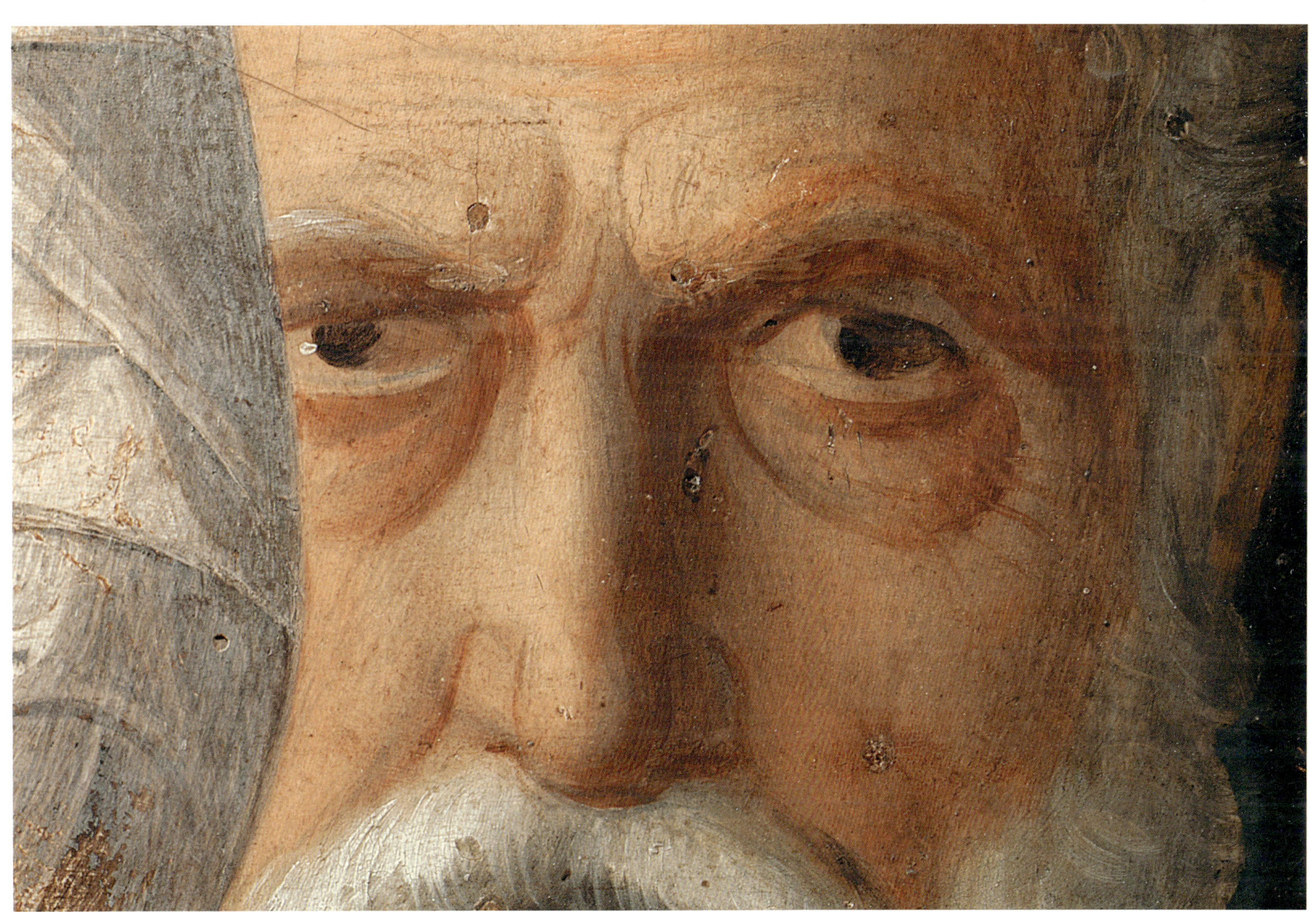

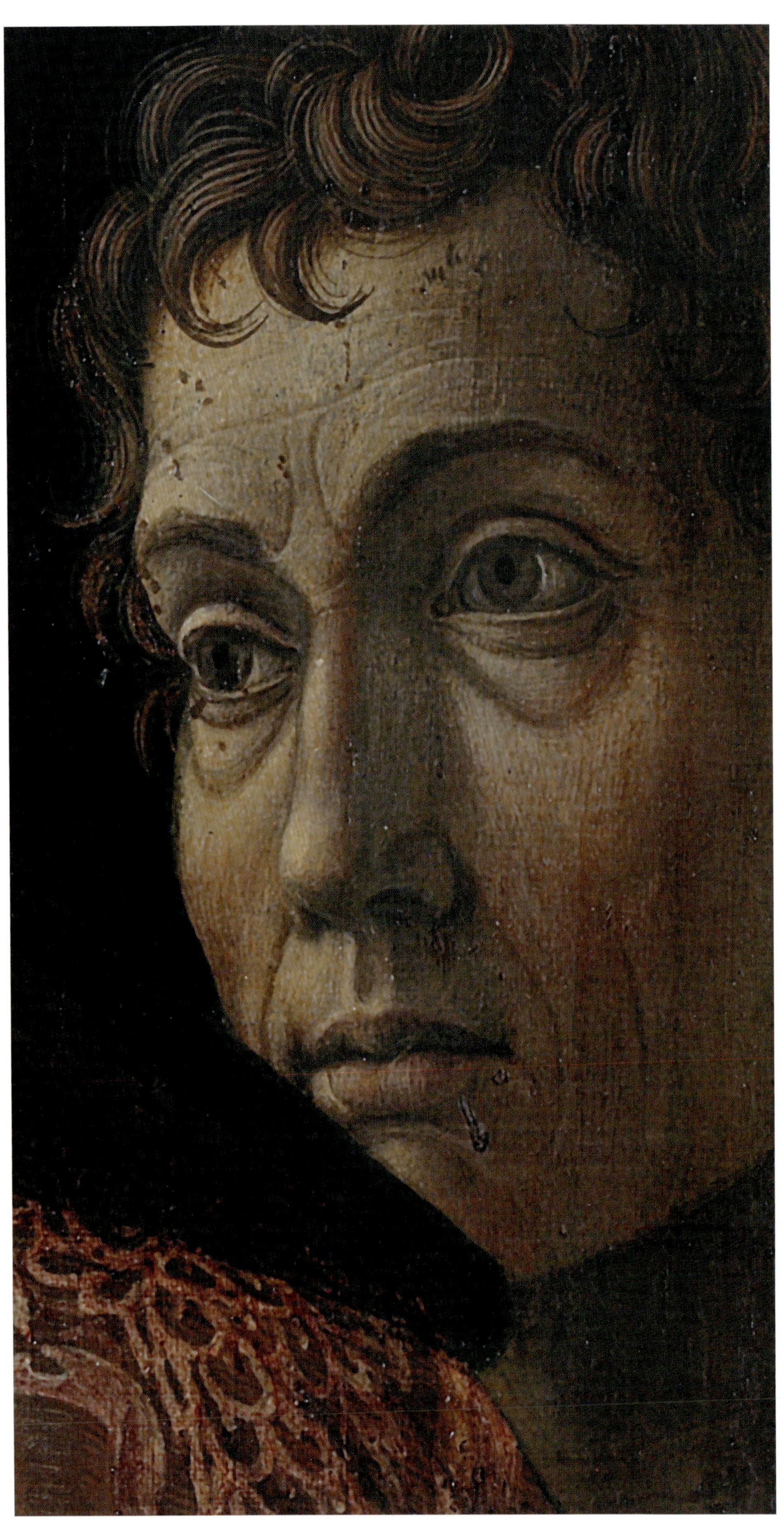

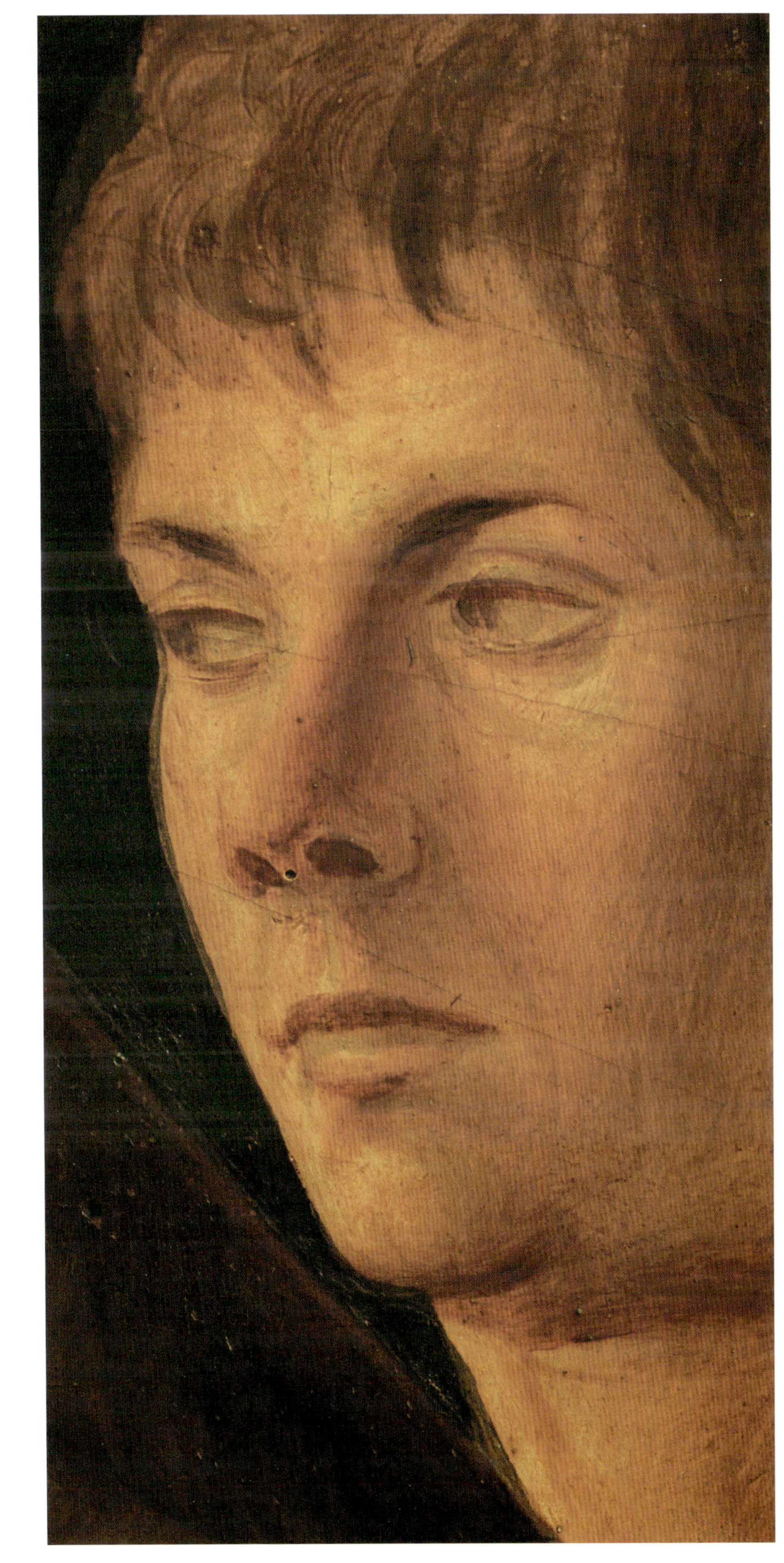

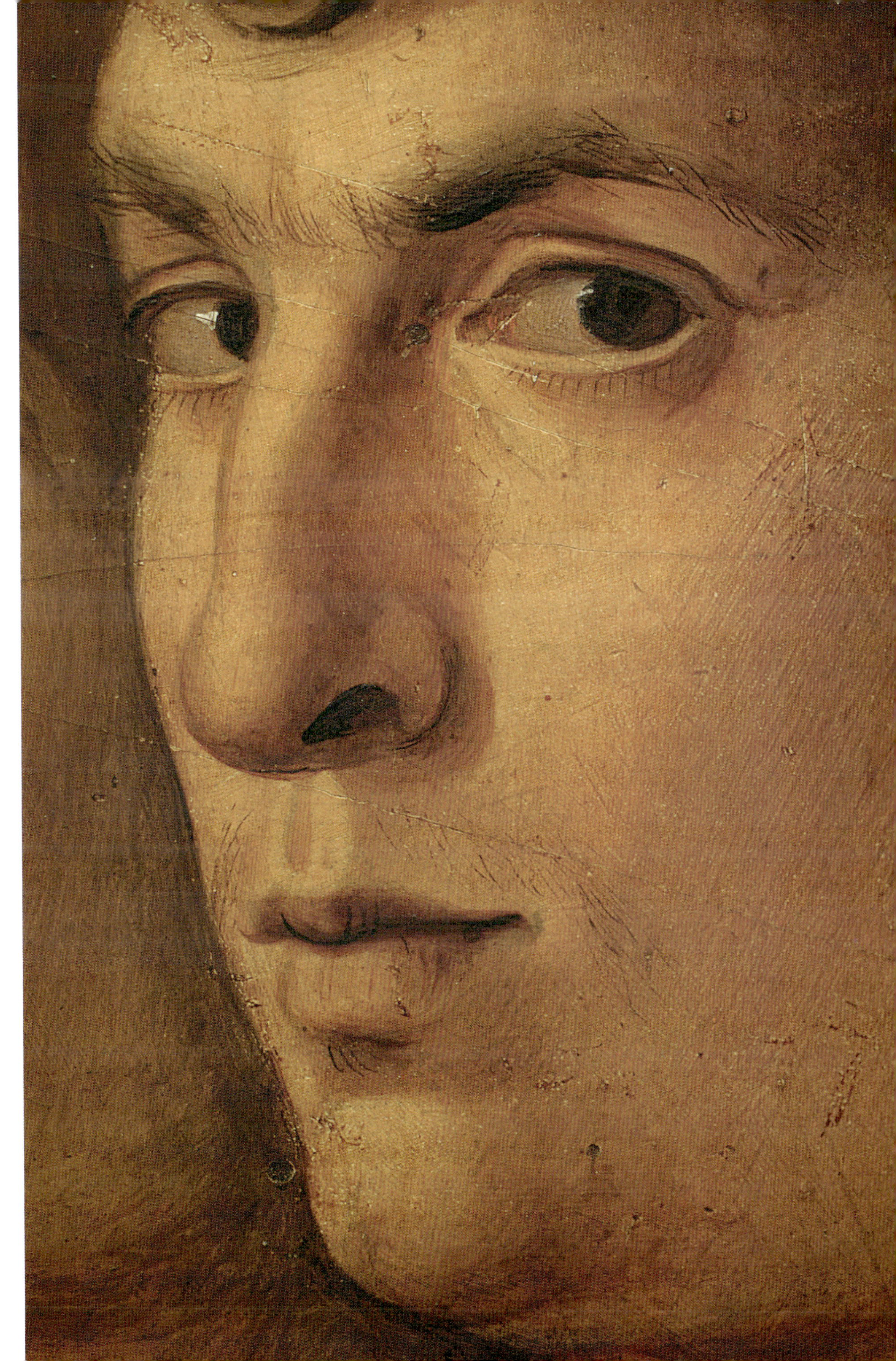

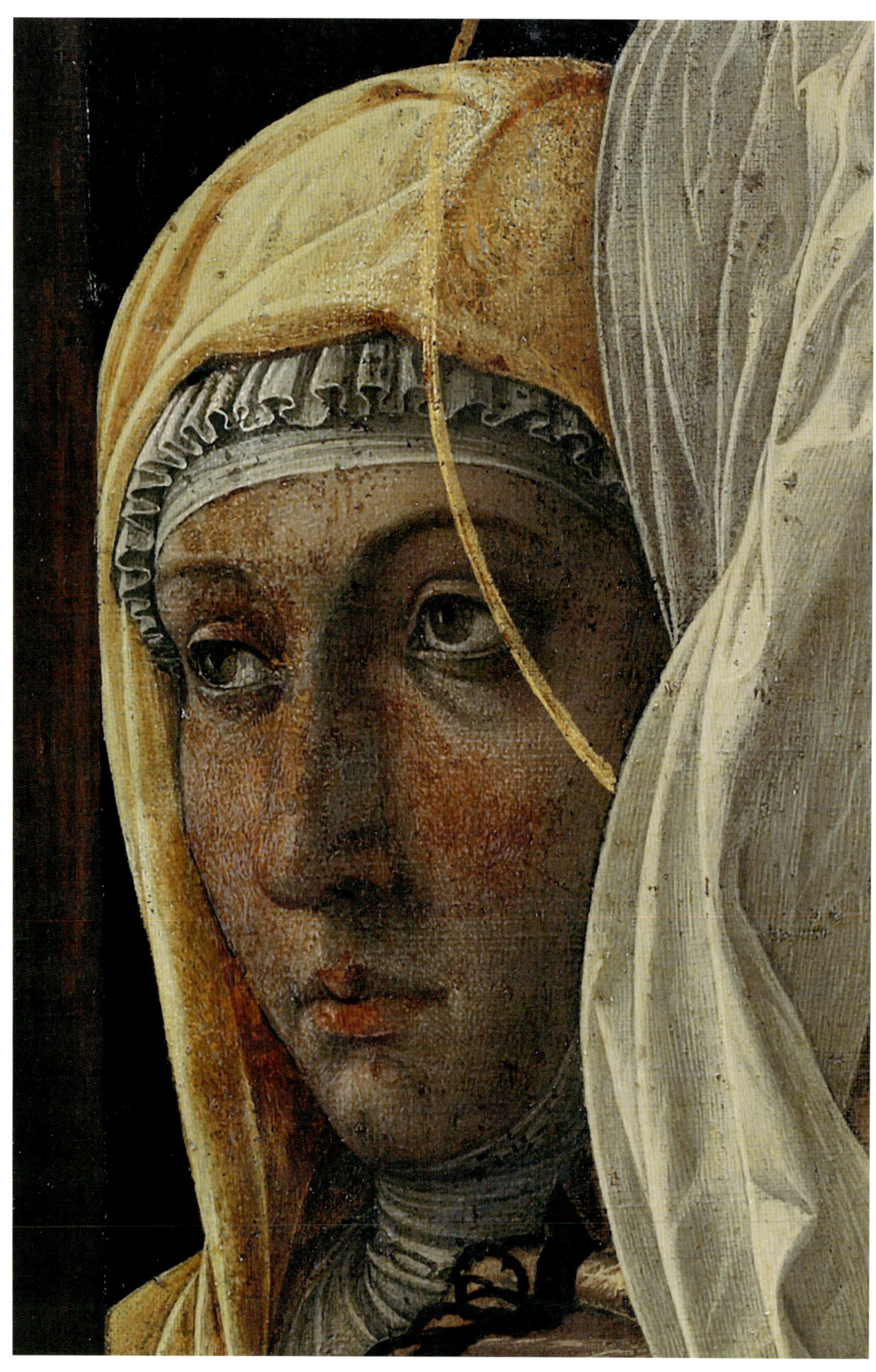

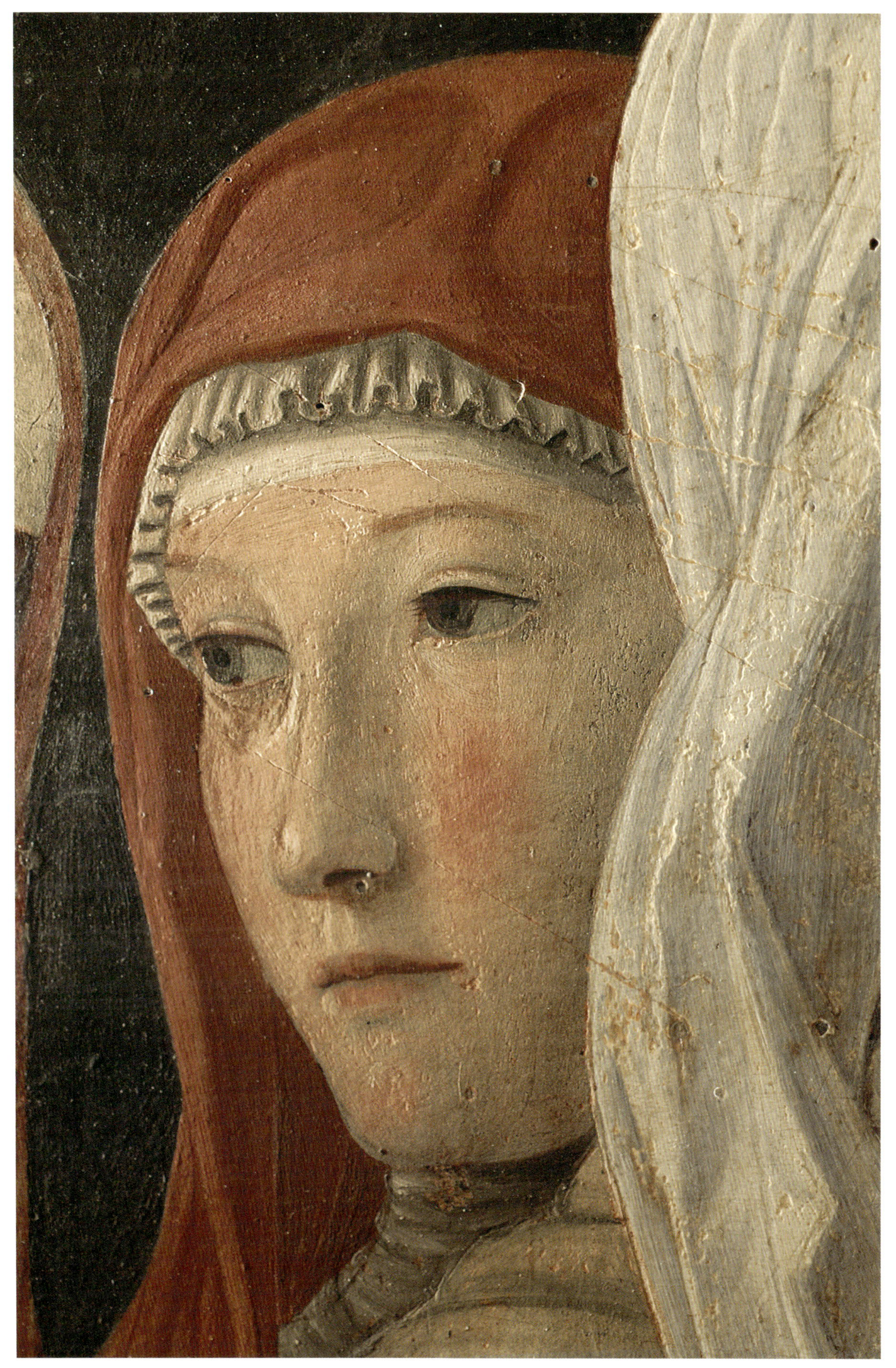

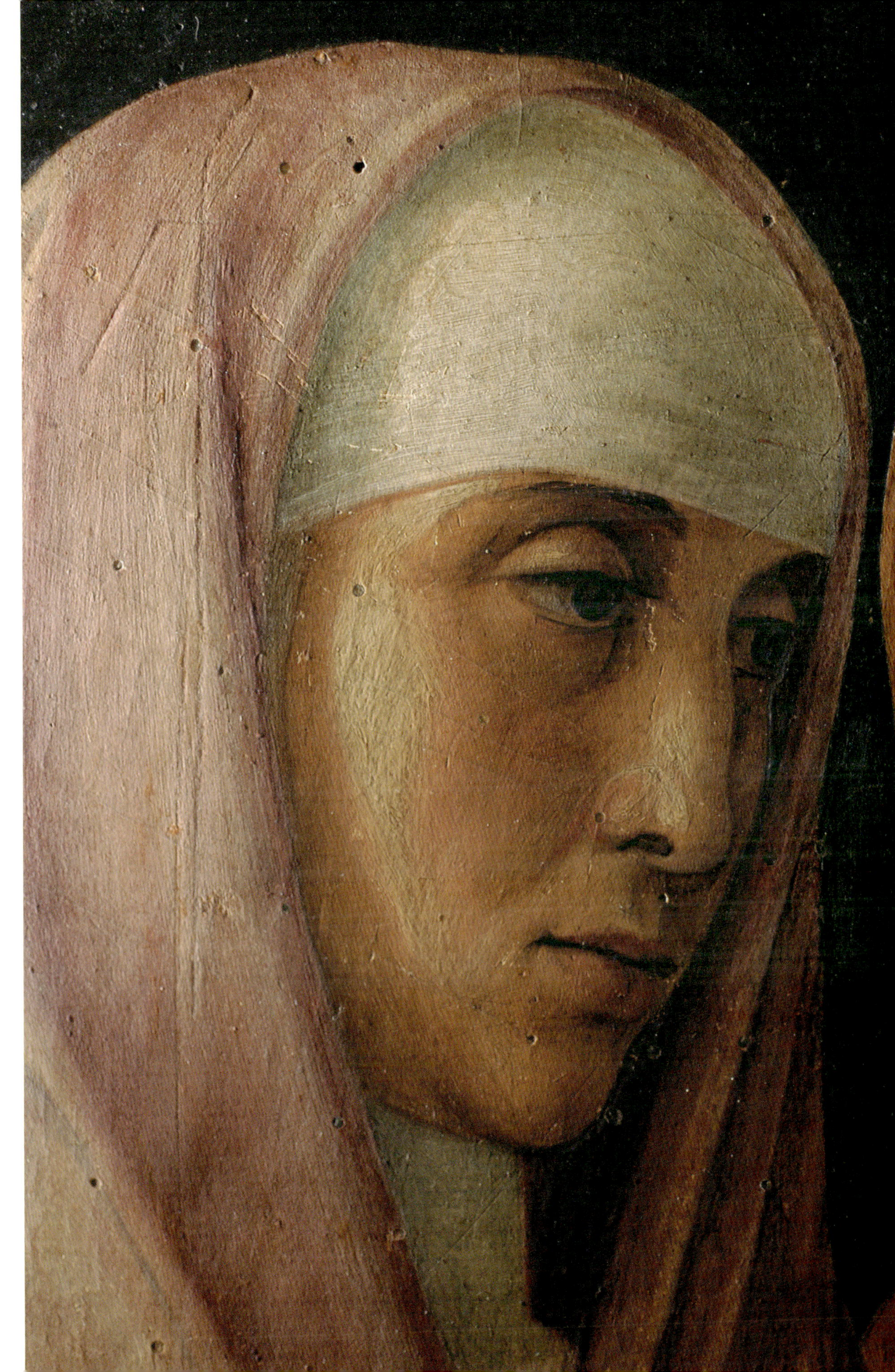

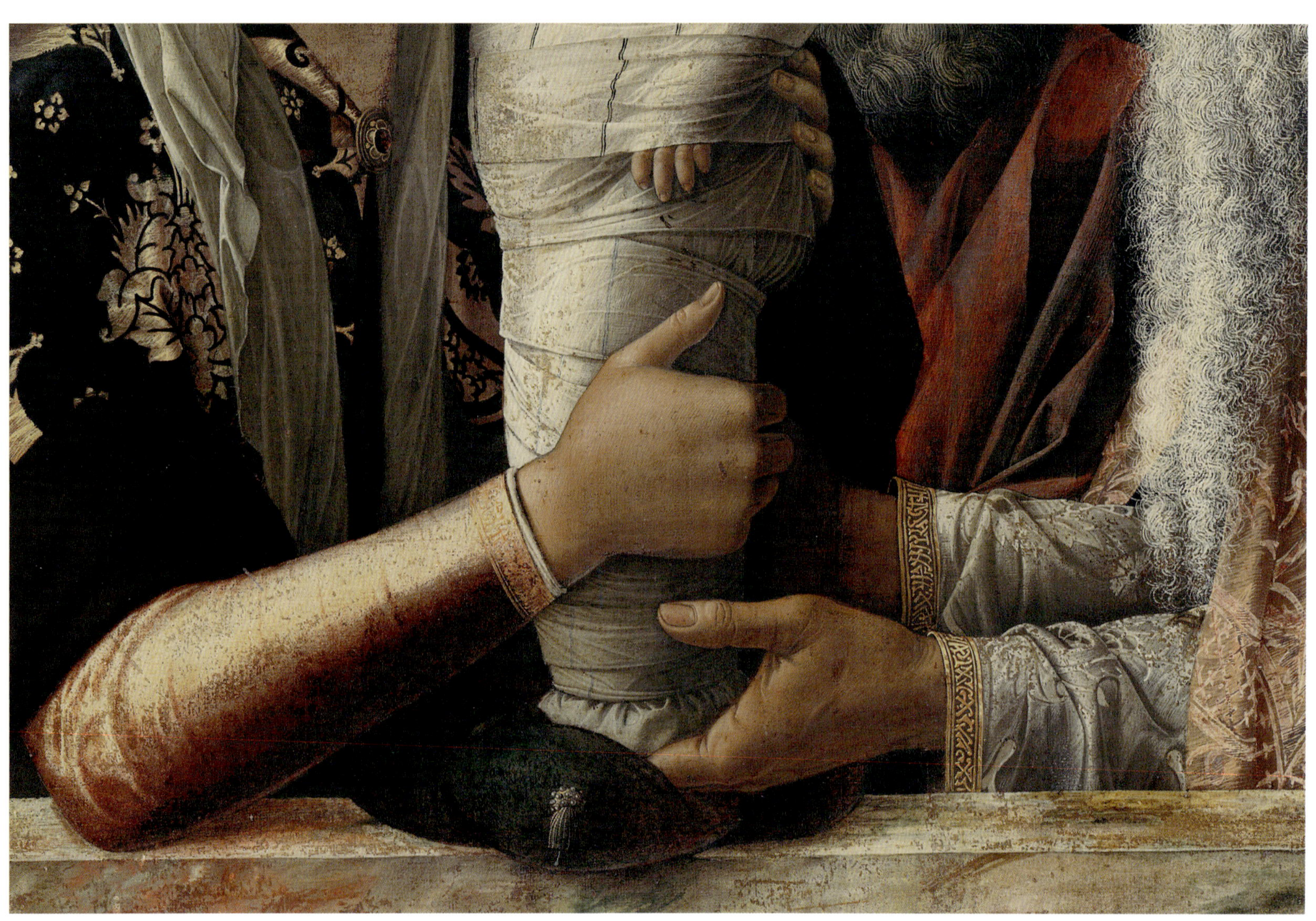

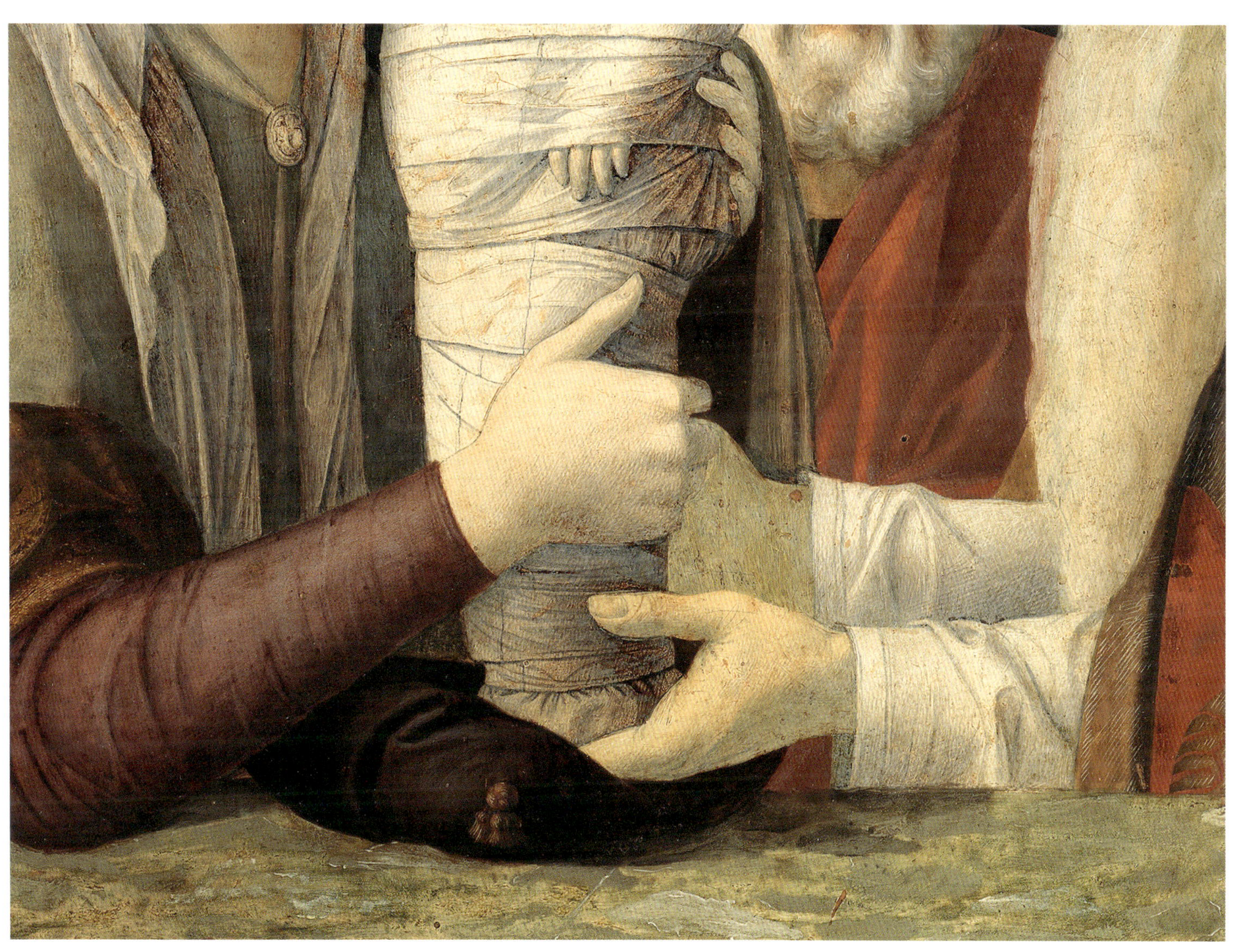

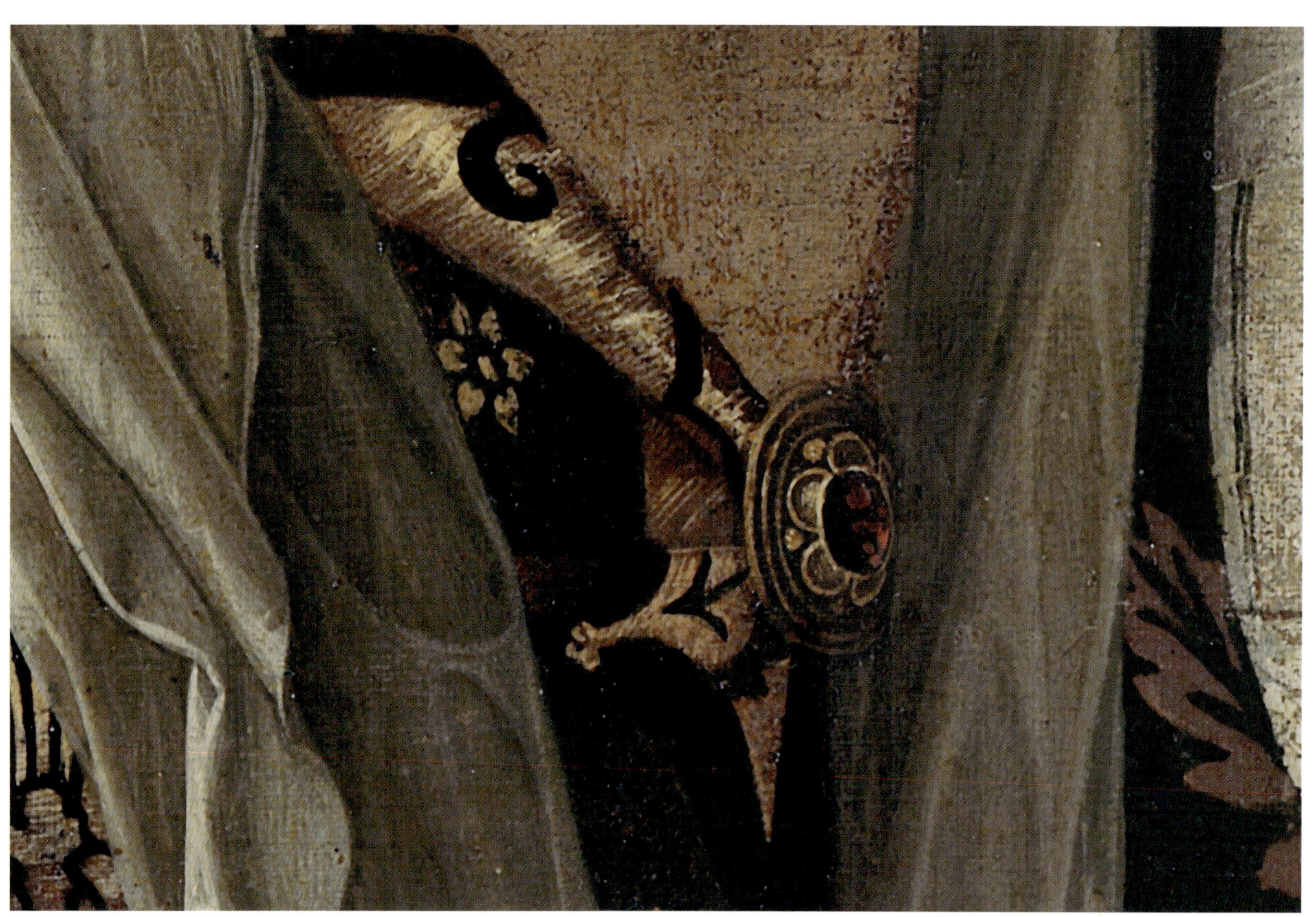

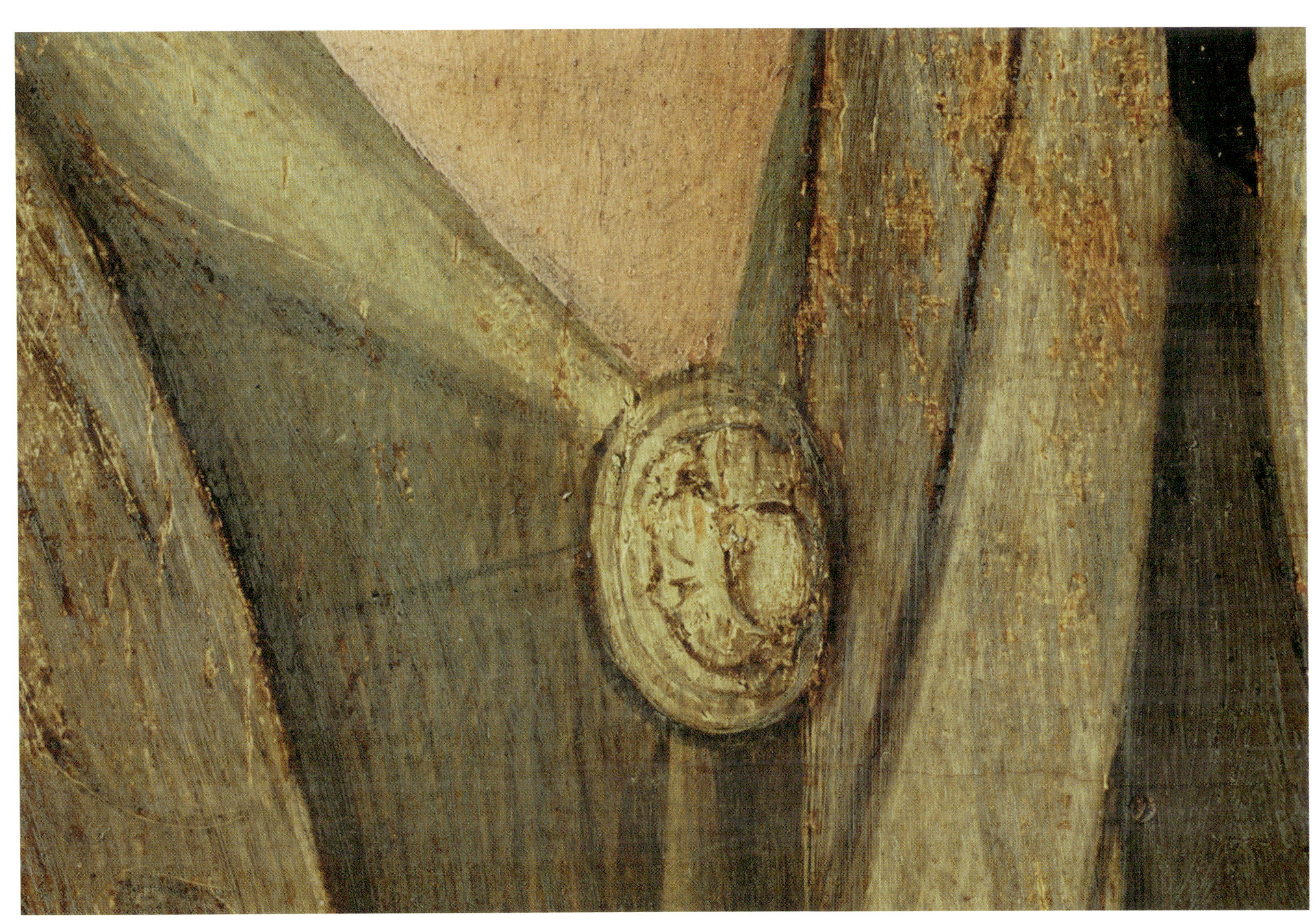

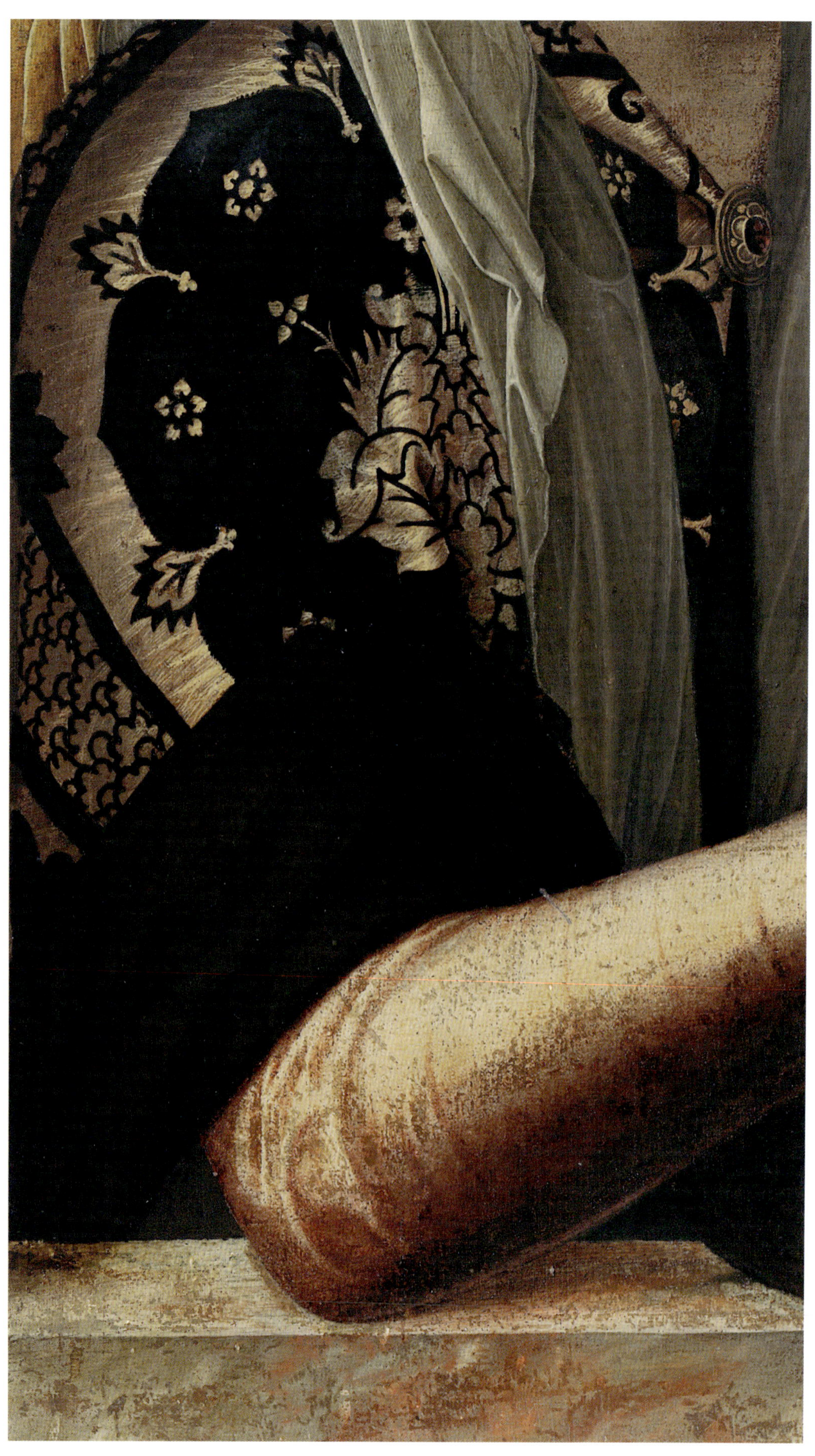

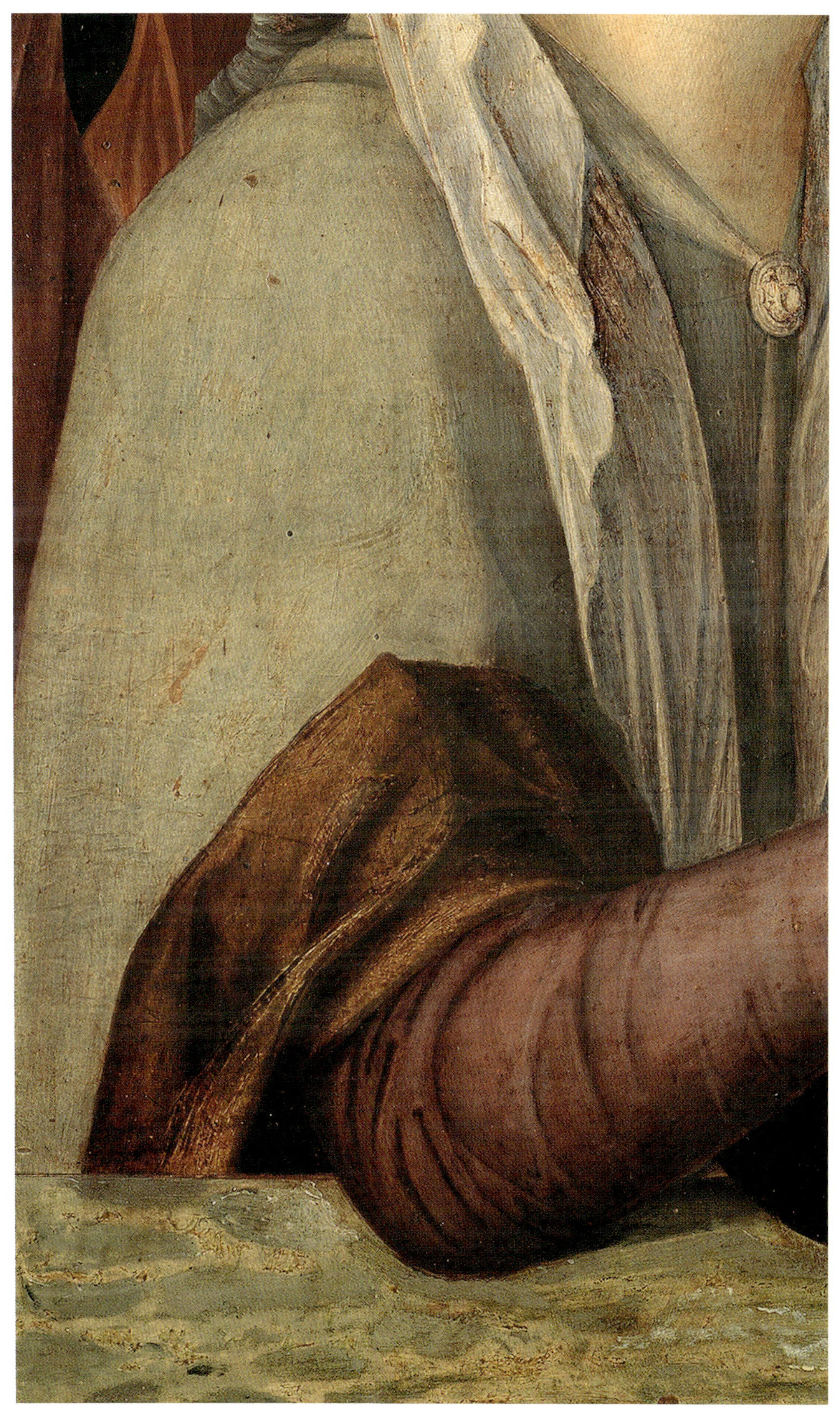

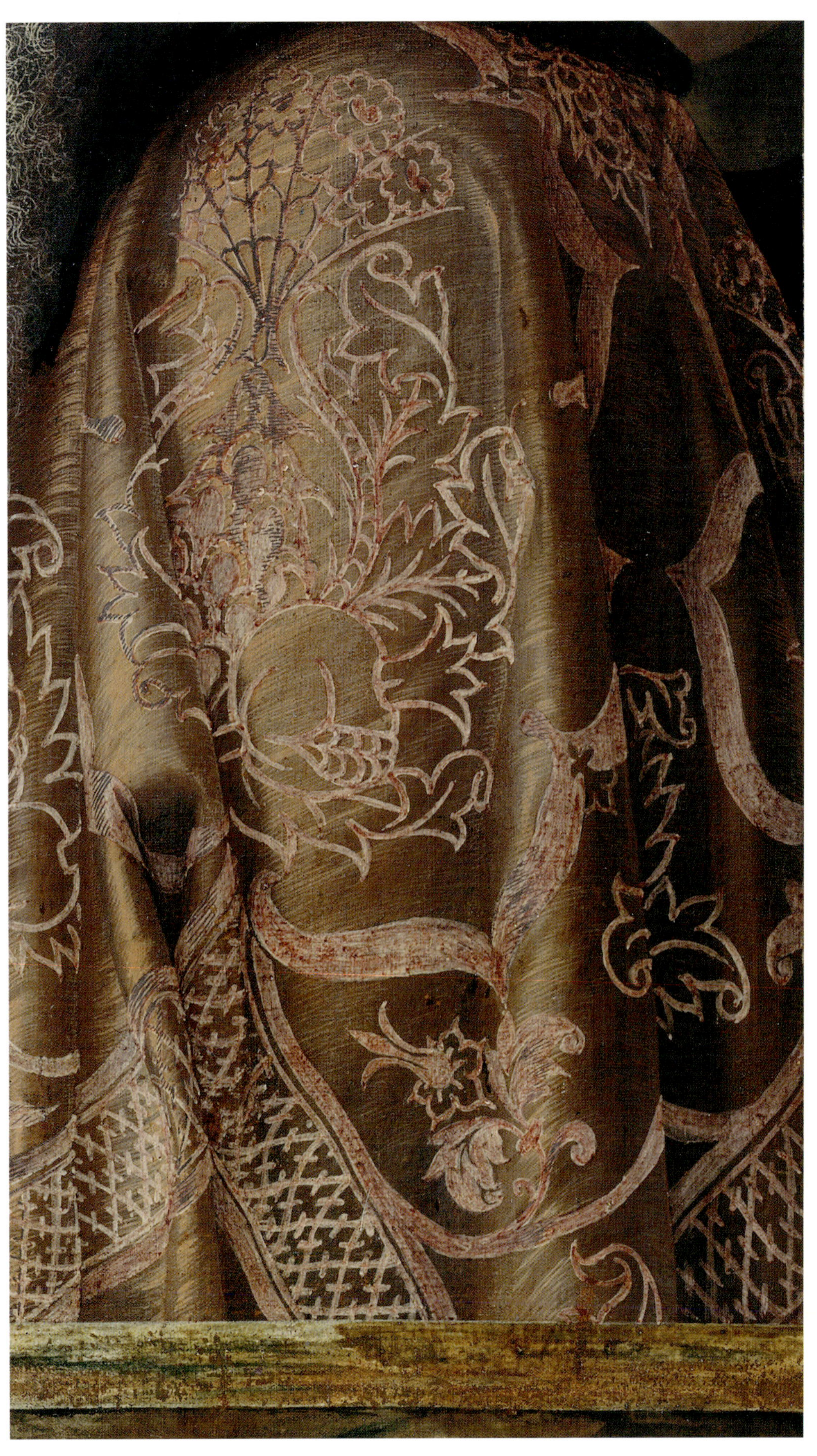

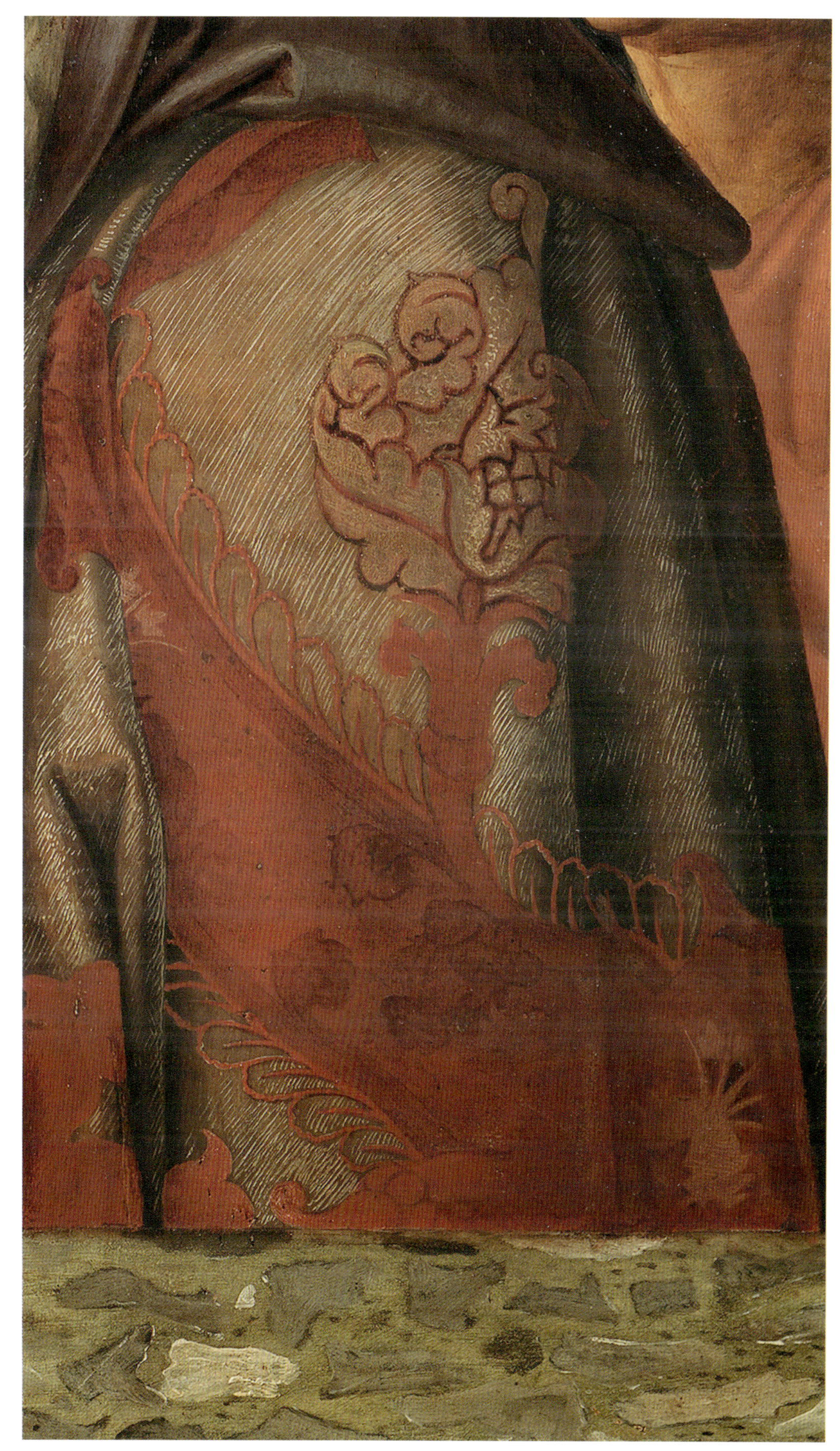

Appendix

Giovanni Bellini. A Biography

Giovanni C.F. Villa

The birth of Giovanni Bellini is a complete mystery because no documents of any kind refer to it. The son of Jacopo, a successful painter, his mother is unknown as is the year of his birth. He was not the son of Anna, Jacopo's wife, who did not name him in her will. He was probably younger than his half-brother Gentile, born no earlier than 1433, so Giovanni is likely to have been born between 1438 and 1440. He was undoubtedly educated in his father's workshop and was of age by 1459, when he was a witness to a notary act in Rialto on 30 January 1458 (according to the Venetian calendar, that is 1459) and resided in the San Lio parish, while his father with his family belonged to the San Geminiano parish. These were the years when the relationships of the Bellini workshop, the most important in Venice together with that of the Vivarini of Murano, branched out after the marriage of his sister Nicolosia to Andrea Mantegna, whom she followed to Mantua. Painter, together with his father and brother, it is certain that together all three signed the *St John the Evangelist* altar-piece for the Santa Maria della Carità church in Venice between 1468 and 1471. He reached full autonomy, when he was over thirty years of age, when on 24 April 1470 the Scuola Grande di San Marco gave him a commission for a large canvas, unknown today. He must therefore have been appreciated at least as much as his brother, with whom he is at times confused or superimposed. Jacopo died at the start of the 1470s and was soon followed by his widow, Anna Rinversi. During the following decade, Giovanni who was in the prime of his liberty and creative talent, realized the *Pietà* for Palazzo Ducale in Venice, the *Portrait of Jörg Fugger* at the Norton Simon Museum in Pasadena and the *Transfiguration* at Capodimonte in Naples – the dates of which were once legible. Around 1475, Giovanni met Antonello da Messina who realized the important altar-piece of San Cassiano during his stay in Venice. The encounter between the two painters was very compelling not only for the development of Venetian art, but for all of Italy.

Giovanni's fame was by this time so well consolidated that he was called on to substitute his half-brother Gentile (on 29 August 1479) as director of the reproduction on canvas of the frescoes in the Sala del Maggior Consiglio at Palazzo Ducale. Gentile departed for a long and prestigious stay in Istanbul, sent by the Republic to the court of Mehmed II (the Conqueror) where he painted a famous portrait of the sultan, the only one in Muslim history.

Subsequently, from 1480, there are several documents that refer directly to important commissions conferred on Giovanni. On 26 February 1483, he was nominated the official painter of the Republic and was exempted from payment of the annual tax levied by the Fraglia dei Pittori (painters' guild). However, very little is known about his private life, even during the period of his notoriety, other than that he had married Ginevra Bocheta (he had issued a receipt for her dowry of 500 gold ducats in 1485). It was only in 1487, when he was over fifty years of age (a fact that is strikingly extraordinary), that the date and his signature appeared on the *Madonna degli alberetti* (Madonna of the Small Trees) of the Gallerie dell'Accademia di Venezia. The following year he signed and dated the official votive canvas, *Doge Agostino Barbarigo opposite the Virgin*, today at San Pietro Martire a Murano. The same date appears on the *Triptych of the Friars*, which also has the date 23 February 1489 written on the back of the canvas, perhaps referring to the date of installation.

That year marks another private event. On 23 September 1489, Ginevra Bocheta made her will; however, the date of her death is not known. It is certain that Giovanni's only son, Alvise (who was not a painter), lived alone with him for a few years before dying in turn by the end of the century. A life that had already been dedicated only to his work must have been even more austere for a man who was honoured and accepted by the Venetian aristocracy. Beginning in these years, more consistent traces in available documents reveal some of his psychological traits. The source is Giovanni's long correspondence, direct on one occasion and through an intermediary on the others, with Isabella d'Este, Marchesa of Mantua, from 1496. Her husband, Francesco Gonzaga, was also in contact with Giovanni Bellini, writing on 4 October 1497 that he would accept the artist's judgement after the latter had refused to depict the city of Paris in a painting because he had never seen it. Giovanni immediately replied that he would undertake to realize another subject with the greatest care.

We know that Bellini's main commitment was always the decoration of the Palazzo Ducale, but also that he received abundant private and ecclesiastic commissions. His workshop was full of young talents and was capable of working on a quantity of devotional images, especially the famous Madonnas. In 1505, Giovanni produced the important *San Zaccaria* altar-piece in Venice, the smaller *Madonna and Child with Saints and Donor* altar-piece in the City Art Museum of Birmingham, and the *St Jerome Reading* at the National Gallery of Art in Washington, D.C. This was the time when another decisive encounter between two artists occurred. Albrecht Dürer came to Venice where he realized the *Rosary* altar-piece (now at the National Gallery in Prague) and, in private letters, expressed all his respect for the man he called "still the best in painting". In successive years, Giovanni finished the Dolfin *Sacra Conversazione* in the church of San Francesco della Vigna in Venice and the *Doge Loredan and Four Councillors* at the Gemäldegalerie in Berlin.

On 18 February 1507, Gentile Bellini made his will, nominating his half-brother Giovanni as one of the executors and asking him to complete the works undertaken for the Scuola Grande di San Marco in Venice. For that operation, he was to inherit the volume of drawings made by his father Jacopo. The other volume of drawings still extant today had been a noble and prestigious gift from Gentile to Mehmet II. Giovanni also terminated the large canvas of the *St Mark Preaching in Alexandria, Egypt*, today at the Pinacoteca di Brera in Milan. At the same time, the Council of Ten also entrusted Giovanni with a commission for three paintings to hang in the Sala del Maggior Consiglio, one of which had been started by Alvise Vivarini, recently deceased. To accelerate completion, he was assigned three assistants, namely Carpaccio, Vittore Belliniano and a certain Girolamo, perhaps Girolamo da Santacroce. Giorgione and Tiziano also passed through Giovanni's workshop.

Another brief document of 1512 exists, in which Isabella d'Este asked to examine an ancient head of Plato with a wax nose that Niccolò Bellini together with his brother Giovanni had proposed for her to acquire for 15 ducats. It is also known that on 16 November 1514, 85 ducats were registered as the balance of payment due from Alfonso d'Este to Giovanni Bellini for the *Feast of the Gods*, today at the National Gallery of Art in Washington, D.C. More prestigious activity followed, marked by the *Naked Young Woman in Front of the Mirror* at the Kunsthistorisches Museum in Vienna, the *San Domenico* at the National Gallery in London and the *Noah* in Besançon. He was also working on a large canvas of the *Martyrdom of St Mark* for the Scuola Grande di San Marco that was to be positioned above the door of the council hall or *albergo grande*. The work, which still exists, was completed by Vittore Belliniano in 1526. He was also working on a commission for the sister of the king of France, Francis I.

Finally, the notice of his death provided by the chronicler Marin Snudo, leaving his age blank, is accompanied by a very brief but intense epitaph: 1516 "Today the 29th of November [...] We learned this morning of the death of *Zuan Belin* a very fine painter, at the age of ** whose fame is known around the world and who, as old as he was, painted excellently. He was buried at San Zane Polo in his tomb, where his brother *Zentil Belin*, also a very fine painter was buried [...]".

Andrea Mantegna. A Biography

Giovanni C.F. Villa

Son of Biagio the carpenter, Andrea Mantegna was born in Isola di Carturo, then part of Vicenza, probably in around 1431, as we can infer from an inscription on the lost altarpiece of the church of Santa Sofia in Padua transcribed in 1560 by Bernardino Scardeone: "Andreas Mantinea Pat. an. septem et decem natus sua manu pinxit M.CCCC.XLVIII." From 1445 onwards he was recorded among the registered members of the painters' guild in Padua as the 'son' of Francesco Squarcione, remaining in the workshop of his adoptive father for around six years, from 1441–42 to 1448. He severed his ties with the workshop on 16 October of that year, when his brother Tomaso Mantegna signed the contract on his behalf for the frescoes commissioned by Imperatrice Ovetari for her chapel in the church of the Eremitani in Padua. Over the years he went on to become the only artist working on the monumental and heroic *Stories of St James and of St Christopher*, completed by 1457, although all that remains of them today are a few fragments pieced back together following the senseless Allied bombing of 11 March 1944.

His period of work in Padua was extremely intense. Mantegna immediately made a name for himself as a great interpreter of the classical style, so much so that he came to the attention of Mauro de' Folperti of Pavia, abbot of the rich and powerful Black Benedictines of the abbey of Santa Giustina: their encounter resulted in the *St Luke Polyptych* (1453-54, now at the Pinacoteca di Brera), emblematic of the personality of a highly precocious artist, whose work was technically exemplary from the very start and whose fine art can be attributed to an unbridled inventive and narrative ability, clearly demonstrated in these early pieces.

His fame spread rapidly. By 1449 Andrea was already working in Ferrara for Leonello d'Este and had recently established a dialogue with the Bellini family, which he joined through his marriage to Nicolosia, sister of Gentile and Giovanni and daughter of Jacopo, to whose wonderful drawings Andrea must have had direct access. News of his work at the Eremitani and Santa Giustina echoed far and wide. In 1457, the artist was in negotiations with Gregorio Correr, abbot of the basilica of San Zeno in Verona, regarding the creation of the altarpiece for the main chapel in the choir of the upper church, above the crypt: a grandiose and austere *sacra conversazione* set within an architectural structure with solemn perspective, inspired by Donatello's high altar at the basilica of Sant'Antonio in Padua. This work was completed by 1460, when Mantegna had already moved to the Mantuan court, having given in to the pressing demands of Ludovico Gonzaga, with whom he had reached an agreement back in January 1457. The marquis had tried everything to get him there, from censure to expressing the concern "that Padua was full of the plague!", before dying of the epidemic himself in 1478.

Mantegna's arrival in Mantua marked the start of his most productive season, becoming familiar with two generations of the Gonzaga family and teacher to three of them: Ludovico, Federico (in power from 1478 to 1484) and Francesco II (1484-1519). He became court artist to these lords, in a city that still conserved the memory of the courtly Gothic period of Pisanello, working as an engraver and perhaps also a sculptor, devoting himself to illuminations and interior decoration, producing cartoons for tapestries and designing jewellery. However, it was a 'group portrait' that really marked his first season on the banks of the River Mincio, starting in 1465 when he was working on the *Camera Picta* (Painted Chamber), also known as the *Camera degli Sposi* (Bridal Chamber), in the Castle of San Giorgio. The frescoes, completed in 1474, celebrate Ludovico Gonzaga and his wife Barbara of Brandenburg together with their courtiers, while also sanctioning the family's adoption of another role in the scene in which the marquis receives his second-born son, Cardinal Francesco Gonzaga, upon his return from Rome. With the famous illusionistic background and the dizzying use of perspective, the room set a fundamental example for generations to come.

This was followed by another important undertaking, in which Mantegna made full use of his taste for classical antiquity, starting work in 1486 on the cycle of canvases dedicated to the *Triumphs of Caesar*, now in the Royal Collection at Hampton Court Palace, revealed to the public from 1501 and described by Giorgio Vasari as "the best thing Mantegna ever painted." With their clear-cut and austere figures and their confident lines, they document the height of an interpretation of classicism that the artist also studied during a stay in Rome, when working between 1489 and 1490 on a lost cycle of frescoes for the chapel of Pope Innocent VIII at the Belvedere. On 6 July 1496, a procession "with more men and women than have ever before been seen in Mantua" (from a *Letter from Sigismondo Gonzaga to Francesco Gonzaga*, 6 July 1496), accompanied what was to become the *Madonna della Vittoria* to the church of Santa Maria della Vittoria. Mantegna worked on this large altarpiece from November 1495 to June 1496 - an immediate glorification of the Battle of Fornovo of 6 July 1495, when Francesco's cavalry was overwhelmed by the swollen River Taro, but were still seemingly the victors – which is characterised by the spectacular plant-filled apse that surrounds the figures. It is now conserved in the Louvre, which also houses the two masterpieces painted for the study of Francesco II's wife, Isabella d'Este. This small chamber (5.28 x 2.72 x 5 metres high), originally in one of the towers of the Castle of San Giorgio, had walls painted to resemble marble and hosted the dance of the muses to the sound of Apollo's harp, portrayed in *Parnassus* and *Triumph of the Virtues*. The latter owes a debt to *De Pictura* by Leon Battista Alberti, to which the narrative in the canvas refers, accompanied by a series of scrolls and inscriptions to remove any doubts regarding its interpretation. The former was completed in around 1497 and the latter in around 1502. They mark the culmination of all the artist's inventive power and technical scrupulousness, from the pond with aquatic plants to the espaliered citrus plants that open onto the distant landscape that forms a backdrop to the scene. The fantastical figures that animate them are truly breathtaking due to their stunning precision and absolute formal control, and to the creative tension that always enabled Mantegna to control every aspect without any stylistic concessions.

The artist's last, involuntary dialogue with his brother-in-law Giovanni Bellini took place in 1505, when Francesco Corner asked the Gonzaga family about the possibility of commissioning Mantegna to paint the canvases for his *camerino*, obtaining *The Introduction of the Cult of Cybele in Rome* (London, The National Gallery) from the painter.

After producing around one hundred works during a career that spanned more than fifty years – almost all of which was spent between Padua, Verona and Mantua – Mantegna died on 13 September 1506. He was buried in the Mantuan church of Sant'Andrea, where his funerary chapel was decorated with the *Holy Family and the Family of St John the Baptist* and the *Baptism of Christ*, cited by his son Ludovico Mantegna as being among the works remaining in his father's studio. Next to them was a bronze bust, a *Self-portrait* that was perhaps the final example of his almost unknown output as a sculptor.

Bibliography

Alberti [1435–1436] 1975
L.B. Alberti, *De pictura*, C. Grayson (ed.) (Rome, 1975).

Neumayr 1807
A. Neumayr, *Illustrazione del Prato della Valle ossia della Piazza delle Statue di Padova* (Padua, 1807).

Campori 1866
G. Campori, *Lettere artistiche inedite* (Modena, 1866).

Michiel [1525–1528] 1800
[M. Michiel], *Notizia d'opere di disegno nella prima metà del secolo XVI* (Bassano, 1800).

Vasari [1550–1568] 1849
G. Vasari, *Le Vite de' più eccellenti pittori, scultori e architetti*, V (Florence, 1849).

Vasari [1550–1568] 1967–1987
G. Vasari, *Le vite de' più eccellenti pittori, scultori e architettori* [1550/1568], R. Bettarini, P. Barocchi (eds.) (Florence, 1967–1987).

Waagen 1830
G.F. Waagen, *Verzeichniss der Gemälde-Sammlung des Königlichen Museums zu Berlin* (Berlin, 1830).

Campori 1866
G. Campori, *Lettere artistiche inedite* (Modena, 1866).

Frizzoni 1870
G. Frizzoni, 'Saggio critico intorno alle opere di pittura dell'epoca del Rinascimento esistenti nella R. Gallerie di Berlino', in *Jahrbücher für Kunstwissenschaft*, 3 (1870).

Crowe, Cavalcaselle 1871
J.A. Crowe, G.B. Cavalcaselle, *A History of Painting in North Italy* (London, 1871).

Catalogo degli oggetti 1872
Catalogo degli oggetti d'arte della pia Fondazione Querini Stampalia preceduto da brevi parole intorno ad essa (Venice, 1872).

Lermolieff [Morelli] 1880
I. Lermolieff [Giovanni Morelli], *Die Werke Italienischer Meister in den Galerien von München, Dresden und Berlin* (Leipzig, 1880).

Guida artistica 1881
Guida artistica e storica di Venezia e delle isole circonvicine (Venice, 1881).

Michiel [1525–1528] 1884
[M. Michiel], *Notizia d'opere di disegno pubblicata e illustrata da D. Jacopo Morelli*, G. Frizzoni (ed.) (Bologna, 1884).

Cennini (Ilg) 1888
C. Cennini, *Das Buch von der Kunst, mit Einleitung, Noten und Register versehen von Albert Ilg, Quellenschriften für Kunstgeschichte und Kunsttechnik des Mittelalters und der Renaissance* (Vienna, 1888).

Bode 1889a
W. Bode, 'Die Bronzebüste des Battista Spagnoli im Königlichen Museum zu Berlin, ein Werk mutmasslich des Gian Marco Cavalli', in *Jahrbuch der Königlich Preußischen Kunstsammlungen*, X (1889), pp. 211–216.

Bode 1889b
W. Bode, 'La Renaissance au musée de Berlin (septième article)', in *Gazette des Beaux-Arts*, 3rd series, XXXI, 1 (1889), pp. 107–120.

Beschreibendes Verzeichnis 1891
Beschreibendes Verzeichnis der Gemälde. Dritte Auflage (Berlin, 1891).

Lermolieff [Morelli] 1893
I. Lermolieff [G. Morelli], *Kunstkritische Studien über Italienische Malerei. Die Galerie zu Berlin*, G. Frizzoni, F.A. Brockhaus (eds.) (Leipzig, 1893).

Kristeller 1901
P. Kristeller, *Andrea Mantegna* (London–New York–Bombay, 1901).

Kristeller 1902
P. Kristeller, *Andrea Mantegna* (Berlin–Leipzig, 1902).

Logan 1902
M. Logan, 'Bibliographie', in *Gazette des Beaux-Arts*, 3rd series, XLIV, 28 (1902), pp. 255–261.

Bode 1903–1904
W. Bode, 'Mantegna und sein neuester Biograph', in *Kunstchronik*, n.s., XV, 8 (1903–1904), coll. 129–135.

Lazzarini, Moschetti 1908 [1974]
V. Lazzarini, A. Moschetti, 'Documenti relativi alla pittura padovana', in *Archivio Veneto*, n.s., XV (1908), pp. 72–190, 249–321; XVI (1908), pp. 68–102 (separated ed. Venice 1908, re-ed. of the anastatic expanded reprint by M. Muraro, [Sala Bolognese 1974]).

Bode *et al.* 1888–1909
W. Bode *et al.*, *Die Gemälde-Galerie der Königlichen Museen zu Berlin*, G. Grote'sche Verlagsbuchhandlung (Berlin, 1888–1909).

Querini Stampalia 1914
G. Querini Stampalia, *Testamento in data 11 decembre 1868 e codicillo in data 17 decembre 1868 del conte Giovanni Querini Stampalia: in atti del veneto notajo Daniele Gaspari* (Venice, 1914).

Venturi 1914
A. Venturi, *Storia dell'arte italiana. VII. La pittura del Quattrocento. Parte III* (Milan, 1914).

Berenson 1916
B. Berenson, *Venetian Painting in America* (New York, 1916).

Venezia e dintorni 1932
Venezia e dintorni (Novi Ligure, 1932).

Dussler 1935
L. Dussler, *Giovanni Bellini* (Frankfurt am Mein, 1935).

Fiocco 1937
G. Fiocco, *Mantegna* (Milan, 1937).

Venezia e dintorni 1937
Venezia e dintorni. Nuova guida illustrata con pianta topografica della città e dell'estuario (Milan, 1937).

Collobi 1939–1940
L. Collobi, 'Lazzaro Bastiani', in *Critica d'arte*, IV-V (1939–1940), pp. 33–53.

Panofsky [1943] 1948
E. Panofsky, *Albrecht Dürer* [1943] (Princeton, 1948).

Galleria Querini Stampalia 1946
Galleria Querini Stampalia. Itinerario delle sale d'esposizione (Vicenza, 1946).

Birkmeyer 1949
K.M. Birkmeyer, *Bericht über 202 Bilder aus Berliner Museen in den Vereinigten Staaten von Amerika*, Gemäldegalerie, Art technologies and restorations department, archive (New York, 22 April 1949).

Dazzi 1949
M. Dazzi, 'La 'Presentazione' della Querini-Stampalia', in *Arte veneta*, III (1949), pp. 153–158.

Dussler 1949
L. Dussler, *Giovanni Bellini* (Vienna, 1949).

Longhi 1949 [1978]
R. Longhi, *The Giovanni Bellini Exhibition* (1949) (now in *Edizione delle Opere Complete di Roberto Longhi, 10. Ricerche sulla pittura Veneta*, [Florence, 1978], pp. 99–109).

Zorzi 1949
E. Zorzi, 'Un rabdomante dei colori scopre il vero Giambellino', in *Corriere d'Informazione* (July 28, 1949).

Venezia e dintorni 1951
Venezia e dintorni (Milan, 1951).

Gilbert 1952
C. Gilbert, 'Sante Zago e la cultura artistica del suo tempo', in *Arte Veneta*, VI (1952), pp. 21–24.

Coletti 1953
L. Coletti, *Pittura veneta del Quattrocento* (Novara, 1953).

Arslan 1953
W. Arslan, 'Il politico di San Zanipolo', in *Bollettino d'Arte*, XXXVI (1952), pp. 127–146.

Venezia e dintorni 1953
Venezia e dintorni (Milan, 1953).

Lorenzetti 1956
G. Lorenzetti, *Venezia e il suo estuario* (Rome, 1956).

Meiss 1957
M. Meiss, *Andrea Mantegna as Illuminator. An Episode of Renaissance Art, Humanism and Diplomacy* (New York, 1957).

Wolters 1960
C. Wolters, in ICOM Commission for the Care of Paintings (ed.), 'The care of paintings: fabric paint supports', in *Museum*, 12 (1960), p. 161.

Davies 1961
M. Davies, *The Earlier Italian Schools* (London, 1961).

Mantua 1961
G. Paccagnini (ed.), *Andrea Mantegna*, exhibition catalogue (Mantua, Palazzo Ducale, September–October 1961) (Venice, 1961).

Heinemann 1962
F.H. Heinemann, *Giovanni Bellini e Belliniani*, I (Venice, 1962).

Longhi 1962 [1978]
R. Longhi, 'Crivelli e Mantegna: due mostre interferenti e la cultura artistica nel 1961', in *Paragone* 145 (1962), pp. 18, 20 (now in *Edizione delle Opere Complete di Roberto Longhi. 10. Ricerche sulla pittura Veneta* [Florence, 1978], pp. 143–154).

Prinz 1962
W. Prinz, 'Die Darstellung Christi im Tempel und die Bildnisse des Andrea Mantegna', in *Berliner Museen*, n.s., XII (1962), pp. 50–54.

Ringbom 1965 [1984]
S. Ringbom, *Icon to Narrative. The Rise of the Dramatic Close-Up in Fifteenth-Century Devotional Painting* (Åbo, 1965) (II ed. 1984).

Longhi [1926] 1967
R. Longhi, *Lettera pittorica a Giuseppe Fiocco*, in Id., *Saggi e ricerche. 1925-1928*, works complete edition by R. Longhi, II (Florence, 1967), 2 vols.

Robertson 1968
G. Robertson, *Giovanni Bellini* (Oxford, 1968).

Delbourgo, Rioux, Martin 1975
S. Delbourgo, J.P. Rioux, E. Martin, 'L'analyse des peintures du Studiolo d'Isabelle d'Este. Etude analytique de la matière picturale', in *Annales des Laboratoires de Recherche des Musées de France* (1975).

Goffen 1975
R. Goffen, 'Icon and Vision: Giovanni Bellini's Half-Length Madonnas', in *The Art Bulletin*, 57 (1975), pp. 487–518.

Vickers 1976
M. Vickers, 'Mantegna and Constantinople', in *The Burlington Magazine*, no. 883, vol. 118 (October 1976), pp. 680–87.

Christie, Manson & Woods 1978
Christie, Manson & Woods International, Inc., *Important Paintings by Old Masters* (New York, January 12, 1978).

Catalogo della Pinacoteca 1979
Catalogo della Pinacoteca della Fondazione Scientifica Querini Stampalia (Venice, 1979).

Dall'Acqua 1980
M. Dall'Acqua, 'Mecenatisimo e collezionismo dei Gonzaga da Ludovico a Isabella d'Este: la nascita dell'esperto e del dilettante', in A. Prosperi (ed.), *La Corte e il 'Cortegiano' II. Un modello europeo* (Rome, 1980), pp. 295–319.

Belting 1981
H. Belting, *Das Bild und sein Publikum im Mittelalter. Form und*

Funktion früher Bildtafeln der Passion (Berlin, 1981).

Straub 1984
R.E. Straub, 'Farbmittel, Buchmalerei, Tafel- und Leinwandmalerei', in *Reclams Handbuch der künstlerischen Techniken* (Stuttgart, 1984), vol. 1, pp. 125–260.

Eisler 1985 (1986)
C. Eisler, 'Saints Anthony Abbot and Bernardino of Siena" designed by Jacopo and painted by Gentile Bellini', in *Arte veneta*, 39 (1985 [1986]), pp. 32–40.

Lightbown 1986
R. Lightbown, *Mantegna with a Complete Catalogue of the Paintings, Drawings and Prints* (Oxford, 1986).

Merkel 1987
E. Merkel, 'Il mecenatismo ed il collezionismo artistico dei Querini Stampalia dalle origini al Settecento', in G. Busetto, M. Gambier (eds.), *Querini Stampalia. Un ritratto di famiglia nel Settecento veneziano* (Venice 1987), pp. 133–153.

Rylands 1988
P. Rylands, *Palma il Vecchio. L'opera completa* (Milan, 1988).

Anderson 1989
J. Anderson, 'Collezioni e collezionisti della pittura veneta del Quattrocento: storia, sfortuna e fortuna', in M. Lucco (ed.), *La pittura nel Veneto. Il Quattrocento* (Milan, 1989), pp. 271–294.
Goffen 1989
R. Goffen, *Giovanni Bellini* (New Haven-London, 1989).

Walter 1989
I. Walter, 'Andrea Mantegnas "Darbringung Jesu im Tempel". Ein Bild der Befreiung und des Aufbruchs', in *Städel-Jahrbuch*, n.s., XII (1989), pp. 59–70.

Degenhart, Schmitt 1990
B. Degenhart, A. Schmitt, *Corpus der italienischen Zeichnungen 1300-1450*, II, 5–8: *Jacopo Bellini*, 4 vols. (Berlin, 1990).

Pietro Brandolese 1990
V. Sgarbi (ed.), *Pietro Brandolese del genio de' Lendiranesi per la pittura* (Lendinara, 1990).

Anderson 1991
J. Anderson, 'Dietro lo pseudonimo', in G. Morelli, *Della pittura italiana. Studii storico-critici. Le Gallerie Borghese e Doria-Pamphili in Roma*, J. Anderson (ed.) (Milan, 1991), pp. 493–578.

Dunkerton *et al.* 1991
J. Dunkerton, S. Foister, D. Gordon, N. Penny, *Giotto to Dürer. Early Renaissance Painting in the National Gallery* (London–New Haven, 1991).

Morelli 1991
G. Morelli, *Della pittura italiana. Studii storico-critici. Le Gallerie Borghese e Doria-Pamphili in Roma*, J. Anderson (ed.) (Milan, 1991).

Christiansen 1992a
K. Christiansen, *Some Observations on Mantegna's Painting Technique*, in J. Martineau (ed.), *Andrea Mantegna*, exhibition catalogue (London, Royal Academy of Art – New York, Metropolitan Museum of Art, January–July 1992) (Milan, 1992), pp. 68–78.

Christiansen 1992b
K. Christiansen, 'St Mark', in J. Martineau (ed.), *Andrea Mantegna*, exhibition catalgoue (London, Royal Academy of Art – New York, Metropolitan Museum of Art, January–July 1992) (Milan, 1992), pp. 119–121.

Christiansen 1992c
K. Christiansen, 'Devotional Works: Mantua', in J. Martineau (ed.), *Andrea Mantegna*, exhibition catalogue (London, Royal Academy of Art-New York, Metropolitan Museum of Art, Janaury–July 1992) (Milan, 1992), pp. 150–158.

Greenstein 1992
J.M. Greenstein, *Mantegna and Painting as Historical Narrative* (Chicago–London, 1992).

London–New York 1992
J. Martineau (ed.), *Andrea Mantegna*, exhibition catalogue (London, Royal Academy of Art – New York, Metropolitan Museum of Art, January–July, 1992) (Milan, 1992).

Rothe 1992
A. Rothe, *Mantegna's Paintings in Distemper*, in J. Martineau (ed.) *Andrea Mantegna*, exhibition catalogue (London, Royal Academy of Art – New York, Metropolitan Museum of Art, Janaury–July 1992) (Milan, 1992), pp. 80–88.

Tempestini 1992
A. Tempestini, *Giovanni Bellini. Catalogo completo* (Florence, 1992).

Dunkerton 1993
J. Dunkerton, 'Mantegna's Painting Techniques', in F. Ames-Lewis, A. Bednarek (eds.), *Mantegna and Fifteenth-Century Court Culture* (London, 1993).

Davanzo Poli, Moronato 1994
D. Davanzo Poli, S. Moronato, *Le stoffe dei veneziani* (Venice, 1994).

Cordellier 1995
D. Cordellier (ed.), 'Documenti e Fonti su Pisanello (1395–1581 circa)', in *Verona Illustrata. Rivista del Museo di Castelvecchio*, 8 (1995).

Venice 1995
G. Busetto (ed.), *Cento scene di vita veneziana Pietro Longhi e Gabriel Bella alla Querini Stampalia*, exhibition catalogue (Venice, 1995).

Anderson 1996
J. Anderson, 'The Political Power of Connoisseurship in Nineteenth-Century Europe: Wilhelm von Bode versus Giovanni Morelli', in *Jahrbuch der Berliner Museen*, XXXVIII (1996), supplement, pp. 107–119.

Brown 1996
D.A. Brown, 'Bode and Berenson: Berlin and Boston', in *Jahrbuch der Berliner Museen*, XXXVIII (1996), supplement, pp. 101–106.

Arasse 1997 [2015]
D. Arasse, 'Signé Mantegna', in Id., *Le sujet dans le tableau. Essais d'iconographie analytique*, (Paris, 1997), pp. 57–77 (now in S.J. Campbell, J. Koering [eds.], *Andrea Mantegna. Making Art [History]*) (Chichester, 2015), pp. 55–74.

Carr 1997
D. Carr, *Andrea Mantegna:*

The Adoration of the Magi (Los Angeles, 1997).

Tempestini 1997
A. Tempestini, *Giovanni Bellini* (Milan, 1997).

Blass-Simmen 1998
B. Blass-Simmen, *Pisanello e l'enluminure ferraraise*, in D. Cordellier (ed.), *Pisanello. Actes du colloque organisé au musée du Louvre les 26,27 et 28 juin 1996* (Paris, 1998), vol. II, pp. 577–615.

Galassi 1998
M.C. Galassi, *Il disegno svelato. Progetto e immagine nella pittura italiana del primo Rinascimento* (Nuoro, 1998).

Venice 1998
E. Dal Carlo (ed.), *Le porcellane dell'ambasciatore*, exhibition catalogue (Arsenale, Venice, 1998) (Venice, 1998).

Bambach 1999
C.L. Bambach, *Drawing and Painting in the Italian Renaissance Workshop: Theory and Practice, 1300-1600* (Cambridge, 1999).

Hiller von Gaertringen 1999
R. Hiller von Gaertringen, *Raffaels Lernerfahrung in der Werkstatt Peruginos. Kartonverwendung und Motivübernahme im Wandel* (München–Berlin, 1999).

Padua 1999
A. de Nicolò Salmazo (ed.), *Francesco Squarcione: "pictorum gymnasiarcha singularis"*, conference proceedings (Università di Padova, Dipartimento di Storia delle Arti Visive e della Musica, 10–11 February, 1998) (Padua, 1999).

Bagarotto *et al.* 2000
R. Bagarotto *et al.*, 'La tecnica pittorica di Giovanni Bellini', in R. Goffen, G. Nepi Scirè (eds.), *Il colore ritrovato. Bellini a Venezia*, exhibition catalogue (Venice, Gallerie dell'Accademia, September 2000 – January 2001) (Milan, 2000), pp. 184–202.

Bottacin 2000
F. Bottacin, '*Tiberio Tinelli: un artista veneziano del Seicento nel suo studio*', in *Studi Veneziani*, XL (2000), pp. 239–255.

Caburlotto 2000
L. Caburlotto, 'Presentazione di Gesù al Tempio', in R. Goffen, G. Nepi Scirè (eds.), *Il colore ritrovato. Bellini a Venezia*, exhibition catalogue (Venice, Gallerie dell'Accademia, September 2000 – Janaury 2001) (Milan, 2000), pp. 149–152.

Farmer 2000
W.I. Farmer, *The Safekeepers. A Memoir of the Arts at the End of World War II* (Berlin–New York, 2000).

Tempestini 2000
A. Tempestini, *Giovanni Bellini* (Milan, 2000).

Venice 2000
R. Goffen, G. Nepi Scirè (eds.), *Il colore ritrovato. Bellini a Venezia*, exhibition catalogue (Venice, Gallerie dell'Accademia, September 2000 – Janaury 2001) (Milan, 2000).

Caburlotto 2001
L. Caburlotto, 'Private passioni e pubblico bene. Studio, collezionismo, tutela e promozione delle arti in Giovanni de Lazara (1744-1833)', in *Saggi e memorie di Storia dell'arte*, 25 (2001), pp. 123–217.

Hockney 2001
D. Hockney, *Secret Knowledge: Rediscovering the Lost Techniques oft the Old Masters* (London, 2001).

Krüger 2001
K. Krüger, *Das Bild als Schleier des Unsichtbaren. Ästhetische Illusion in der Kunst der Frühen Neuzeit in Italien* (München, 2001).

Olivari 2001
M. Olivari, 'Tecnica pittorica e disegno preparatorio in Giovanni Bellini e Mario Basaiti', in G. Buccellati, A. Marchi (eds.), *Oltre il visibile, indagini riflettografiche* (Milan, 2001).

Saramago 2002
J. Saramago, *Andrea Mantegna. Un'etica, un'estetica* (Genoa, 2002).

Boskovits, Brown 2003
M. Boskovits, D.A. Brown, *Italian Paintings of the Fifteenth Century. The Collections of the National Gallery of Art. A Systematic Catalogue* (New York–Oxford, 2003).

Schmitter 2003
M. Schmitter, 'The Dating of Marcantonio Michiel's "Notizia" on works of art in Padua', in *The Burlington Magazine*, CXLV, 1205 (2003), pp. 564–571.

Villa 2003
G.C.F. Villa, *Un Bellini in chiaroscuro: indagini infrarosse e problemi cronologici*, in F. Rigon, E.M. Maria Dal Pozzolo (eds.), *Capolavori che ritornano. Bellini e Vicenza*, exhibition catalogue (Vicenza, Palazzo Thiene, 5 December 2003 – 25 January 2004) (Cittadella [Padua], 2003), pp. 73–85.

Busetto 2004
G. Busetto, 'Notizie sulle collezioni d'arte dei Querini Stampalia', in *Dei ed eroi del barocco veneziano. Dal Padovanino a Luca Giordano e Sebastiano Ricci* (Catania, 2004).

Casu 2004
S. Casu, '"Veluti Caesar triumphans": Ciriaco d'Ancona e la statuaria equestre', in *Paragone*, 55, 3 (2004), pp. 3–46.

Christiansen 2004a
K. Christiansen, 'Bellini and Mantegna', in P. Humfrey (ed.), *The Cambridge Companion to Giovanni Bellini* (Cambridge, 2004), pp. 48–74.

Christiansen 2004b
K. Christiansen, 'Giovanni Bellini and the Practice of Devotional Painting', in R. Kasl (ed.), *Giovanni Bellini and the Art of Devotion* (Indianapolis, 2004), pp. 7–57.

Dunkerton 2004
J. Dunkerton, 'Bellini's Technique', in P. Humfrey (ed.), *The Cambridge Companion to Giovanni Bellini* (Cambridge, 2004), pp. 195–225.

Fletcher 2004
J. Fletcher, 'Bellini's Social World', in P. Humfrey (ed.), *The Cambridge Companion to Giovanni Bellini* (Cambridge, 2004), pp. 13–47.

Gentili 2004
A. Gentili, 'Bellini and Landscape', in P. Humfrey (ed.), *The Cambridge Companion to Giovanni Bellini* (Cambridge, 2004), pp. 167–81.

Golden 2004
A. Golden, 'Creating and Re-Creating: The Practice of Replication in the Workshop of Giovanni Bellini', in R. Dasl (ed.),*Giovanni Bellini and the Art of Devotion* (Indianapolis, 2004), pp. 90–127.

Goldner 2004
G. Goldner, 'Bellini's Drawings', in P. Humfrey (ed.), *The Cambridge Companion to Giovanni Bellini* (Cambridge, 2004), pp. 226–255.

Sander 2004
J. Sander, *Italienische Gemälde im Städel 1300-1550. Oberitalien, die Marken und Rom* (Mainz, 2004).

Strehlke 2004
C.B. Strehlke, *Italian Paintings 1250–1450 in the John G. Johnson Collection and the Philadelphia Museum of Art* (Philadelphia, 2004).

Rollandini 2005
E. Rollandini, 'Paolo Fabris "Intelligente di cose d'arte e pregevole artista"', in *Archivio Storico di Belluno, Feltre e Cadore*, LXXIV, 327 (2005), pp. 51–68.

Agosti 2006
G. Agosti, *Mantegna 1961 Mantova* (Mantua, 2006).

Faietti 2006
M. Faietti, 'Andrea, disegnatore con "maschera"', in D. Banzato, A. De Nicolò Salmazo, A.M. Maria Spiazzi (eds.), *Mantegna e Padova: 1445–1460*, exhibition catalogue (Padua, 2006) (Milan, 2006), pp. 81–89.

Knopp 2006
W. Knopp, *Einst und jetzt*, in *Kaiser Friedrich-Museums-Verein. Tradition, Leidenschaft, Kunstverstand* (Berlin, 2006), pp. 10–18.

Poldi, Villa 2006
G. Poldi, G.C.F. Villa, *Appunti di cantiere per il Mantegna sottopelle*, in *Mantegna a Mantova (1460-1506)*, M. Lucco (ed.), exhibition catalogue (Mantua, Galleria civica di Palazzo Te, September 2006 – Janaury 2007) (Milan, 2006), pp. 47–61.

Villa, Poldi 2006
'Giovanni Bellini e dintorni, ovvero Appunti veneziani', in G. Poldi, G.C.F. Villa, *Dalla conservazione alla storia dell'arte. Riflettografia e analisi non invasive per lo studio dei dipinti* (Pisa, 2006), pp. 308–398.

Guerriero 2007
S. Guerriero, 'Il collezionismo di sculture moderne', in L. Borean, S. Mason (eds.) *Il collezionismo d'arte a Venezia. Il Seicento* (Venice, 2007).

Villa 2007
G.C.F. Villa, *Indagando Mantegna* (Mantua, 2007).

Barausse 2008
M. Barausse, *Giovanni Bellini. I documenti*, in M. Lucco, G.C.F. Villa (eds.), *Giovanni Bellini*, exhibition catalogue (Rome, Scuderie del Quirinale, September 2008 – Janaury 2009) (Cinisello Balsamo, 2008), pp. 327–359.

Bellosi 2008
L. Bellosi, *Giovanni Bellini et Andrea Mantegna*, in G. Agosti, D. Thiébaut (eds.), *Mantegna 1431-1506*, exhibition catalogue (Paris, Musée du Louvre, September 2008 – Janaury 2009) (Paris, 2008), pp. 103–109.

De Marchi 2008
A. De Marchi, 'Autour du triptyque de San Zeno de Vérone', in G. Agosti, D. Thiébaut (eds.), *Mantegna 1431-1506*, exhibition catalogue (Paris, Musée du Louvre, 2008–2009) (Paris–Milan, 2008), pp. 153–157.

Nova 2008
A. Nova, 'Icona, racconto e dramatic close-up nei dipinti devozionali di Giovanni Bellini', in M. Lucco, G.C.F. Villa (eds.), *Giovanni Bellini*, exhibition catalogue (Rome, Scuderie del Quirinale, September 2008 – Janaury 2009) (Cinisello Balsamo, 2008), pp. 105–115.

Paris 2008
G. Agosti, D. Thiébaut (eds.), *Mantegna 1431-1506*, exhibition catalgoue (Paris, Musée du Louvre, 2008–2009) (Paris–Milan, 2008).

Pilo 2008
G.M. Pilo, *'Giovanni Bellini'*, in *Arte documento*, 24 (2008), pp. 82–87.

Poldi, Villa 2008
G. Poldi, G.C.F. Villa, *Bellini a Venezia. Sette opere indagate nel loro contesto* (Cinisello Balsamo, 2008).

Rome 2008
M. Lucco, G.C.F. Villa (eds.), *Giovanni Bellini*, exhibition catalogue (Rome, Scuderie del Quirinale, September 2008 – Janaury 2009) (Cinisello Balsamo–Rome, 2008).

Skwirblies 2008
R. Skwirblies, *Die Sammlung Solly in Preußen. Eine Privatsammlung wird Grundlage der Berliner Gemäldegalerie*, graduation thesis (Freie Universität Berlin, 2008).

Trevisan 2008
B. Trevisan, 'Presentazione di Gesù al Tempio', in M. Lucco, G.C.F. Villa (eds.), *Giovanni Bellini*, exhibition catalogue (Rome, Scuderie del Quirinale, September 2008 – Janaury 2009) (Cinisello Balsamo, 2008), pp. 176–177, no. 31.

Villa 2008a
G.C.F. Villa, 'L'arte della ricerca, il primato del disegno. "L'altra luce" di Giovanni Bellini', in M. Lucco, G.C.F. Villa (eds.) *Giovanni Bellini*, exhibition catalogue (Rome, Scuderie del Quirinale, September 2008 – Janaury 2009) (Cinisello Balsamo, 2008), p. 39–51.

Villa 2008b
G.C.F. Villa, 'Dall'underdrawing al disegno. Il caso Giovanni Bellini', in M. Faietti, L. Melli, A. Nova (eds.), *Le tecniche del disegno rinascimentale. Dai materiali allo stile*, international conference proceedings (Florence, Kunsthistorisches Institut, 22–23 September 2008), "Mitteilungen des Kunsthistorischen Institutes in Florenz", LII. (Band 2008), Heft 2/3, pp. 73-87.

Ciatti, Marini 2009
M. Ciatti, P. Marini (eds.), *La Pala di San Zeno di Andrea Mantegna. Studio e conservazione* (Florence, 2009).

Menu, Ravaud 2009
M. Menu, É. Ravaud (eds.), *La*

technique picturale d'Andrea Mantegna ("Technè" hors-série) (Paris, 2009).

Poldi, Villa 2009
G. Poldi, G.C. F. Villa, *Indagando Bellini* (Milan, 2009).

Villa 2009
G.C.F. Villa, 'Indagando Bellini', in G. Poldi, G.C.F. Villa, *Indagando Bellini* (Milan, 2009), pp. 9–160.

Ravaud *et al.* 2009
E. Ravaud, M. Eveno, S. Mirabaud, E. Lambert, 'Matériaux et techniques de quatre toiles d'Andrea Mantegna', in M. Menu, É. Ravaud (eds.), *La technique picturale d'Andrea Mantegna* ("Technè" hors-série) (Paris, 2009), pp. 27–34.

Skwirblies 2009
R. Skwirblies, 'Ein Nationalgut, auf das jeder Einwohner stolz sein dürfte: die Sammlung Solly als Grundlage der Berliner Gemäldegalerie', in *Jahrbuch der Berliner Museen*, 51 (2009), pp. 69–99.

Syson 2009
L. Syson, 'Reflections on the Mantegna Exhibition in Paris', in *The Burlington Magazine*, CLI (2009), pp. 526–535.

Trevisan 2009
B. Trevisan, 'Querini Stampalia collezione', in L. Borean, S. Mason (eds.) *Il collezionismo d'arte a Venezia. Il Settecento* (Venice, 2009), pp. 292–294.

Rome 2010
I grandi veneti. Da Pisanello a Tiziano, da Tintoretto a Tiepolo. Capolavori dell'Accademia Carrara di Bergamo, G. Valagussa, G.C.F. Villa (eds.), exhibition catalogue, (Rome, Chiostro del Bramante, October 2010 – Janaury 2011) (Cinisello Balsamo, 2010).

Rowley 2010
N. Rowley, *"Pittura di luce". La manière claire dans la peinture du Quattrocento*, doctorate thesis (Université Paris-Sorbonne, 2010).

Marinelli 2011
S. Marinelli, *Pietro Bembo nella storia della pittura*, in G. Beltrami, H. Burns, D. Gasparotto (eds.) *Pietro Bembo e le arti*, meetings (Padua, 24–26 February 2011) (Venice, 2013), pp. 465–478.

Dietemann *et al.* 2012
P. Dietemann *et al.*, 'Die Bindemittel der Altkölner Malerei in der ersten Hälfte des 15. Jahrhunderts', in *Zeitschrift für Kunsttechnologie und Konservierung*, XXVI, 1 (2012), pp. 80–87, 286–289.

Stehr 2012
U. Stehr, 'Johann Jakob Schlesinger (1792-1855) - Künstler - Kopist - Restaurator', in *Jahrbuch der Berliner Museen*, 53 (2011), supplement.

Beltramini 2013
G. Beltramini, 'La residenza di Pietro Bembo in contrada di San Bartolomeo a Padova', in G. Beltramini, H. Burns, D. Gasparotto (eds.), *Pietro Bembo e le arti*, meetings (Padua, 24–26 February 2011) (Venice, 2013), pp. 375–406.

Gasparotto 2013
D. Gasparotto, 'Il mito della collezione', in G. Beltramini, D. Gasparotto, A. Tura (eds.) *Pietro Bembo e l'invenzione del Rinascimento*, exhibition catalogue (Padua, Palazzo del Monte di Pietà, February–May 2013), Venice 2013, pp. 48-65.

Grabowski 2013
J. Grabowski, '*Versäumen Sie Ihre arischen Nachweis nicht!' Die Staatliche Museen zu Berlin und ihr Umgang mit Bürgern jüdischer Abkunft 1933-1939*, in *Zwischen Politik und Kunst. Die Staatlichen Museen zu Berlin in der Zeit des Nationalsozialismus*, J. Grabowski, P. Winter (eds.) (Köln–Weimar–Vienna, 2013), pp. 29–51.

Lauber 2013
R. Lauber, '"In casa di messer Pietro Bembo". Riflessioni su Pietro Bembo e Marcantonio Michiel', in G. Beltrami, H. Burns, D. Gasparotto (eds.), *Pietro Bembo e le arti*, meetings (Padua, 24–26 February 2011) (Venice 2013), pp. 441–464.

Lucco 2013
M. Lucco, *Mantegna* (Milan, 2013).

Marinelli 2013
S. Marinelli, *Pietro Bembo nella storia della pittura*, in G. Beltramini, D. Gasparotto, A. Tura (eds.), *Pietro Bembo e l'invenzione del Rinascimento*, exhibition catalogue (Padua, Palazzo del Monte di Pietà, February-May 2013) (Venice, 2013), pp. 465–478.

Van Duijn 2013
E.E. van Duijn, *All What Glitters is not Gold. The Depiction of Gold-Brocaded Velvets in Fifteenth- and Early Sixteenth-Century Netherlandish Paintings*, doctorate thesis (University of Amsterdam, 2013).

Wallace Maze 2013
D. Wallace Maze, 'Giovanni Bellini: Birth, Parentage and Independence', in *Renaissance Quarterly*, 66 (2013), pp. 783–823.

Brown, Pizzati 2014
D.A. Brown, A. Pizzati, '"Meum amantissimum nepotem" a new document concerning Giovanni Bellini', in *The Burlington Magazine* CLVI, 1332 (2014), pp. 148–152.

De Marchi 2014
A. De Marchi, 'Giovanni Bellini, Andrea Mantegna e la tenerezza della Madre', in E. Daffra (ed.), *Giovanni Bellini. La nascita della pittura devozionale umanistica. Gli studi*, exhibition catalogue (Milan, Pinacoteca di Brera, 9 April – 13 July 2014) (Milan, 2104), pp. 73–82.

Faietti 2014
M. Faietti, 'From Solomon's Temple to Hagia Sophia: A Metaphorical Journey for Andrea Mantegna', in A. Payne (ed.), *Dalmatia and the Mediterrranean* (Leiden, 2014), pp. 115–144.

Zimmer 2014
J. Zimmer, 'Von Rom nach Berlin', in A. Fendt, C. Sedlarz, J. Zimmer (eds.), *Aloys Hirt in Berlin. Kulturmanagement im frühen 19. Jahrhundert* (Berlin–München, 2014), pp. 11–58.

Berlin 2015
J. Chapuis, S. Kemperdick (eds.),

Das verschwundene Museum: Die Verluste der Berliner Gemälde- und Skulpturensammlungen 70 Jahre nach Kriegsende, exhibition catalogue (Berlin, Bode-Museum, March–September 2015) (Berlin–Petersberg, 2015).

Cassegrain 2015
G. Cassegrain, 'Mantegna the Grammarian', in S.J. Campbell, J. Koering (eds.) *Andrea Mantegna. Making Art (History)* (Chichester, 2015), pp. 77–92.

Godla, Allen 2015
J. Godla, D. Allen, '"St. Francis in the Desert" and the Art of Linear Perspective', in S. Rutherglen, C. Hale (eds.), *In a New Light. Giovanni Bellini's "St. Francis in the Desert"*, (London [2015]), pp. 133–153.

Hartwieg 2015
B. Hartwieg, 'Kunsttechnologische Analyse des Göttinger Barfüßerretabels mit Schlussfolgerungen zu Charakteristika und Struktur der Werkstatt', in *Niederdeutsche Beiträge zur Kunstgeschichte*, n.s., 1 (2015), pp. 321–380 (*Das Göttinger Barfüßerretabel von 1424*).

Hauser 2015
A. Hauser, 'The Griffin's Gaze and the Mask of Medusa: Self-Referential Motifs in Andrea Mantegna's Trial of St James', in S.J. Campbell, J. Koering (eds.), *Andrea Mantegna. Making Art (History)* (Chichester, 2015), pp. 135–151.

Schmidt Arcangeli 2015
C. Schmidt Arcangeli, *Giovanni Bellini e la pittura veneta a Berlino. Le collezioni di James Simon e Edward Solly alla Gemäldegalerie* (Verona, 2015).

Winter 2015
P. Winter, *Zum Schicksal der Kunstwerke in den Bergungsorten außerhalb Berlins*, in J. Chapuis, S. Kemperdick (eds.), *Das verschwundene Museum: Die Verluste der Berliner Gemälde- und Skulpturensammlungen 70 Jahre nach Kriegsende*, exhibition catalogue (Berlin, Bode-Museum, March–September 2015) (Berlin–Petersberg, 2015), p. 23.

Frankfurt 2016
Maniera. Pontormo, Bronzino und das Florenz der Medici, B. Eclercy (ed.), exhibition catalogue (Frankfurt, Städel Museum, 24 February – 5 June 2016) (München, 2016).

Hammond 2016
J. Hammond, 'Five Jacopo Bellinis: the lives of Christ and the Virgin at the Scuola Grande di S. Giovanni Evangelista, Venice', in *The Burlington Magazine* (1361), vol. 158 (August 2016), pp. 601–609.

Hockney, Grayford 2016
D. Hockney, M. Gayford, *A History of Pictures: From the Cave to the Computer Screen* (London, 2016).

Blake-McHam 2017
S. Blake-McHam, 'The Eclectic Taste of the Gattemelata Family', in B. Blass-Simmen, S. Weppelmann (eds.), *Padua and Venice. Transcultural Exchange in the Early Modern Age* (Berlin–Boston, 2017), pp. 29–40.

Blass-Simmen 2017
B. Blass-Simmen, 'Cultural Transfer in Microcosm', in B. Blass-Simmen, S. Weppelmann (eds.), *Padua and Venice. Transcultural Exchange in the Early Modern Age* (Berlin–Boston, 2017), pp. 1–18.

Blass-Simmen, Weppelmann 2017
B. Blass-Simmen, S. Weppelmann (eds.), *Padua and Venice. Transcultural Exchange in the Early Modern Age* (Berlin–Boston, 2017).

Dietemann, Fischer, Karl 2017
P. Dietemann, U. Fischer, D. Karl, 'Die Bindemittel der Florentiner Malerei', in A. Schumacher, A. Kranz, A. Hojer, *Florentiner Malerei Alte Pinakothek. Die Gemälde des 14. Bis 16. Jahrhunderts* (Berlin, 2017), pp. 92–105.

Gentili 2017
A. Gentili, *Devote meditazioni*, in *Bellini e i belliniani dall'Accademia dei Concordi di Rovigo*, G. Romanelli, F. Lugato (eds.), exhibition catalogue (Conegliano, Palazzo Sarcinelli 25 February –18 June 2017) (Venice, 2017), pp. 108–135.

London 2017
M. Wivel (ed.), *Michelangelo & Sebastiano*, exhibition catalogue (London, National Gallery, 15 March – 25 June 2017) (London 2017).

Los Angeles 2017
D. Gasparotto (ed.), *Giovanni Bellini. Landscapes of Faith in Renaissance Venice*, exhibition catalogue (Los Angeles, J. Paul Getty Museum, October 2017 – Janaury 2018) (Los Angeles, 2017).

Maze 2017
D.L.W. Maze, 'The Life of Giovanni Bellini', in D. Gasparotto (ed.), *Giovanni Bellini. Landscapes of Faith in Renaissance Venice*, exhibition catalogue (Los Angeles, J. Paul Getty Museum, October 2017 – Janaury 2018) (Los Angeles, 2017), pp. 37–56.

New York 2017
C. Bambach (ed.), *Michelangelo: Divine Drafsman & Designer*, exhibition catalogue (New York, The Metropolitan Museum of Art, 13 November 2017 – 12 February 2018) (New York, 2017).

Rowley 2017
N. Rowley, *Domenico Veneziano 1925: una predella ricomposta*, in A.M. Ambrosini Massari, A. Bacchi, D. Benati, A. Galli (eds.), *Il mestiere del conoscitore. Roberto Longhi*, conference proceedings (Bologna, Fondazione Zeri, September 2015) (Bologna, 2017), pp. 103–121.

Skwirblies 2017
R. Skwirblies, *Altitalienische Malerei als preußisches Kulturgut. Gemäldesammlungen, Kunsthandel und Museumspolitik 1797-1830* (Berlin–Boston, 2017).

Villa 2017
G.C.F. Villa, *Andrea Mantegna and Giovanni Bellini-The Hidden Dialogue*, in B. Blass-Simmen, S. Weppelmann (eds.), *Padua and Venice. Transcultural Exchange in the Early Modern Age* (Berlin–Boston, 2017), pp. 79–92.

Campbell 2018
C. Campbell, 'A tale of two artists and two cities: Mantegna and Bellini; Padua and Venice', in C. Campbell, D. Korbacher, N. Rowley *et al.* (eds.), *Mantegna and Bellini*,

exhibition catalogue (London, National Gallery; Berlin, Staatliche Museen zu Berlin, October 2018 – June 2019) (London, 2018).

De Marchi 2018
A. De Marchi, 'Tone and inventio/elegy and historia: Bellini vs. Mantegna', in C. Campbell, D. Korbacher, N. Rowley *et al.* (eds.), *Mantegna and Bellini*, exhibition catalogue (London, National Gallery; Berlin, Staatliche Museen zu Berlin, October 2018 – June 2019) (London, 2018).

Dunkerton *et al.* 2018
J. Dunkerton, R. Billinge, M. Spring, C. Campbell, 'Giovanni Bellini', in *National Gallery Technical Bulletin*, special issue, vol. 39 (2018).

Dunkerton, Hartwieg 2018
J. Dunkerton, B. Hartwieg, 'Mantegna and Bellini: contrasting approaches to technique', in *Mantegna-Bellini. Exhibition Catalogue London-Berlin*, forthcoming (2018).

London–Berlin 2018
Mantegna-Bellini. Exhibition Catalogue London-Berlin, forthcoming (2018).

Mazzotta 2018
A. Mazzotta, 'Giovanni Bellini and the early "teleri" for the Scuola di San Giovanni Evangelista in Venice', in *The Burlington Magazine*, 1381, vol. 160 forthcoming (April 2018).

Rowley 2018
N. Rowley, *Bellini stands higher [...] than Mantegna*, in C. Campbell, D. Korbacher, N. Rowley *et al.* (eds.), *Mantegna and Bellini*, exhibition catalogue (London, National Gallery; Berlino, Staatliche Museen zu Berlin, October 2018 – June 2019) (London, 2018).

Dunkerton, Billinge, Wivel in press
J. Dunkerton, R. Billinge, M. Wivel, 'Sebastiano and Michelangelo: Infrared Insights into their Collaboration', in *National Gallery Technical Bulletin*, vol. 38, pp. 32–55, forthcoming.

Pinacoteca Querini Stampalia n.d.
Pinacoteca Querini Stampalia. Catalogo (Venice, n.d.).

Trevisan n.d.
B. Trevisan, *La "Presentazione di Gesù al tempio" di Giovanni Bellini* (Venice, n.d.).

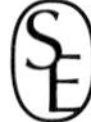

Silvana Editoriale

Direction
Dario Cimorelli

Art Director
Giacomo Merli

Editorial Coordinator
Sergio Di Stefano

Copy Editors
Clelia Palmese, Paola Rossi

Layout
Letizia Abbate

Translations
From Italian to English:
Sonia Hill for Scriptum, Rome
Gordon Fisher
Contextus S.r.l., Pavia
From German into English:
Calum Short for Contextus S.r.l., Pavia

Production Coordinator
Antonio Micelli

Editorial Assistant
Ondina Granato

Photo Editor
Alessandra Olivari, Silvia Sala

Press Office
Lidia Masolini, press@silvanaeditoriale.it

Silvana Editoriale S.p.A.
via dei Lavoratori, 78
20092 Cinisello Balsamo, Milano
tel. 02 453 951 01
fax 02 453 951 51
www.silvanaeditoriale.it

Reproductions, printing and binding in Italy
Printed by Tipostampa, Moncalieri (To)
March 2018

Credits
Archivi Alinari, Florence
Fondazione Querini Stampalia, Venice
© The National Gallery, London
Jörg P. Anders
Marco Beck Peccoz
Brigit Blass-Simmen
Serge Domingie
Babette Hartwieg
Mauro Magliani
Luciano Pedicini
Staatliche Museen zu Berlin - Preußischer Kulturbesitz, Gemäldegalerie. Photo: Christoph Schmidt
Giovanni C.F. Villa, Università degli Studi di Bergamo, Centro di Ateneo di Arti Visive
Antje Voigt, Staatliche Museen zu Berlin